"...exciting, revealing and convincing!"

"With an eloquence that is direct and informative, Henry Bolduc tells us the difference between channeling, mediumship and past-life regression. And how channeling brings an awareness that brings you to the truth. As he changed his life, so can all, he says, by making the same journey within."

— Jess Stearn
author of
Edgar Cayce: The Sleeping Prophet

"...substantial and meaningful contributions to our understanding of the mind."

"My own experiences using hypnosis as a medical therapeutic tool since 1950 corroborates Henry Bolduc's cases. A high percentage of my patients found the original source of their symptoms in an earlier life and obtained complete relief when the source event was relived or reviewed and the old emotions released.

He carefully includes descriptions of guiding techniques which serve as safeguards to avoid difficulties that might be encountered by those who venture into unexplored territory.

I commend him for his untiring efforts in adding this book to the field of hypnotherapy."

— Irene Hickman, D.O.
author of *Mind Probe* and
founder of Hickman Systems

By the Same Author

SELF-HYPNOSIS
Creating Your Own Destiny

THE JOURNEY WITHIN

Past-Life Regression and Channeling

By

Henry Leo Bolduc

INNER VISION
Virginia Beach, Virginia

Cover painting by
James Francis Yax
Amsterdam, Holland

FIRST EDITION
Copyright © 1988 by Henry Leo Bolduc

This book is published by:
        Inner Vision Publishing Co.
        Box 1117 Seapines
        Virginia Beach, Virginia 23451
        Phone (804) 671-1777

This book is printed in the United States of America.

First Printing, April 1988
Second Printing, June 1989

ISBN 0-917483-14-6

CONTENTS

ILLUSTRATIONS

ACKNOWLEDGMENTS

This book tells about real events involving real people. The facts have not been altered nor the names changed. It is a pleasure to write those names – to thank those people who have helped me on my long journey within.

I am grateful to the friends of my youth for their desire to reach out into the unknown – to seek answers when even the questions were unclear. I thank you, dear friends: Calvin, Heikki, Brenda, Susie, Jon, Veijo, Dave, and Annette. I thank Philip for teaching me how to make good recordings. And, in memorium, Tom, a fine friend.

It is difficult to single out my teachers, for life offers many teachers in many guises. The two educators most influential in my youth were Dan Kelly for English and Melvin Bitter for psychology. My high school apple orchard job financed my hypnosis courses and recording equipment; I thank Elmer S. Fitzgerald Jr. for teaching valuable work habits and management skills. He showed me that good habits, learned young, last a lifetime (or maybe several!).

With great appreciation I thank my friends and fellow students of the "Adventure Years." This was a time of intense learning, growing, and maturing. I enjoyed the company of all: thank you, Patricia, Scott, Loren, Fred, Rick, Louis, Carol, George and Steve, and I thank the people of the community for their patience – which they needed if only because of the constant traffic generated by our wonderful visitors.

In New England I hold in highest esteem Paul and Geraldine Pearle for encouraging and sponsoring my early outreach programs. I thank the staff of the Providence Hypnosis Center while I was director – Deborah Cannity, George Parker, Mary Swajian, Robert Fenster, and Richard Simmons. A warm thanks to Bob Bow, the previous director, who was an important link in the chain of events bringing this book to fruition.

Sharon Fowler and Diane Davidson Cayce helped make my Texas year a big success.

For research and enlightenment, I heartily thank the Edgar Cayce Foundation and the Association for Research and Enlightenment, Inc. (A.R.E.). The A.R.E. library in Virginia Beach is a treasure of information and the staff a wealth of generosity and help. I thank the library staff, especially Steve Jordan, the manager, and my particular friend, Geraldine McDowell. I thank the entire staff of the A.R.E., the Foundation, and Atlantic University for their help with a previous book and also with my lectures, workshops, and tapes. I especially thank the president of the A.R.E., Charles Thomas Cayce; and, in memorium, Hugh Lynn Cayce.

Near my present home in Virginia's Blue Ridge Mountains, I thank the staff of the Wythe-Grayson Regional Library and Joyce Roberts, the acting director.

The most valuable contributors to this book are the many friends who live nearby and who read, evaluate, type, proofread, laugh, critique, nurture, and encourage my work. Other people have attended unusual and innovative sessions at my home. In random order, these fine mountain folk are: Suzanne, Dan, Richard, Donnie, Diane, Sandy, Jonathan, Gordon, Dick, Sylvia, Peter, Margaret, Susan, Gerry, Larry, Nancy, Rosemary, Mark, Lenora, Roger, Sue, Don, Billy, Kim, Michael and Jackie. Bless you, dear friends and neighbors, for your indefatigable goodness and energy.

With the greatest love I thank the following friends for their special gifts.

Ann Phelan Adams, my wife, for her support, encouragement, and generous help.

Daniel Clay Pugh, for the original inspiration to duplicate

the Cayce experiment. He continues to give profound readings and is a courageous explorer of the inner mind.

Eileen Rota and I shared the vision of this book. We wrote, transcribed, and compiled the original 950 pages of manuscript during a two-week vacation that evolved into a two-month marathon. She presently writes and channels the gentle soul of Pretty Flower.

Brock Hood has continued to work with Eileen as her guide. He also channels and has been most helpful in applying the principles and showing that the procedures in this book are clearly spelled out and easy for others to follow.

D. Sue Jones drew the helpful illustrations.

Evagene H. Bond, my editor, has brought structure to the unwieldy early manuscript. Evagene did everything a good editor should – and much more – to make the narrative clear, succinct, and readable. It was an exciting and educational experience to work with her.

Henry Leo Bolduc
Independence, VA
December, 1986

An author may conceive a book and sometimes even birth it. But the editor is the one who nurtures and refines it and presents it to the world. I thank Doris Dean, Editor at Inner Vision Publishing, for her dedication and enthusiasm, and for condensing the vast manuscript into a beautiful book.

Henry
March 1988

PROLOGUE

I once heard a delightful story that the ancients came to earth, bringing with them the secrets of eternity. The ancients worried about how to hide these great secrets until mankind was spiritually ready to appreciate and appropriately use them. One lamented, "If we hide them on land, people will conquer the land and discover them." Another commented, "If we hide them in the sea, mankind will reach the very bottom of the sea." A third observed, "If we hide them in space, men and women will one day soar into space."

They pondered. Then the wisest said, "Let us hide these secrets in the last place they will think to search. Let us hide the secrets in their own minds." And this proved to be the perfect hiding place.

Not until recently has mankind dared to explore this final frontier; people are now searching their minds for the secrets of eternity. I am part of this exploration. I am a past-life researcher. I do hypno-regression to help people experience episodes of past lives. I also help people become channels through which voices speak from eternity. This is a book about how, and why, I do it. I have few theories to offer, but I have a quarter of a century of exploration, exhaustive testing and research to share with you.

I didn't set out to be a past-life researcher. In fact, when I was young the word didn't even exist. I did have an early desire to be a priest, to help people achieve their spiritual goals. Later, in junior high school, I thought I'd be a detective, a goal implanted by watching far too much television. Now I have become a detective of a sort, investigating clues to the mysteries of time and the soul. And I sincerely hope my work helps people grow spiritually.

My work takes a scientific and humanistic approach to previously uncharted areas of the inner mind. The belief in past lives is centuries old, but the methods of exploring and testing this belief are modern.

One of the things I have realized over time is the spiritual significance of the human mind that is not to be linked or confused with religion. Religion has an important place in the community, but it oversteps common sense or becomes dogmatic if it says, "Only our religion and church have the answers; God is on our side only." No one owns an exclusive franchise on God or truth. God and the spirit are universal – known to all people of all ages and places, if sometimes under different names.

Naive people say jokingly, "Oh, when you talk of past lives, why is everybody Cleopatra or Mark Anthony?" But I say from experience that we were not Cleopatras or Mark Anthonys. We were street sweepers, murderers, cutthroats, rogues, and whores. We were also priests, priestesses, healers, helpers, nurturing mothers, and providing fathers. We were varied people with varied life experiences, just as we are today. Within this context, only cynics will declare that we were all famous personalities and only egotists will hope so.

As a past-life researcher, my primary tool is hypnosis – a mind-awake-body-asleep process. Unfortunately, the word is loaded with meanings, not all of them favorable. As I see it, there are three kinds of hypnotists, each using hypnosis for different purposes.

The first group comprises the stage entertainers. They use hypnosis almost entirely for entertainment, working with a person's mind to show one can do more things, or different ones, than one normally could. My early courses were in stage hypnosis and they taught me good techniques. I learned to work in front of an audience and I learned self-confidence; it was impressive to me to see people respond to things I was asking them to do.

The next group of professional hypnotists uses hypnosis as a therapeutic tool for stress management, cigarette cessation, weight and habit control, building self-esteem, and other manifestations of a positive personality and a healthy lifestyle. In my years working at a hypnosis clinic, that was the kind of hypnosis I did; I gave suggestions to clients to encourage them to respond in certain specific ways. In this type of work, the hypnotist gives what is needed, whether a formula of exercises, suggestions, key words, visualizations or metaphors, to get subjects to respond in ways they need and want – to produce a desired therapeutic result.

The third group of professional hypnotists believes that the best way to enrich lives is to enrich minds. They work to bring out information and feelings already in the mind or subconscious of people. This information can be from a present life, a past life, or both. This is how I use hypnosis now; I induce a trance and guide my subjects to reexperience past lives or to open themselves to the eternal. The object is to gain access to the subconscious by using hypnotic techniques for the purpose of allowing what is stored in the mind to come forth. I am not a magician; I put nothing in, but simply draw out what is already there. For those with a technical bent, I include information in this book on my methods.

There is not always a therapeutic intent; the subject may merely want information – you can never learn too much about yourself. Other subjects do have therapeutic aims. This kind of person believes an unsolved past problem is affecting the present life. By bringing the problem into awareness it can be dealt with and let go, the first step toward solving the present-day problem. I have found that merely taking this first step is sometimes enough to solve the problem; on the other hand, success can come after multiple sessions.

Early in my career, I had to decide how to approach my research into the subconscious. I could enter the academic world, as did Dr. Milton Erickson, a pioneer of modern hypnosis, and Dr. Ian Stevenson, whose research on reincarnation is unique. Or I could go in the direction of the spiritual entrepreneur, like Edgar Cayce, the preeminent American psychic, or Jane Roberts, whose channeling of the entity Seth made them both widely known. Even a world-renowned, respected, and meticulous reincarnation researcher like Dr. Stevenson, with impressive academic credentials, has encountered resistance from his peers. So I realized that to have the freedom I wanted to pursue my hypnosis exploration goals I would have to work apart from the establishment. The academic world or even a structured organization could be stifling to my desire to map the mind and pursue truth wherever I saw it, wherever it led me.

In later years I realized that the academic world and life as a scientist in "the system" were in the words of those already there: "...tenure wars, grant skimming, departmental cocktail parties, Byzantine academic politics, Department of Defense contracts, jealous colleagues, not to mention the work of actually doing the science. It turns out that 'doing science' is quite a bit different from studying it."[1]

On the other hand, choosing the path of the entrepreneur meant that I would receive no financing from anyone; without grants I would have to fund all my research myself. But this is the path I chose and it has offered far greater freedom. It has been years since I've been to a cocktail party, and I'm a pacifist in the tenure wars. To compensate for lack of funding I worked slowly and used whatever resources were available. I learned patience and kept careful records of procedures and results.

I suggest to others who wish to follow this path, this quest, that they first learn to keep an open mind – but not so open that their brains fall out! Build trust – not blind trust – but trust for those people worthy of trust, whether individuals or organizations. Later, when I explain the procedures I followed in my own search, I will welcome you to test and duplicate the experiments. These experiments can easily be conducted in any quiet home setting. You do not need stainless steel labs with state-of-the-art technology, only honest questioning minds and the desire to learn and to experience.

The journey within is different for everyone, so you will want to evaluate your results for yourself. Then do accept the validity of *your own* experience. See for yourself if this work answers any inner questions, satisfies any inner needs, or resolves any inner conflicts.

I find past-life-regression work does satisfy deep needs for me. Here are some reasons I do what I do. I have found my goal is to understand and to be understood, then to inspire others. I like to unravel the mysteries of the past through self-examination to appreciate the incredible sagas of the soul's journey. I like to awaken to awareness of my life's mission and the knowledge of my spiritual evolution, and to help others to do so. I like to recognize past friends and soul mates — echoes of the heart from some enchanted time and place; to find reasons to laugh at human folly and reasons to cry for human weakness; to realize how extraordinary every person is now and to appreciate the magnitude of their shared memories and experience.

As I give talks, seminars, and workshops around the country, I discuss the latest discoveries in the field of past lives. So much information is being discovered by other researchers every day that our vocabulary and understanding change and grow rapidly.

Part of my work is to simplify these complicated new ideas. I strive to translate new ideas and concepts into familiar words and images. One of these new words and concepts is "channeling." My hypnosis and regression work led me to this exciting new field. Again, I will clearly spell out my channeling procedures so you can test and replicate these experiences also.

Hypnosis is the tool I use to guide both regression and channeling sessions. In regression work I guide people into their own inner minds. They journey deep within to examine memory imprints that we call "past lives." Whether these visions are always actual past lifetimes or whether they are metaphoric or symbolic doesn't really matter to me. What matters is that the person experiences new insight and self-understanding. The regression session focuses on a person's stored memory banks, deep within.

The channeling session is completely different. It guides a person to other sources of information. These sources seem to come from "outside" the person; that is, an entity enters the body, or vessel, and speaks through it. In this book, Daniel and Eileen are the vessels; they become channels for the entities of The Eternals and Pretty Flower. These latter entities seem separate from Daniel and Eileen – "outside" them, as it were. Yet both The Eternals and Pretty Flower stress the oneness of the entity and the channeler and, indeed, of the whole universe.

What can we say, then? Are the entities real? Or are they figments of the imagination? Manifestations of the subconscious? Does it matter?

I think it does not. I believe channeling tunes in to a person's superconscious mind – a kind of universal mind or infinite universal intelligence. Going to this higher state of consciousness is opening new channels to divinity, accessing the soul's mind – what some people call "angelic communication," the "compassionate mind," or the "God Force." Channeling does not originate in the conscious or subconcious mind but transcends them to the superconscious. That at least is how I understand it now. I have much to learn, as we all do, about the process.

Of course I have had questions, doubt, and self-criticism about my work. I wish to help everyone, but experience has taught me that I can only help those who first ask for help, and then I have time only for a small number of those. I see my role more as a door opener and teacher to encourage and inspire other people to become guides and channels so they, in turn, can help even greater numbers – like being a teacher of teachers.

Only one minor problem has arisen from my search into

the secrets of the mind. Some few people heard it rumored that my work was "speaking to the dead." Such a description is born of ignorance. Had anyone said such a thing directly to me (these things always seem to come second or third hand), I would surely have explained that *anyone* can speak to the dead. Getting the dead to answer back is the hard part.

Well, that is a very old joke, born perhaps of the days of seances and mysterious tappings by unseen hands. We work differently now, I hope. I myself have been fortunate to have received favorable notice from other explorers of the human mind. I have met and made friends with some of the advanced thinkers of our time. I consider it a great honor just to be a part of this new movement and the exciting time of enlightenment in which we live and learn.

My 25-year search is a long time in which to realize how much I still have to learn. My search is still just beginning, it seems. All the secrets of the ages are not revealed in the blink of an eye of cosmic time. But in these years I have gained profound insight and experienced peak episodes that I am about to share with you in this book. I will present my story without embellishment. I do not pretend to be more than I am, nor do I hide in false modesty. This is a story of youthful curiosity and my eager search for answers.

The adventure quickens! Working with the mind is like opening a window into eternity. Every mind is like an entire living universe, a mother lode of information. When we search deep within and travel the pathways of our minds and souls there is a joy of accomplishment. Like buried treasure, mankind is finding and unlocking the secrets of the ancients – mining them, at last, from their hiding places within us.

Endnotes:

[1]Jane Hooper, "Hard Science," *Omni Magazine*, October (1985): p. 116.

NOTE ON THE EDITING OF
THE TRANSCRIBED MATERIAL

Much material in this book is quoted directly from audio tapes made during both regression and channeling sessions.

The channeled and regression material is presented almost exactly as it was spoken. I have not corrected grammar, syntax, or diction. Some words are necessarily spelled phonetically. In rare cases I have added a few words for clarity or inserted an explanatory note; these are indicated by brackets [ ].

I have made a few omissions, again for clarity; these are indicated by dots, either three (...), for a deletion within a sentence, or four (....), for a deletion at the beginning or end of a sentence.

Pauses, where the speaker hesitates or changes the subject abruptly, are indicated with dashes (–).

I have added capital letters where they seem necessary.

Regression and channeling sessions are printed in a special type face. The questions are italicized.

Of the vast material from both the Teachings (The Eternals) and the Gatherings (Pretty Flower), I have used what seems of highest general interest and what best represents the messages of the souls who speak. I have not, however, included any material on health issues, since answers to health questions are specific to individuals.

Chapter One

MY SEARCH BEGINS

The heart knoweth, the soul never forgetteth.
Edgar Cayce, Reading 5351-1

In the late 1950s, when I was a teenager, my brother went to a hospital fair and spent five cents on a used book. That nickel changed my life. I was overwhelmed by excitement as I turned its tattered pages. The story added a whole new level to life. If the premise was correct, that we had lived many lives prior to our present one, then life was now a *series* of adventures rather than a single episode!

The book was *The Search for Bridey Murphy*,[1] the story which unfolds from the author's hypnotically directed sessions with his friend Ruth. He had begun in the traditional format, asking Ruth to reexperience episodes from her childhood. Then he asked her to experience her prenatal state. And then he asked her to go beyond. Now Ruth began speaking of herself in another lifetime in Cork, Ireland. The book continues with their captivating search for knowledge of lives before the one we experience "now" — reincarnation, in fact.

In its heyday, this book was a best seller and stirred up controversy and conversation. Newspapers and magazines

15

sent reporters to Ireland to try to check out the story. But I thought that the press had missed the point. For me, the question was not "Is every single detail accurate?" I accepted the book's truth. Its basic principles felt right, touched some hidden core in my being. Maybe I just wanted it to be right.

No matter. What *I* wanted to know was, "Can this experiment be duplicated?" And, more important, "Can *I* do it?" I knew I would have to try. So, in my high school years, the adventure began.

Because Bernstein had used hypnosis to bring Ruth back to past lives, I said to myself, "Well, I will simply have to learn hypnosis." I realized that hypnosis was just the first step — the tool that would enable me to get to the important thing, the regression experiment. So, with the drive that fills explorers, I devoured information about hypnosis. I took courses, attended lectures, and listened to tapes. Most information available then was about stage hypnosis techniques, though I found some serious material — a course for doctors, dentists, and psychologists, for example, that taught me more useful therapeutic hypnotic procedures.

At 15, I was hypnotizing willing friends. By the time I was 16, I felt I knew enough to start experiments in hypnotic regression.

At a time when most of my friends were buying their first cars, I bought my first tape recording system. (At this point I was following Bernstein — a good model, by the way. I needed the tape recorder to record every session, as he did.) With this equipment and with interested volunteers, I was ready to begin.

My friend, Calvin, volunteered to be my first subject. Earlier, Cal and I had practiced stage hypnosis exercises and I could tell when he was in a deep trance. On this particular evening, he and I entered the dimly lit room we had chosen for the session. Other friends sat around us in a half circle. A hushed silence fell as we began our first experiment. After inducing a trance, I repeated the techniques used in *The Search for Bridey Murphy*. I asked Cal to write his name, first in the present and then again as we went back a year at a time to the very first time he wrote his name. We watched in amazement; Cal wrote his name differently with each year. With the last, or youngest, signature, he described his grandfather placing a hand on his, guiding the pencil and showing him how to write his name. This is a copy of Cal's actual writing. (See illustration #1)

The success of this experiment encouraged me to venture further into the past. Cal was receptive and ready to work. I will report the results of our work later in this chapter.

Meanwhile, I continued working with friends, guiding other hypnosis sessions. I was learning to use this tool, hypnosis, that would help me achieve my goal: to duplicate the Bridey Murphy experiments.

My biggest needs were for guidance and practice. There were no books or courses on methods of past-life exploration. Fortunately, my high school psychology teacher encouraged me to learn hypnosis and even allowed me to guide a group hypnosis session in our class. The students who participated enjoyed themselves, so their evaluation sheets said.

But I was often puzzled or discouraged. For instance, once, in a trance, a friend described one of his earliest present-life memories: his aunt dropped him from the top of a bureau. Later, when I asked his mother, she denied the incident had taken place. I jumped to the conclusion that my friend was "making up" the episode. I questioned the validity of what I was doing, and nearly gave up regression work altogether.

Now, of course, I am glad I didn't, especially because years later, when I was visiting my friend's older sister, the full story emerged. As I was telling the story of her brother's regression, she blurted out that *she* had been the one who had dropped her little brother and had covered up the incident as best she could! This was my first big lession that not everything in a regression session is exactly "accurate." I have learned to allow every subject to tell his or her story without interrupting the flow of information. There is plenty of time after the session for analysis and judgment if accuracy is an issue.

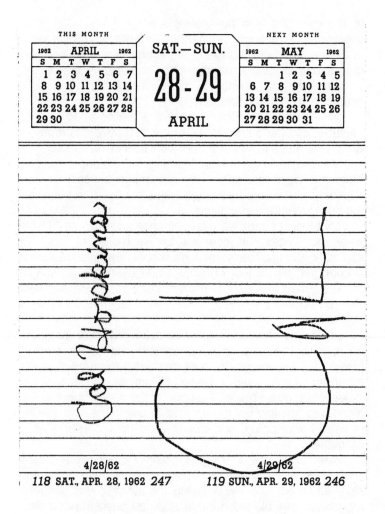

Illustration #1, Front & Back
Cal's writing in a hypnotic regression. It was fortunate
that our only scrap of paper was a desk calendar, conven-
iently dating the event.

Cal Hopkins
Cal Hopkins 8
Cal Hopkins 7
Cal Hopkins 6
Cal Hopkins 5
Cal Hopkins 4
Cal Hopkins 3
CAL HOPKINS 2
CAL HOPKINS 1

THE FIRST PAST-LIFE REGRESSION

Until now, I had experimented with hypnosis as a way of helping people recall experiences from their present lives. It was time to see if we could go deeper into the past. Although I was young, I wanted to work slowly and carefully and to make a sincere, in-depth study. Somehow I knew, or had a premonition, that this was something far more than a single experiment. This was something that would become part of my lifework.

Many of my friends wanted to "go first" on this journey, my first attempt to help someone experience past-life recall. I chose Cal because I liked his receptivity and felt our earlier success augured well for this experiment.

Now my preparation in learning hypnosis and regression techniques was about to pay off — or fail. Cal and I agreed on the date, time and place for our first past-life session. I felt both eager and apprehensive. The day ticked by slowly. Evening came and we gathered at Cal's. Earlier that summer a group of us had built a room in the large barn attached to Cal's house. This room, separated from the activity of the home, gave us an ideal place to work. Cal lay on the sofa as the group of friends and observers sat in a half circle. I dimmed the lights and turned on the tape recorder. Here is an excerpt from that first, hour-long session.

CALVIN
August 19, 1962
Ashby, Massachusetts

You are in a past lifetime. Everything is so completely clear. Your mouth is nice and moist. Now I want you to tell me about the scene you can see.[2]

I'm standing in front of a house. I'm — it's a wooden house and it's got some kind of a grass roof — something like that. And there is two big trees in front of the house. I'm leaning against one of them. I got a beard and — ah — a grey beard. And there's a dog — a dog standing beside me. I don't know, never seen the dog, but he's [a] good dog. And um —

You will quickly note, I'm sure, that Cal's first words were not particularly profound. Their value is admittedly personal: these were the first words spoken in the first past-life regression I ever conducted. And to my delight, Cal went on to describe a life he lived as John O'Hara in 1762 near Berkshire County, England!

After the session we were hushed into a long silence. We had all witnessed something profound and exciting. When we did start talking, we asked Cal if he remembered anything of the session. He did. In fact, he was able to add details of the lifetime he had just reexperienced. I was very surprised by this fact, as other subjects I had read about had no conscious recall after the session. Cal appeared fine — reenergized, even — after the experience. Our success encouraged us to schedule another session a week later.

I knew that something important had happened that summer evening in 1962. I realized that my lifework had taken its first big step forward. But I had no conception whatsoever of the phenomenal events that were to come of it.

For the next three years Cal and I continued to work together. In his second session, while returning him to the present, I specifically gave him the suggestion, "You will retain in your conscious mind only that which is important and beneficial for you to retain at this time." I was trying to guide Cal not to have memory after awakening if it was not good for him. Nonetheless, Cal did continue to recall much information; I have since found recall after the regression to be a normal and natural occurrence for many people. I also discovered that it was possible to have Cal explore more than one lifetime during each session. He could easily review and relive two, three, and four lives in a single session.

THE WORD SPREADS

I lived in a small town. It didn't take long for word to spread. Soon I was flooded with volunteers eager to experience what Cal had. The friends who sat in on Cal's sessions saw that it was safe and interesting, so they wanted to try — and they told their friends. Even I wanted to

21

experience regression, but there was no one prepared to guide me.

Cal and I listened to his recorded sessions, I to perfect my techniques and he to fill in the gaps in his conscious memory from subconscious recall. We soon realized that there were curious things about his past lives; Cal observed this first. One day he said, "Have you noticed that in every one of my past lives I died a violent death?" I had typed out the material on the tapes, and went to study the transcripts. Sure enough, Cal was right. There was a form or a design — a kind of thread woven through his lives — a pattern that might warn him to be careful of possible violent death in his present life, if that's possible.

A few sessions are necessary for patterns like this to begin to show. Two years later, a man came along who was to teach me the vital importance of understanding past-life patterns. This man, Tom, heard of my work and asked me to work with him. He did not say if he wanted to learn more about himself or if he was just curious, and I didn't ask. Whatever his reasons, Tom proved to be an excellent subject.

On October 21, 1964, Tom and I worked together for the first time. During that session, Tom relived his life as Mokoutu, and talked of living on a smoking volcanic island, Ponjupo. With a smile of love, Mokoutu spoke of his mother, Moko. Then his story turned to pain and sadness as he remembered the drowning of his beautiful woman, Byutu.

He often spoke in a language no one in our area had ever heard. He called houses "kieyoshuto" and described their structure of sticks and clay. He talked of his people's washing their clothes in the river, of the hard work in the garden, and of his dog.

Mokoutu and his friends took their "kelia" (boats) to the deep water to net whitefish and rockfish. They returned from these expeditions as quickly as possible because the Monokis, their enemies on another island, might attack their homes in their absence. "Don't go to the islands!" Mokoutu shouted. "Go halfway between! Never all the way!"

Mokoutu's father had died in war, when enemies came in war boats to destroy their homes, to steal, to trample their gardens, to kill his dog. Mokoutu and his people fought bravely and fiercely, killing some of the war men. The rest fled.

"How old did you live to be?" I asked.

"Lived to be old — forty — fifty."

I had learned from Cal and others that death is often as important to a person's memory and development as life. I guided him to the time just before his death.

"Men standing," he said. "Old women weeping. Crying. Men sad. Presents — gifts — for me to take." He saw the young men leave, while the old men remained to "take a smoke." The old men stayed with him and told the story of the village. "Time," he said.

"Time for what?" I asked.

"To go." That was his simple description of his death, "Time to go."

As I questioned him about his death state he described a "blue darkness" and then "swift movement." After a moment, he said spontaneously, "Leap! Move quickly!"

I now guided him back to his childhood as Mokoutu and then to a life "before." This concept of lives "before" or your "next life" is probably not always chronologically accurate. But the sequence of lifetimes is confusing. For example, is your "first" life your present life or does it start the first time you enter flesh?

This life "before" was in Belgium, where in his childhood he was with his mother, picking grapes. His father worked in a cotton factory. He talked about how he was too small to work in the "Allen Tavern." "Too small — too small to work in tavern. Steins — floor — broke and I got mad. Men drag me — stab." Tom's face contorted with intense pain and his body jerked.

As a guide I feel my duty is to protect my subject, so I guided him forward to detach him from his pain. "It's something of the past, " I said. "What happened after?"

He said that he died and after death was "clear." I did not

23

know what he meant, but he continued, "Clearness — waiting — very clear — sky was very clear." Upon returning to the present and waking, he had little recollection of the session.

TOM'S OTHER LIVES

This two-year period gave me confidence. I knew now that the Bridey Murphy experiment could be duplicated and that I could do it. I continued my work.

Tom was a Marine, which meant scheduling was difficult, but on February 7, 1965, we were able to meet again.

Apart from the vivid description of his death state and his speaking a foreign language, our first session had been quite ordinary. Now, in Tom's second session, his past-life patterns start to emerge.

In this session he reexperienced two lives. The first was in 1912 in Norway and was not remarkable. There was no discussion of his death or the cause of death. The second, an earlier life chronologically, took place in France.

Tom, now "Peter Foulke," described the beautiful countryside as he traveled through many towns and forests. He said, for example, that "Bradfire" forest was one of the nicest places he had ever seen.

In questioning, no events of any import seemed to occur until we moved to the death scene. This dialogue followed:

How old were you when you died? Do you see a scene now when you left this life?
Not old — forties — about forty.
How did you die?
Died in bed.
Of old age?
No, heart trouble; drinking.
And what happened after you died? Do you want to tell me about this?
Go away from the building — going north — just leaving.
What form are you in?
Well, white — silver form. It's pretty good. Going away — getting away from everything. This happened. Leaving people

24

that hated. Just leave.

What's the purpose of death? Why do we die?

Purpose? We just die. Things don't go away. We die and we — can go on.

Why should the body die and the soul live?

Well, the body is just the soul's shield. It takes all the blows and everything caused by the human hate, despise. The body dies — it has to.

Is there anything else?

Move on.

Which way?

Toward better things — you move to improvement — trying to look for happiness — not so much just achievement. You have to move. If you stayed in one place, you wouldn't be progressive. Move on and you see and live more full — better.

LEARNING FROM OUR SESSIONS

At the time of these sessions, I could only observe and learn. I faithfully transcribed the tapes and read and reread the material. Learning to grasp the valuable clues hidden in each and every regression session would come with experience. For instance, at the time I did not understand the implications of the past-life material about alcohol Tom was presenting. In two lives, his deaths, one from the tavern stabbing and one from heart disease, involved alcohol. At the time of our sessions, Tom was already a heavy drinker. He died suddenly in 1979, killed instantly in an alcohol-related car accident. Had I been more aware of the patterns that can occur from lifetime to lifetime, I might have seen the obvious correlation of Tom's present life with his past lives in regard to alcohol use. Perhaps I could have helped him bring about the changes he needed to make to avoid a repetition of his destructive alcohol use. But perhaps not. I had so very much to learn about the patterns and lessons of lifetimes.

Of course, this brings us to the more expansive issues of fatalism and predestination which are certainly worthy of a greater discussion than what can be covered briefly here. Admittedly, I don't have all the answers. In the grand scheme of the karmic pattern and the infusion of Grace, I simply don't know how fixed one's time of death is, nor whether the conditions surrounding it will necessarily follow predictable patterns from past-life experiences. Where there are clues given, such as alcohol abuse related to violent death in Tom's case, surely we should act upon them. Even with a predetermined time of death, the quality of his life until that point could have been greatly enhanced had he come to terms with his alcohol abuse. I have come to believe that past-life regression has therapeutic value if it helps us to understand our present lives and to make the changes necessary to clear away the wreckage of past lives.

AFTER-SESSION EVENTS

Reading about a regression experience is completely different from being there in person. The body movements of a subject being regressed are sometimes unusual and almost always different from those made in the conscious state. Subjects wring their hands, smile and laugh, cry and sob.

Often after the session, the memory door is still open and the subject will continue to talk in great detail about the events he or she has experienced. For instance, during a regression, one woman thought she was a servant in a house; afterwards, as she continued to "live" the experience, she realized she was the wife of the man she had served.

Sometimes the memory door closes but the subject continues to behave for a little while as if still in the regressed state. This was the case with a young man who experienced a past life as a leper. Others considered him — and he considered himself — unclean; he was disgusted with his body, which the disease caused to rot away before his eyes. After the session, he immediately got up and went over to the sink, where he washed his hands over and over. I watched and asked, "What are you doing?" Only then did he realize he was doing something unusual. There was still the need to wash his hands after being considered unclean. He was quite unaware of his action. He was astonished when I told him he had been washing his hands for almost 10 minutes.

The repellent nature of leprosy and the subject's reaction brings up the question of dealing with "disagreeable" episodes in past lives. If the session brings forward a violent or traumatic life or episode, the subject tends not to recall it consciously when brought out of hypnosis. His or her subconscious protector takes over. In these cases I doubt if it is necessary or beneficial to share the content of the session with the subject, and I rarely do so, except when a subject makes a serious request, and then only after a month or two has passed. Odd as this sounds, no subject has demanded to hear the tape if I explained it was a tragic or difficult lifetime. Perhaps some inner voice or guidance reassures them that the experience of the regression in itself is enough. The subject who experienced himself as a leper followed that life's experience into and through death and achieved peace and understanding. He had little need for conscious recall in this life. It seems to be true that reexperiencing past lives, no matter how traumatic or violent, can have positive effects.

Another time, I guided a woman into a past life as an American Indian. She came to me, she said, because her life had always been sad. She had a good job and enough money and a loving husband and child, yet she always felt sad. The recall opened dramatically. Her small band was attacked by another tribe while the men were away. The older women, the old men, and all the children were slaughtered. A few of the desirable younger women and maidens were taken as slaves. The subject watched her two children being killed. She was taken captive and barely survived the trek to her new home and a warrior husband. The subject was able to tell this much; the remainder of the hour session was filled with floods of tears. She cried for 40 minutes. Not knowing what else to do, I simply let her cry. As her anguish subsided, I gave positive suggestions about forgiveness and about closing the door to the past. Then I brought her back to the present.

When I saw the woman and her husband months after the session I hardly recognized her. It was as if a giant weight of resentment had been lifted. She talked differently; she laughed; she walked more lightly. I believe she made a major breakthrough in changing her pattern of habitual sadness. She said she felt wonderful about the session, and had no need or desire to hear the tape; I saw no reason to give her a copy or to play it for her.

Except for floods of tears, I have had no real problems in regression work. Not everyone has instant success either. This is a new field, a new science, a new study. There are no guarantees whatsoever. My early years were experimental; there were no manuals or courses. But I strove always for high standards of ethics and professionalism.

As past-life regression becomes more accepted as therapy, there will be the need for more schools and the sharing of knowledge. There is great need for therapeutic responsibility; when dealing with any trauma there are risks.

In these early years I had only the vaguest idea of the challenge I was accepting. This is human *reality*, with all the shadows and all the joy. Past-life regression is looking into the most secret, complicated inner workings and the profound simplicity of the soul. There is far more to humanity than behavior and statistics.

The psyche is the human soul. Psychology, as I see it, is the study or the science of the soul. Past-life exploration is, to me, in-depth soul study, the real essence and the real meaning of tomorrow's psychology.

The psychology of the past — and unfortunately, of the present — has sometimes concentrated on behavior to the exclusion of other things. I believe this produces a narrow and stunted view of the soul. There is more to people than mere behavior. Working with past lives shows me how much more there is to a person's psyche than old-school psychologists will admit. The behaviorist view of an earlier generation of psychologists seems to me too distant and cold compared with the enriching humanism of the past-lives approach.

Through the continuous thread of lifetimes, with their patterns and lessons, I am beginning to view humanity in a clear new light. Deep within each of us is a timeless, sensitive soul seeking to unfold and open into the light. This unfolding I call the "human adventure."

Endnotes:

[1]Morey Bernstein, *The Search for Bridey Murphy* (Garden City, NY: Doubleday, 1956.)

[2]"Now I want you to tell me..." is an outdated method of questioning a subject. I would not use such a directive approach today; modern hypnosis uses indirect, open-ended questioning. For examples of the newer method, see "Accessing Your Soul's Memory" in the Appendix.

Chapter Two

MOVING INTO ACTION

The class philosopher, Henry has no use for pseudo-intellectuals.
He enjoys life, death, adventure, and beauty.
Included in his future plans are hypnosis, travel, and writing.
Ashby High School Yearbook, 1964

Watatic 1964, the Ashby High School yearbook, had it right. After two years of regression experiments I knew where my life was going and what the next adventure would be.

I had taken all the courses I could take and read all the books I could read. For instance, in high school I devoured books about Franz Anton Mesmer, the father of hypnotism.[1] Now I needed more, and the only place to get it was the Edgar Cayce Foundation in Virginia Beach, Virginia, home of the Association for Research and Enlightenment (A.R.E.).[2]

I sold or gave away almost all my possessions — my record albums and recording equipment, even my car. (This paring down was to become a pattern marking periods of major change and growth.) I lingered in Massachusetts until Thanksgiving so I could spend the holiday with my family. Then, taking only traveling clothes and my tapes, notes, and transcripts of regression sessions, along with the money I had saved by working weekends and evenings in an apple orchard, I got on a bus for "college." I matriculated, unannounced, one December night in 1964. I didn't have a plan; I didn't even know where I could sleep.

I did know one thing: I needed to learn more about past-life regression work. My technique as a hypnotist had improved, and I had kept accurate transcripts and case studies.

I was acquainted — barely — with Edgar Cayce; I had read about him in the Bridey Murphy book. I knew he was America's preeminent psychic and that he had conducted "readings," or discourses, given in a self-induced hypnotic sleep. I knew that he was a recognized source of documented past-life information, and although he did not conduct "regressions," he did speak of people's past lives.[3]

I also knew the name of his son. I had been impressed by one of Hugh Lynn Cayce's taped lectures on reincarnation. So when I got to Virginia Beach I looked up Hugh Lynn's address in the telephone book, cadged a ride to his house, and rang his bell.

"Here I am," I announced. "I've been doing past-life regressions. I have tapes and transcripts. Teach me." Or words to that effect.

It was evening. Hugh Lynn and his wife, Sally, were just leaving for a dinner engagement. Instead of laughing at this, a naive, brash teenager on their doorstep, they kindly arranged for me to stay at the A.R.E. headquarters building, where I could also study.

The next day I had the first of many talks with Hugh Lynn. He seemed interested in my work and asked me to give a talk and demonstration to a large group of the members, but I had sense enough to know I wasn't ready. Years later I was to give speeches and workshops at the A.R.E.; now, I was a student.

I was full of doubts and questions. I had tried to ignore them, but they would not go away. What could past-life study teach? What could be gained from knowledge of the unconscious mind? Where was I going and how? Did people think I was crazy for pursuing this "stuff?" Was I wasting my time and money? Did people want to know about past lives? Sometimes I doubted it. I wondered, "What am I doing this for? What do I do with this information, anyway? Is it all just wishful thinking? What if it *is* real? Will we have to return again and again and again until we get our lives 'right?'"

In 1964, the Cayce Foundation headquarters was in a big white building that had been donated by Cayce supporters as a hospital where healing procedures from the Cayce readings could be utilized. The building is a Virginia Beach landmark, perched high on a hill overlooking the Atlantic Ocean. In 1964 it contained offices, a small rack of books for sale, and a library that housed thousands of books on topics that paralleled the Cayce readings. It was and is one of the most important libraries in the world in parapsychology. In addition, the library contains all 14,253 readings, cross-referenced for anyone to read and study.

The upper floors of the building, where I stayed, had a number of rooms which members of the A.R.E. could use while doing research and study. An adjacent building housed a print shop and an auditorium for conferences. (Since then, the guest rooms have been turned into offices; the library has been moved to a new library/conference center; the single rack of books has grown into a large and active bookstore. The presses are still rolling and computers help the A.R.E. keep in touch with a membership of more than 76,000.)

THE CAYCE READINGS

The more than 14,000 Cayce readings are a fascinating but difficult study. The technical language and vocabulary were far beyond my high school comprehension. Also, the flow of subconscious, psychic, channeled material was a whole new world for me. I could not just sit and read it as I would a storybook; it was hard even to understand most sentences. I am a good reader, but the material was very deep and unfamiliar, and written in a complicated syntax.

I also read just about every book in the library on hypnosis and age-regression experiments. I averaged about

Illustration #2
The landmark building in Virginia Beach, Virginia,
where I stayed on my first sojourn at the Association for
Research and Enlightenment, Inc., in 1964. The modern
building is the library, conference center and classroom
building of Atlantic University, which offers a master's
degree in transpersonal studies.

one book per day, reading late into the night during the month I stayed at the A.R.E.

Here are some of the key questions I explored.

Can we remember past lives?

Yes, we can recall past lives. But if I could prove it absolutely there would be no need for this book. Reincarnation, which is what we are talking about, would be accepted by everyone — or almost everyone, as almost everyone now accepts that the world is round.

We use electricity every day, but no one can define it. We fall in love, and who can define that? We accept many beliefs we cannot prove, and that does not affect their reality.

Here is a parable from Kahlil Gibran that illustrates my point.

Other Seas

A fish said to another fish, "Above this sea of ours there is another sea, with creatures swimming in it — and they live there even as we live here."

The fish replied, "Pure fancy! Pure fancy! When you know that everything that leaves our sea by even an inch, and stays out of it, dies. What proof have you of other lives in other seas?"[4]

Are we making it all up?

I remembered my youth and the Santa Claus myth that all adults seemed to be in conspiracy to protect. I wanted real answers; I did not want fairy tales. I had peeked on Christmas Eve and discovered that Santa had an amazing resemblance to my dad. (And his helper was dressed in a bathrobe just like my mom's!) That's when I started questioning how many other things were not what people said — and not just the obvious ones.

So in the library I read books by other serious researchers who had done regression work that paralleled my experiments.

Answers began to unfold slowly. There was no great

flash of light nor instant revelation; it was not like that. Some things did not fit well and I put them aside. But slowly, bit by bit, things began to fit together. As it turned out, it took a few more years of living, learning, and growing before I proved to my own satisfaction that people just do not make up past lives — that consensus reality (which would be, for example, the traditional rejection of the concept of reincarnation in Western culture) isn't always "the way it is." Even when no one *believed* it, the world was still round.

Meanwhile, I delved for the answers in the Cayce readings.[5] Surprisingly, Cayce was quite wary of reincarnation in his conscious state; but in his subconscious state he was an outspoken advocate. His readings convey that we can discover our talents and strengths in past lives; that recalling them is part of soul development. Two resulting major benefits of past-life recall are thus peace (that could not have come from merely trying to *understand* current difficulties) and the realization that life is continuous.[6]

These were fine explanations of the advantages of understanding past lives. But I could not find anything by Cayce that said we could prove their existence to anyone but ourselves. This dilemma led to my biggest question.

What role does imagination play in past-life recall experiences?

In past-life exploration, many people worry that their experiences are "only imagination." At times, I suspect this is so. Nevertheless, further research may reveal that even simple imagination may have strong messages embedded in symbols, as in nocturnal dreams.

Cayce suggests that imagination is the avenue to the visual faculty of the mind. My own experiments suggested that hypnosis enhances the image part of the mind; that is, people who can consciously visualize, imagine, or daydream seem to be better subjects for hypnosis. Years later I was to understand the reason for this: hypnosis stimulates and enhances right-brain activity and visualization is a right-brain activity. There is a definite link between the part of the mind that stores and retrieves images and past-life work. The processing of visual information is one function of the mind; we do this all the time when we recall anything from our experience.

The creation of visual fantasy is another function of the mind; we do this whenever we daydream. The functions are separate and distinct, but they are often confused. Fantasy is fantasy. Retrieval of a stored image, whether the image is conscious or unconscious, is retrieval of a stored image.

But there is a fuzzy border between the two. That overlap is what causes confusion in many people — thinking that all images are fantasy. For instance, consider two Walt Disney movies. Real-story, true-event "imagination" is exemplified in the movie, *The Living Desert*, while fantasy-imagination is exemplified in *Fantasia*.

My own regression experiments had shown me that most people recall events through scenes, pictures, and images, though the other senses can trigger recall of past memories. A few subjects said they "heard" the information in their minds and repeated it. A few others said they "felt" or "sensed" the information that came forward. One said she "smelled the ocean," and much of her recall was triggered by her sense of smell.

But for most, the image facility is the key or the doorway to the past-life memory. Most of my subjects' recall was of images and scenes, and because they had not *consciously* "seen" these images before, I could understand that some thought of it, or mislabeled it, as imagination. But this "imagination" stayed with them long after the session. With time comes the realization of what is valid and meaningful. Time separates the wheat from the chaff in past-life recall; the impressions that last for a long time are more meaningful than passing flights of fantasy.

When I searched the Cayce readings on this question I discovered an entirely new link of the imagination with past-life study. They said that the ability to imagine other places came from having lived there before. I responded to this statement with a surge of enlightenment. The imagination is not in conflict or opposed to past-life memory; it is a helpful tool.

"So that's why my subjects can describe a particular place or time period so vividly," I thought. "Because it is actually remembered from their own past!" People are always so quiet in libraries, but I wanted to shout for joy when I found this nugget. In fact, Cayce told one person specifically to use her imagination to fill in details of a past life and another person to simply imagine what might have been served at dinnertime. One individual was told odors and visions would remind him of a past life in the desert. (This reminded me of the woman who started her regression by smelling the ocean.)

What are the warnings about recalling our past lives?

The Cayce readings caution us not to seek past-life information unless we are balanced in purpose.[7] Also, advice is given not to dwell on the past nor to abuse one's talent for recalling it. One person was cautioned that past-life exploration could cause him to be "sidetracked" from his present life.

I heartily agree. My concern was not that a person would get "stuck" in the past, because that has never happened in my experience,[8] but that someone might dwell on the past or, worse, take it too seriously. I was beginning to realize that we are given a series of lives specifically to be able to start anew — that we are born again to be free of the past, not sentenced by it. Insight and self-knowledge of our past can bring benefit, can sometimes help us change and grow. But the past is *past*. The readings encourage people to study themselves and their past lives and caution only of the "abuse" of recall. I had faith that if my intent was unconditional love in helping others there was nothing to be afraid of.

Why can't everyone recall past lives?

In one reading, Cayce answered that it was simply *doubt*. To me, that summed it up in a neat, one-word package. But really, there are many more factors than that. Some people are afraid of what they will uncover. Some people still think hypnosis is like a truth serum that will cause them to blurt out some deep secret. (Actually, a subject will reveal only what he or she wants to reveal.) Perhaps a bigger block than either of these is over-anxiousness. Some people are too eager and try to rush the process. The best subjects are neither too apprehensive nor too zealous. The qualities I value most are honest skepticism and an open and honest mind that is willing to accept new experience.

What are other recall techniques?

If using the imagination can help recapture past-life experience, are there other methods? Looking into water, a mirror, a crystal ball, or one's own mind can be good tools for meditation. But a more practical method to enhance past-life recall is to study the time period. Naturally, the Cayce readings were able to state *which* time periods to study for the individuals who expressed interest. But we are all drawn to certain eras of history and that's a good starting place for study.

When I read this material in the A.R.E. library, I wondered how many people already subconsciously study a certain era or place because of their earlier ties there. The readings give sound advice; anyone can get insight into themselves by studying times and places that deeply interest them. To me, this gave clues as to why some friends only read a certain era of history and others studied only certain places. And the opposite: why some people disliked a particular time or place — because of negative experiences, perhaps? One young woman I had recently regressed had had a sad and tragic life in China. After the session, she confided that she hated Chinese food and disliked everything Chinese. In her present life she had no ties whatsoever to the Orient.

Travel can also help us get in touch with past lives by stimulating recall through familiarity, say the Cayce readings. To various individuals he mentioned, respectively, travels to Williamsburg (where a woman would then be able to remember a past life with her present husband), to Jamestown, to Palestine (which would remind the person of a crusade experience as well as an earlier incarnation) and to the Connecticut coast (which would be reminiscent of an early settlement experience). Another was told that merely sitting on the sand would bring up Persian memories. The readings even suggested the combination of travel and activity to reexperience events.

I loved the suggestions for travel. I took the advice and launched a new career of extensive travel. Studying was a nice, passive approach to past lives. Actual travel to other lands suited me better. There are feelings and vibrations that can only be lived; I do not find them in books. Little did I realize it then, but I was destined to fill a number of passports and to live in and travel to many countries. I love travel and recommend it as an exciting, if sometimes difficult, method of stimulating inner experience.

Reading is a memory stimulant, Cayce said. Among the many books he recommended were historical novels and several books of the Bible, such as the stories of John the Baptist and Mary Magdalene and the first chapters of Acts.

Many readings recommend meditation to stimulate visions of past lives and/or to recall specific details from a lifetime past.

What about dreams of past lives?

The Cayce readings suggest that dreams can help us recall past-life information. People were told that dreams recall major events in other lives — Egyptian, American Indian, and Roman, for example. The study of our dreams, along with daily prayer and meditation, is one of the main paths on the road to the spiritual, according to the readings.

MY DAYS AT THE A.R.E.

Soon after my arrival at the A.R.E. I started my personal dream journal. I put a notebook and pen by my bed. Before retiring I gave myself a suggestion to recall my dreams and write them down immediately upon awakening. There were many people, both staff and visitors, to help me interpret them — dreams are symbols that must be translated into words and ideas.

There are many kinds of dreams, I learned: dreams to relieve stress, sexual dreams, dreams of fear, dreams of flying and, occasionally, dreams of past lives. Some dreams have personal meanings that apply only to ourselves. Studying my dreams was fun and I achieved some new, past-life insights, but to me this method was more haphazard than a guided regression.

The dreams that have the most significance are recurring dreams because, as a Cayce reading explains, they can validate past-life information. The recurrence of a dream definitely means a message is trying to reach the dreamer. To me, such a dream (even, or especially, a frightening one) needs to be discussed, explored, looked at, studied, meditated upon or prayed about in order that its message be fully understood. If the message is from a past life, a combination of dream analysis and regression can help understand the memory.

The link between dreams and other lifetimes is not yet fully understood, but I think it is clear that dreams and daydreams are a key to unlocking the mystery of the subconsious. Carl G. Jung said, "The unconscious helps by communicating things to us, or making figurative allusions. It has other ways, too, of informing us of things which by all logic we could not possibly know. Consider synchronistic phenomena, premonitions, and dreams that come true."[9]

MANY KINDS OF EDUCATION

My mind was filling with ideas and inspiration. To balance so much mental exercise, I did yoga exercises in my room. I washed my clothes in the bathroom in the evening and hung them to dry near the radiator. I cooked my meals in the kitchen (everyone cooked for himself) and shared many a stimulating conversation with staff and visitors at mealtimes. I walked on the beach. Virginia Beach was then quite open, with ample dunes to explore. The years have brought in more hotels and condominiums. But the spirit of the A.R.E. has remained the same — there are usually sensitive souls around to share sparkling conversation and experiences.

In fact, the biggest benefit I received at the Foundation in the mid-1960s was the meetings with other seeking people. In daily conversation with people living or working at the Cayce Foundation, I began to see honest minds with valid questions. These were not carnival psychics but real people with real experiences. Not only had Cayce questioned what this work was all about, those after him did also. I was not alone with my questions.

The A.R.E. confirmed my research and gave substantiation to my work. I was excited by the readings and realized I was not alone; I was not "weird." Some people were there to study Cayce's information on holistic health. Some came to test their extrasensory perception. Many came to study the prehistoric past; others, to look into the future. People came from all over the world with searching minds and most found the answers they craved. Even skeptics were welcome and many broadened their views. The Cayce material taught me that I could now look at life in a much fuller way. The information broadened my horizons and confirmed my own research that there is continuity to life. It now seemed that five or six lifetimes was no more miraculous than just one. To hear honest and sincere people discussing their previous lives as openly as talking about last year's trip to Europe was comforting.

SOUTH AND NORTH

As the weather got colder, I felt the call of warm, sunny beaches. Staff members at the A.R.E. gave me the names of a delightful Florida chiropractor husband-and-wife team to contact who were active in using hypnotherapy.

While in Miami Beach, I gladly received a series of psychic firsts: meeting my very first psychics; my first psychic reading; my first palm reading, an impressive one; and before I left, being guided by the chiropractor through the deepest and best session of hypnosis I had experienced until then.

41

In New England there had been no one to work with me to guide me as a subject. I had experienced good sessions by using pre-recorded tapes and made a couple of tapes myself, but this was my first "live" session of hypnosis.

Traveling back north in the spring I was in Norfolk, Virginia, and ran out of cash. I had an out-of-state personal check that I kept for emergency use, but because it was a weekend no bank was open. A sign on a bar said "checks cashed," and although I was too young to drink, I went in and explained my situation. The bartender asked for my local address, but I had none. He asked if I knew anyone locally; I did not.

He said, "I would like to cash this for you, but I can't."

I said, "Well, I *was* staying at the Cayce Foundation a few months ago; it's about 20 miles away."

His face lighted up and he said, "Well, then, of course I'll cash it for you." I thought he was kidding. But he told me to sign it, and counted out the cash. "They're all real good people over there," he said. Or something close to that; I was so full of appreciation I still don't recall his exact words.

To me, this experience explains better than almost anything else what the Cayce Foundation is all about. The Cayce material taught me a great deal; the Cayce philosophy and way of life, with its motto above the main entrance, "That we may make manifest the love of God and man," taught me even more.

I believed I could gain still more understanding of soul development. The way to do it was clear: do the work. I could whole-heartedly welcome the field of inner exploration. If I did the work, went in and explored, if I were willing to take the steps, the answers would come. If I were willing to learn, if I had patience, if I were determined to understand the secrets of the mind, what the mind is, and to uncover my purpose and spiritual destiny, then I would *have* to do the work.

Other people might misunderstand or reject this type of search; that must not be my attitude. I would search. If I were hurt or others were hurt, then I would put it down and stop. But if I could gain understanding and knowledge and realization of self ... if I could know myself through the exploration of past lives ... if I could attain insight, then that would be the course I had to follow. To dive in. To search. To learn.

Endnotes:

[1]Franz Anton Mesmer (1734-1815), Austrian physician. He believed that "animal magnetism," a mysterious inner fluid, had healing properties. It could sometimes be transferred from person to person by touch, inducing a sleeplike state from which the patients awoke cured or much improved. Mesmerism was discredited by the hostile 18th century medical establishment and Mesmer died in obscurity, but some doctors continued to experiment and improve his techniques. One was a Scottish physician, Dr. James Braid, working in the 1840s, who coined the word "hypnosis," from the Greek root, *hypnos* (sleep). Interest in hypnosis reawakened in the late 19th century and has continued until today.

[2]Three organizations have been created to express and promote the worthy ideals which were articulated through Edgar Cayce: the Association for Research and Englightenment, the Edgar Cayce Foundation, and Atlantic University.

The Association (A.R.E.) was founded to promote activities for individuals to interact with information in the readings. It is an open membership organization dedicated to making available to all interested persons the readings of Edgar Cayce, and related materials and experiences, through publications, lectures, conferences, home study, group study and specialized programs. They consider Search for God Study Groups their most significant work.

The Foundation serves as the custodian of the Edgar Cayce readings and related materials, which it makes available to researchers and organizations. It also maintains a collection of books and journals in parapsychology, comparative religion, and mysticism.

Atlantic University, which reopened in 1985, offers a Master of Arts in Transpersonal Studies, emphasizing the integration of body, mind and spirit; and of Eastern and Western thought. Residential and independent study courses are offered. Atlantic University's role is to provide a suitable environment for the study of questions of ultimate meaning and personal growth.

[3]Edgar Cayce (1877-1945) manifested one of the truly remarkable psychic talents of all time. Widely known today through the scores of books published about his work, he was able to enter self-hypnosis and give accurate and helpful information on a virtually unlimited range of subjects. The transcripts of this psychically given information are called "readings." For many years the information requested of Edgar Cayce related mainly to physical ills. The repeated accuracy of his diagnoses and the effectiveness of the sometimes unorthodox treatments he prescribed made him a medical phenomenon. The fact that he needed only the name and current location of an individual anywhere in the world in order to give a careful diagnosis of the physical condition compounded the mystery. Eventually the scope of his work expanded to include information and advice on thousands of subjects, including mental and spiritual counsel, metaphysics, parapsychology, religion, reincarnation, and prophecy of personal and world events.

[4]Kahlil Gibran, *The Forerunner: His Parables and Poems* (New York: Alfred A. Knopf, 1961).

[5]The Cayce readings are arranged numerically. The first number is the one assigned to the person who received the reading, for confidentiality, and the second is the reading number given this person. Thus Reading 294-19 refers to a person, Cayce himself, and to his 19th reading.

[6]The first mention of past lives is usually said to have occurred on Aug. 10, 1923. However, it has recently been discovered that there is an earlier one, on April 22, 1911, when his secretary, Gladys Davis, made a notation in Reading

4841-1. This reference, being so unexpected and about a topic unknown to those present, must have slipped by without anyone's remarking of it or understanding its significance.

[7]I heartily agree with the Cayce admonition, "Beware unless you are balanced in purpose." If you are a balanced person, and your purpose is balanced with your ideals, you can gain great insight from past-life exploration. But if you seriously need psychological or psychiatric help, believing that the solution to your problems lies only in your past-life experiences may be a serious mistake.

[8]No serious or professional hypnotist would allow a subject to get "stuck" in the past. It has never happened to me, nor have I ever heard of such a case. I do have one undocumented story about a stage entertainer who undertook a successful past-life experiment, but did not properly close the door to the subconscious memories at the end of the session. The subject functioned normally but was disoriented for a few days after the experience.

[9]Carl Jung, *Memories, Dreams, Reflections* (New York: Vintage Books, 1965), p. 302.

Chapter Three

THE TURNING POINT

Belief consists in accepting the affirmations of the soul;
Unbelief, in denying them.
Ralph Waldo Emerson, *Representative Men*

In 1974, my friend Patricia and I set out to drive by van through the United States and Mexico. On the first morning, we picked up a young man who was hitchhiking from Boston to Lansdowne, Pennsylvania, a town just south of Philadelphia, where he was due that evening at a church rehearsal where he played the organ. The three of us talked, and joked all day. We all enjoyed the conversation, so much so that we drove a full hour south of Chuck Shiplove's destination.

Turning, we headed back to Lansdowne. During that last hour, Chuck talked about the recent death of a young woman who was very close to him. Her death left him with the feeling that their relationship was incomplete, unfulfilled.

Trust and friendship had developed among the three of us. I wanted to help Chuck. While it is difficult now to reconstruct the sequence of events exactly, I think I simply asked Chuck if he wanted to participate in an exercise that might help him understand the loss of his friend. I must have explained that I had done similar work before. He agreed. I suggested he mentally look into the eyes of the young woman, to send love from his eyes into her eyes, and to allow her to fade away. Chuck responded very well to this exercise.

Then, spontaneously, with his eyes still closed, he held his right knee and talked about a pain he felt there and had — with no apparent cause — felt at other times in his life. I suggested we look for the cause of that pain, and I then guided him through a few steps of a technique for viewing past lives without hypnosis.[1]

I asked Chuck to imagine enlarging himself to twice his normal size; then returning to his normal size; then floating safely a few inches above himself; and then returning to his body. Eventually, after a few more steps, I asked him to come down to Earth once again, place his feet on the Earth, and describe his feet. (In retrospect, this seems very strange and a confusing direction to give in a moving van.) Chuck did the exercise.

What happened next filled me with astonishment and awe.

CHUCK'S EXPERIENCE

Chuck began to talk. In fact, he began a monologue that lasted 45 minutes, and which I stopped only because I knew he was due at his rehearsal.

First he described himself as an old man in an Eskimo-like tribe in a frozen land. His tribe could not support its elderly; there was simply not enough food. Chuck suffered the fate the tribe prescribed in this situation: one of his legs was broken so he couldn't follow the band as it migrated. He was left to die.

Next, without pause, he started to talk about a life in a place he called "Atlantinus" or "Atlanticinus" and later, "Oceanus Atlantis." He was delivering a speech. His message was apocalyptic: he told the people in his audience they had five years left before the land was destroyed, and he begged them to flee with him and other leaders.

As a guide or facilitator I had conducted many past-life regressions. A few were dull, most were good, some were excellent. But what was happening with Chuck, right here in my van, was phenomenal beyond anything I had yet seen or imagined.

Chuck was about five minutes into his speech before I realized we had a tape recorder in the van. I started recording, picking up his speech in mid-sentence.

CHUCK
Spring, 1974
Near Lansdowne, Pennsylvania

First Session

....need to be fed tonight, to be clothed tomorrow, and to love tomorrow after. You will follow every single origin that has been before you, only to follow a conclusion you have not known. You will be part of me. You will be part of ourselves. We are teach[ing] each other. You must follow. Pack up everything you own. Pack up your idols. Pack up your possessions. Tell your children, tell your grandparents you must leave them. Break every tie.

There is a mountain and a valley beyond it. There is a spring. There is everything ever that we have ever had; that we have never had. There is a being within us so strong that you cannot deny it. I will lead you; believe in me. We will go to a valley that no one has ever seen or no one will ever see again. There is a forest, a veritable forest. There is unanimity in our purpose, but our purpose is to be beyond, to a point where people will precede us and antecede us. People who have known us and never known us. Generations of generations will come after us and they will know where we were but they've never been. They will be in places to the north and to the south. They will to be with the fair-skinned people from the East. We will create our own, Atlantinus — Atlantinus — Atlantinus! We will be there! We will die with you so that we will live with you. When our race is with our race, we will be.

We will be what has never been, and we will die, but we will live, and you've got to be with us because that is what Louana was ever.[2]

That's what she pointed. That's why I hurt. I've been among you, but I've been away from you for years. It's Louana. I've come out. She knew. She knew she had to break away so that I would be me, but it's us and it's me, so follow. Will you follow! Will you be with us! Will you be with me! Will you be with the passion and will you be with the purpose! Will you rise above your lowly rags and will you rise above your lowly existence! Will you be something that has never been! Will you dare to conquer what is unconquered! Will you go with me! Then we shall go. Then we shall go. Then we shall go.

[Chuck next spoke quietly in a language I did not know, though I am familiar with Latin and several European languages. With the next question, I was able to guide him back into English. I was relieved, for two reasons: it made the session intelligible and it reassured me that my skills were sufficient to guide him during the session. The possibility that I might not be able to was very real, as Chuck was totally living the experience.]

What's happening now?
People.
What are they doing?
They're following a course that cannot be followed.
Why?
Its conclusion is so soon. They're abandoning what made them what they are to become, something they can never be. Too fast! They don't realize what they are. They can't. If they did, they'd slow down. They'd teach their children, but they're not teaching their children. They're not even teaching themselves.
What are they doing?
They're following a principle that can't be followed.
What principle?
They're selfish. They can't be. They're worshipping, they're worshipping the Power. They can't. It's not the Power they should worship. They should worship what made them powerful.

49

They don't understand the difference.

What made them powerful?

They don't know. They know that they're gifted. They know they've conquered, but they don't know why, and they think they're omnipotent, but they're not. They're human. They're subject to weaknesses. I'm trying to tell them. They won't listen. There's a few. Launch ships. Go places you've never been. Start what we've started, but start it. Start it so they can be themselves and not what they're not. We'll kill each other off; you know it. You know we'll do something we can't ever recover from. You've got to go. You've got to leave. You've got to follow me.

You've got to follow me to places that we've never been. We're explorers! We're adventurers! We're not self-effacing. We're not dignified without our dignity. They will follow themselves until they die. They will create powers they can't control. You can't allow it. We'll kill each other from within. We've got to start over. I know we do. We've got to start slower; we've got to realize what human dignity and value is. We've got to realize behavior. We've got to realize our minds.

Don't you understand that people are worshipping us, but we're not worshipping-ful? They are worshipping us as ultra-beings and we're not. Can it be that we're not? Can it be that we've learned something for not learning?

There are people that have been before us. We've got to find them. We've got to find their secrets. Why are we different? Why are our colors different? Why are our heads bigger, our noses longer? Why are our fingers longer? Why are we taller? It's not from something we've learned. It's from something that's within us. It's inherent. We've got to learn it before we advance any further. We've got to take time to study what we are and what we will become. We can't be powerful without until we're powerful within, and we can't ever be powerful within until we realize our potential.

You who believe me, you've got to follow me and Moran. You've got to follow me and Moran and Estes and Challis. You've got to follow the four of us. We are the Quadrant. We are the ones who are what we were.

If you can see beyond your fingers, if you can see beyond the sunset, you'll know it's not the sun we revolve around. You know it's not ourselves we revolve around. It's a universe. It's a galaxy. You know that we are not the seasons. We're the reasons for the seasons. You don't know the reasons.

You must know that the reason for man and woman is not because of some, some divineness within self. Did we create man and woman? Did we create learning? Did we create our noses, our bodies, our beings? Did we create sexual fulfillment? Did we create learning? No! We *were* created.

We are what our predecessors were and what they built upon. So we must continue to build. Think of the horizons we can expand. Think of the enormous structures, the enormous learning. Think of the philosophy, the etiology. Think of what we are. Think of what we are now. It's one billionth of what we can become, not in our lifetime, not in our children's lifetime, but it's up to us. We must propagate. We must procreate. We must go to our centers of learning. We cannot think that we are the end. We cannot believe that this is the absolute end of what we are. We are a steppingstone.

You're leading to destruction. Don't you understand? There will be mutants. There will be emaciated faces. There will be people who will never arise beyond what half of what we are.

We must go to other lands, other horizons. There are places to the south that we have not ventured to. We must launch ships. We must launch everything that we have. We must build cities. We must build waystones. We must build pointers to where we have never been.

We will build again. We will arise, only slower. We must use every single ounce of mentality. And we must learn what we are so that we can become what we will be. What will our children be? Will they be self-centered egotists? Will they be caught up with their own power? No. They can't be that. We'll never evolve. Think of what we can do. There are civilizations we haven't seen. We must be there. You *must* follow me. See my hand. See my eyes. See what they tell you. Don't listen to my words; see my being! Look at it! Look at it! It trembles! Look at it! We will be! We will conquer what we are to be, what we haven't been! We will reach! There is strength within us that has never been strengthly tested. We must be. We must arrive. If this is the end, we cannot look at ourselves with pride. We must abandon sex. We must abandon bodies. We must be outside our bodies. We must be mind. We must be, we must be mentality and spirit. We will cover oceans. We will cover mountains. We are! Understand that we are! Your politics are worthless. Your physical sensations are needless. Your starving, your hunger, they can be overcome. There will be — there will be people after us. There have been people before us. They are pointing the way to something, to somewhere we must follow. There are pathways that have been made but never recorded, and we will follow.

Look at me! Look at the strength! You know me as a leader. You know me as a strong man. You know me as a man who can move temples with a single word. You know me as someone who has power from within. You know me as parentless, as brotherless, as sisterless, but you do not know me! You must abandon yourself. You must abandon physical being. You must abandon pain and hurt and pleasure and surface. You must be from within. It has come from your very stomach, from your intestines. You must be able to look beyond what is to be seen.

....You will follow because I command it.... I dare command what you are.... what you think you are. I will lead because it is within me to lead and I question it not. I question not! I know that you are with me.... You will go now. You will pack. You will bring your asses, your donkeys, your lambs, your llamas, your goats. You will bring everything that was in you. Everything material, everything financial — you will abandon it! You will follow these hands. They will lay themselves down to the west and to the north. We will cross oceans. We must launch now before the entire Brotherhood abandons itself for power, and they will never do that successfully.

There is a power from underneath that will kill us. We will be abandoned. We will be cast into the ocean. We will die. We will sink. We cannot allow it. I give you five years, five years, 364 days times five. I give you calendars. I give you dates. Follow me. If we die, we die, but we'll die *living*. We will die living instead of dying slowly.

We must be, we must be better than what we are or else — or

else what have we striven for all these years? Our ships that go under, our vehicles that fly over mountains, are they to fly because we command them to fly? Did we invent them because we were the only inventors, or did we invent them so that after we die people will follow them? They will say, "Look at what our predecessors were. That is what we must become."

We must discover why we are so light and others dark. It is because there is a light within us. It is because we have the power that we do not deserve, but that we must continue. You must realize that drunkenness and immorality will never ever sacrifice or never ever replace spiritual immortality.

We will conquer.... We will rise above what we are. It is what Louana was. It is what her parents sanctioned. It is what I must continue and I will bear the burden if only, if only to die and leave you carrying it on. I will die helpless. I will die friendless. I will die, if only so that we can continue.

Do you think that we go underneath the water because we are so gifted that we looked in silver plates for mirrors that told us that we were omnipotent — that we were gods because we have seen others lower than ourselves? No. If all we are here for is self-preservation and for selfishness, then we are here for nothing! We are transient.

Follow me, follow Challis, follow Moran. We are the way. We have given you the knowledge. You must contain within you the need for understanding. Then we will conquer, from worlds beyond, from horizons beyond, we will *overcome* what we are to be — what others before us and after us need to be. And that is why I stand before you, and that is why I ask you: Will you follow? Will you be what our brothers cannot see? Will you be the preservation of a — of a goal? Will you lower yourselves with brothers [others]? Will you continue a race that can never give hope to be what we are? In only a thousand years to be what we are?

Have I reached that much? Is that single chord within you struck enough? Will you follow — Challis! Challis! Challis!

Then let us go to the west and tell them what we were and hope — and hope that those under us will never undermine what we've become, because we are the hope. We are the compassion, we are! And we can never be less than what we are. Let others die underneath rubble. Let others waste themselves in principles that we'll never know. Let us be beyond what we are. Let us rise above flesh to be what our spirits command. Let us leave now. Let us launch. Let us journey. Let us continue. Let us propagate and procreate. Let us carry on those principles of humanity that our brothers have forsaken for power. Let us be — let us continue — let us go!

MY DOUBTS REMOVED

Everyone has doubts, especially about new ideas and new discoveries. When does doubt become belief? At what point does belief become reality? Does a child, for example, believe it can walk when it sees other people walking, or when it takes the first unsure step, or when it can go a certain number of steps without falling? For me, belief in the existence of past lives turned into the reality of acceptance with Chuck. All my previous questioning and doubt suddenly took a quantum leap into unqualified conviction.

I had never met Chuck until the day we worked together, and as far as I can tell, he had nothing to gain by faking any of this recall. When we talked later, I discovered he had virtually no knowledge of the concept of past lives or even of hypnosis. He knew nothing of my previous explorations in mental recall.

Chuck did not know specifically what I was doing — neither did I, for that matter. At this point my sessions were very much learn-as-we-go affairs. So he did not want to please the hypnotist, a phenomenon some people mistakenly assume accounts for behavior under hypnosis.

I was not leading him with questions, nor directing him to a conclusion, as the session was almost all a monologue. My mind was fully occupied simply with trying to understand what was happening; I could hardly formulate questions at all, much less lead him in a preconceived direction.

When we started, I never imagined a full regression. I had only conducted such sessions in a controlled setting with preestablished procedures and at least a few witnesses.

To attempt anything more in an impromptu session in a van on a highway was the farthest thing from my mind; I hoped only for a few basic exercises. But the door opened to a full, in-depth, profound session. One step flowed easily into the next without effort and soon Chuck was in the deepest hypnosis. This was completely against my normal procedures. He was an able subject and seemed to have a flood of information waiting to burst forth — and it did. There was no stopping him. Rather than the usual question and answer approach, he began the monologue I eventually had to stop so he could get to his appointment.

I was astounded not only by Chuck's spontaneous speech, but also by his delivery. He spoke with commanding power and authority, in the voice of a man, not a youth (he was 18 at the time). He accented each important point by pounding on the dash of the van. I could not see his audience, but I could see and feel his pleading to them. There in my van, in the person of an 18-year-old, I was seeing the great leader of a lost people as he warned them of their approaching doom. I believed it would require a phenomenal imagination and vocabulary — more than Chuck had displayed in conversation — to create and deliver such a story.

I believed his Atlantinus to be Atlantis, the fabled lost island civilization, and the effect of his speech was all the more overwhelming because I believed his audience to have been inundated for thousands of years. I asked him later if he knew anything of Atlantis; he had no conscious knowledge of or interest in it. To him it was just a myth, an imaginary colony or a mythical island that had sunk in the ocean. (In the second session [to follow], however, he talks of Atlantis, rather than Atlantinus, adapting the word to fit my vocabulary.) After this session, Chuck had no conscious memory of what he had said. He was, however, shaken by the whole experience and knew that something unusual had happened. He left to go to his organ practice. We agreed to meet the next day.

THE SECOND DAY

When we met again, Chuck still had no recall of the session, and asked me what had happened. I made an exception to my usual practice and played the tape for him. (I made an exception with Chuck because he had no painful personal recall during his first regression.) When we had listened to about a third of the tape, he closed his eyes and started speaking again in a monologue. I sensed that listening to the tape might be enough to propel him back into the past time and asked him to be careful not to do that, since I hoped to discuss the tape with him and then conduct another session. However, he went spontaneously into past time, without detriment to himself or the session.

On this second day, he spoke in a tone of deep resignation about a time that seemed to follow the destruction of Atlantis. He spoke of the destruction; of how the people followed the principles of a person called "Pyramadis"; of what the people did; of the beginnings of the city of Rome. A great deal of history — not all of it history as modern historians recognize it — is related in this session.

CHUCK

Second Session

Conquer — there was no need to conquer. We were teaching, we were building — the principles of Pyramadis. We had constructed them. The ancients worshipped us. Why? Why did we destroy two cities? To prove our power over men, or to prove our power? Was it an accident? It was a tragedy. It couldn't have been our fault. No, we're the gifted. It was meant to be by purpose.

Ah, Challis. How I do respect you — I disagreed with you. I called him a coward in the face of nobility, for the only true patriotic thing to do was to leave. And Ares abandoned. He abandoned his entire principles to save face. He said he would start again, but he didn't. He and I have been warring ever since. No, Ares, your chance will never come again. They've outgrown us, because we outgrew ourselves. We had so much pride in what we were that we refused to look in mirrors for fear it would spoil the image. You know, I often wonder, when you were lecturing, how many people wrote your words, 'cause you were so divinely wrapped up in self, it was beyond you to lift a pen.

That light — what you must have thought when you saw the light. You didn't believe that a light could undermine your world. It was to be a glow. I curse you. I curse you and shall always curse you. The view — you are standing, watching us burn and I can't even feel enough hate to want to kill you. The time when I thought I'd most want to have you between my arms. I cry for you, for what you made yourself and your followers.

To the east they expect us. To the north there is ruin. To the south there is the sun. What would few follow? What did they follow? They don't know why. Maybe it's better. Maybe it's better....

[I told Chuck he had no right to curse anybody and he laughed.]

There is no curse. It is he who has cursed himself, and I am only the physical embodiment of that curse. He will die hating me for something that I am. He will die hating me because I am what he could never be. I am the sight for the blind. He is the sight from the mirror. I am the strength from within. It is in this hand; as long as he can never usurp my strength, he is nothing. He combatted that all his life, you know. He fought the Quadrant. He fought Challis. He hated Challis and despised him because Challis would not fight. He hated me because I would fight and he could not beat me. Yes, Estes, you are right. It is not for me to curse. I beg you forgive that weakness. The curse is beyond destiny. Let us go to the Hall. Let us go. The last vibration will be soon. The fire is ignited. What is there left but to ascend?

What is your name, your full name?

Moran Charras, Challis Karmas. Ares Vilas, Ares Vilas, Ares Vilas.

And what is the name of the land you are leaving?

I am not, I am not leaving. I shall stay, for there is nowhere for me.

What is the name of your land?

[Here he lists, in Atlantian language, what I assume to be all the provinces of Atlantis. He mentioned a ring, and I asked him to tell us about it.]

I remember. There was a large stone to be divided into four, and cut four different segments, and a ring, a large ring. Pinnacle in the center — placed in such a way — the roundness — the oval — the eclipse. It was the eclipse. An eclipse with an orbit. Thirty-nine degrees at parallel five would bring us far to the south.... It was like a map. It was like a geographical, nautical map. That was where the secrets were. We needed all four. Our last point, we buried the last secret so no one could find it — and subjected ourselves to mirrors, so that we would never be able to remember what we did. That's why — that's why Ares Vilas hated us so much. Because we stole the second key. The binary key. He never saw it because he had his friends working on it and had them executed and we knew.

We kept him from destroying the world, but we sacrificed Oceanus Atlantis. That's why I'm free. That is why I'm free. My curse was in making him lost — by losing myself. That is the secret of this ring. That is [pointing] the eclipse, the planet, the orbit, the moon. The orbit pattern 39 to the fifth. One, two, three, four, and five was the dark. I'm sure of it. I'm sure of that. The patterns, every layer is of orbital flight. Every layer is a pattern of air. Levels, by 1,000 [unclear]. Every light being the space between, so no collisions could possibly occur, and every pattern had a vortex. The vortex, there was something about the vortex. Yes, yes, every vortex, here [pointing], was in parallel with Ascension Hall, there [pointing]. It was our guiding; it was a guide. It was natural because we had no records of its creation. It was monolithic in proportions. [pointing] That was for trade; [pointing] that was for dignitary; [pointing] this was uncharted. It was night. The configuration is perfect. Granlandia, Islanda, Sudias Articas, Estes Avilas. Thirty-ninth by the fifth binary sector. Where did we put it? By the spider. Oh, yes, we've put it by the spider.[3] Three degrees from the wing to the arrow — four; Oceanus — four. There was an earthquake there. I remember four Phoenician sailors accidentally drowned because of turbulence caused in Oceanus Four. If only they had known!

Ares Vilas retreated to the west hoping to start again. He

couldn't have made it. The west was uncharted and there was no one there. He and his whitefaces took it. They tried, but they segregated and they split. I remember the accounts. Ten years after the fatality, they had a monolithic war. Souls were dying, but the war continued. They crossed mountains. They crossed valleys, and every time the war would end another segment would start. In the end there was a revolution. And Challis Karmas came out of hiding after 27 years. Told his followers he would have no more to do with war. Promptly retreated to the Mediterranean and he started his sect. It was the same time the ancient Romans began conquering. The Romans under the direction of Montomus Caras and Antonus Romilis, who they said was raised by the heathen, but he wasn't. He was the nephew of General Maros. Estes and I had raised him. He was a fine general. He took after Alexis, who conquered the East.

Netarnius Forests started the underwater colony in hopes that perhaps they could start again underneath and become their own civilization, but it never lasted. I remember — I remember the Wavian telling us all that the pressure was too great, that a large force had cracked the top. And I remember Challis Karmas writing to me at last through the ballast that he had cast his ring into the sea, begging me to do the same. And Ares begged me to keep it in the hopes that one day when our futures were ready, our spirits would be united again, and have the rings together.

It never worked. Ares retreated again into the east, hoping to get what he had buried.... Ares Vilas went, and ran and ran, creating colonies and hoping to band them together, but he couldn't teach them. He could not teach them. So Ares Vilas died in a show of martyrdom, proclaiming himself the last great hero and could not kill himself properly, needed the aid of a Sarian sister, who came back to proclaim her great deed.

[Chuck now speaks in a different tone of voice. He is quieter, introspective, almost reserved.]

We were gods then. We were revered as gods and we were, but only to others. We made ourselves gods in others' eyes because we were so weak in our own. If only we had taken time to realize what we were — that we had had fathers and forefathers. If only we had realized what we were.

Instead, Ares Vilas did the final call. And Atlantis burned for seven years — *seven god-awful years* and collapsed as a nation.

Ares Vilas did one great purpose. He had discipline. His followers had discipline and they had discipline after them. And all we could have was compassion. But that was the secret of the ring. That was the secret. I understand the ring. There are three more like it.

[From here on, Chuck seems to be going in and out of the trance, from past to present life, on his own. By now, he was really guiding his own session. I had very little influence over what was taking place.[4] I was learning that the biggest job of the guide is to protect the subject from external disruption and to gear the session in a certain direction if it needs it, if the subject gets stuck. Chuck seemed to know where he was going, and fortunately I was wise enough to let him go there.]

I don't believe this. This is the Milliyear 1974. I am in the present, as a "Chuck," but I remember what I was. I was somebody else. Somebody else in a different time. There's a voice. It keeps telling me I've dealt enough with origin. I should go to transformation. What else am I? What else am I?

What's the voice saying? What's the inner voice saying?

Yes, yes, I remember. I was there, I remember. I remember the great scene. It was him coming off the boat and all of us laid down our arms. We couldn't fight him. He was one of us. He was the greatest man our country had ever produced. How could we fight this man? I remember going home and telling Juliette, "There will be another war." I remember her crying, but it was happiness, because we were going to be victorious — but we lost. He wasn't the general anymore — and me a mere lieutenant, commanding a cavalry of half-starved men who had lived on pride and sacrifice for months. Disgraced and ashamed and hoping to regain honor by fighting the vilest, filthiest, stinkiest, cruelest, most ludicrous and lewd, vulgar, repulsive army on earth who called themselves "proper, and the true army." We had to fight Prussians to beat the French. I remember.

That's not all I am. That was very short. So confusing. Too

many trials, but not enough tribulation. This cannot be. I can't have been all these things.

You've been all these things and many, many, countless more. They are all within the part of you that goes into the making of what is the you and it's all part of soul development. It's all part of the evolvement, that this voice is saying that you must evolve to, what you must strive to. These are all memories and experiences of things that you have done, you have been.

Frightened. What else was I? Who am I? I'm scared. I sit here now and I see what is, but I'm scared. How do I deal with myself now? What do I say when I look in a mirror? What am I to become this time? Why now?

Look ahead. Look yourself to what you will become, to what you must do in this life. Look ahead now yourself to what you must be, to what you must fulfill and to what you must accomplish in this life. Don't be frightened. Just look ahead. Let it come.

It's clear. It's very clear. We have been fighting a war for thousands of years in different bodies, in different faces, in different times, but it's the same war. It's the Quadrant. It's Ares. It's Napoleon, it's Waterloo, it's every single war. The battle is not yet ended. The lost keep searching for themselves and Challis still roams this Earth trying, trying hard to keep the war from going on — trying to break down that blind obedience — and I keep trying to find compassion in a world that turns heartless. You said it yourself, it was the War of Karmas. It was karma gathering to fight unjustice past, and it's that way ever since. If Atlantis had fought Atlantis, if the victory had been decisive — the Earth [death?] would not have needed to continue. Atlantis would be here. But Atlantis died, not the people, not the karma, not the reasons, not the evil or the good. It is good versus evil. It is the wisdom versus the youth. It is why I could not give my blessing for Atlantis. It was why I could not kill my general. It was why I lived a pauper. It was why I died an alcoholic. It was why I could not see the reason for the hanging of John Wilkes. It is why, it is why the battle will never end.

Look ahead. Look ahead in this life. What must you do? What must you do in this life?

I must find Challis.

How will you recognize him?

I will know him, his eyes. I recognized them before, but we didn't meet. I saw him in passing. It was recognition. It was a half smile. Welcome, brother, to the fight. Welcome, because the fight is continuing and I can't talk with you now, but later.

I must find Challis. In this life, I must find Challis. We must talk. We must put away our hatred and our longing. We must find ourselves here. We must make this the last stand. This must be the last stand.

Moran, Challis, and Estes. Estes had the idea, but he didn't have the strength. He had the knowledge, but he didn't have the ability to carry it. We must unite and be one as we were once *one*.

We must come face to face with Ares, but we cannot, we cannot allow it to battle.

Is Ares on the Earth's planet at this time?

No. Ares was always late with us. He always came later. He was always the late arrival. I could tell. We must await him coming. We must sit down and reconcile, for it's our only hope. There must be a reconciliation, because annihilation will never work. We've used too many people carrying on our cause — carrying on the principles — carrying on a war that should have long ended.

I must find Challis. I must find his eyes.

Where will you look?

Inside myself. If I know myself, then I will know Challis. I will know where he is. I will know what he's thinking, and he then will be able to find me. He's not here. I don't sense him. I remember sensing imminent danger with imminent joy. Challis was that way, a blind man who saw with his fingers. A blind man who glowed in his eyes. They were colors. I could see them at night.

There is such a man. Where is he now? He must be to the south. Yes, he must be to the south. The West isn't ready, and the East is in turmoil. The South is all that's left. I must finish here and I must go to the south. I must find Challis. I must find Estes. We will stand against Ares Vilas. They never could pronounce his name in the West.... They never understood our language.

I am — I is — Ares. He used his name like he used a godhead title. Ares — Ares — Ares — Ares.

Challis: the fountain, the seaman. Moran: morales [morals?], dignity, loyalty, compassion. Estes: always looking, always seeking, always going to the east. Estes, Estes, Foturas.

After the session, we were all hungry, and we went looking for a park in which to have a picnic lunch. Somehow we needed a real lawn to "ground" ourselves after our wrenching soul-traveling experience. We found no park. Instead, a cemetery, strangely appropriate, with green grass on which to sit. (I have never before or since had lunch in a cemetery.)

Chuck's mind was full of memories. He remembered much of the second session. The whole experience was unexpected and fantastic. Truly, Patricia and I didn't know what to say or do. In retrospect, we obviously should have stayed on and continued working with this young man, but we didn't. We simply said goodbye after our picnic and left.

We never saw Chuck again. After our return from a two-month trip in the U.S., we wrote to him, but he had moved, leaving no forwarding address. I was unable to follow up on what he did and what happened to him. I often wonder if he did follow the map that he had outlined for his present life.

Patricia and I resumed our trip, going to the Mayan ruins in the Yucatan, and north to the Oregon and Washington coasts, then back to New England. There, we were to start a whole new adventure.

Endnotes:

[1]In 1974, I attended several classes a week at the New Birth Center in Groton, Massachusetts. It was started in 1972 to educate people in psychic development, health food, and organic gardening; it has since closed.

At the center, I learned a technique called the "Christos

Experience"; I was using variations of this with Chuck. The purpose is to open a subject's awareness — to show him he can reach beyond a limited perception of reality by changing size, floating, etc. The subject is given time to accomplish each step. To send love, the subject is asked to close his eyes, visualize the eyes of another, and then, when this is accomplished, to send love from eyes to eyes. The technique is described more fully in *The Case for Reincarnation* by Joe Fisher (New York: Bantam Books, 1985), pp. 138-143.

[2]I do not know if Louana was the name of Chuck's friend, the girl who died. At the time, so much information was coming through and I was so astonished by its extent and depth, that I did not think to ask, either during the session or the next day.

[3]He may be referring to the giant Earth drawings that appear in many parts of the world; for instance, the spider on the plains of Nazca in southern Peru. See illustration #3.

[4]A subject's taking control of the entering and exiting in hypnosis is rare, but not without precedent. A young woman I had guided a few years earlier described a violent scene in which she was stabbing someone or being stabbed with a knife. She was particularly surprised that there was a definite sound to this act. (From her description the lung cavity was probably punctured by the knife.) She willed herself back to the present and out of hypnosis, refusing to discuss the episode. As I write this 16 years after her session (her first and only one), she still will not discuss the memory with me.

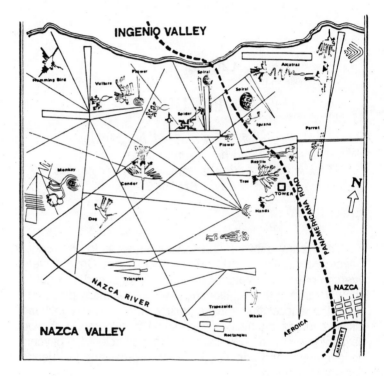

Illustration #3
A map of the "Spider" on the plains of Nazca, Peru.

Chapter Four

THE ADVENTURE YEARS

Begin with that in hand, but begin
if there would be anything accomplished.
Talk is well. Action is wise. Deeds are golden.
Edgar Cayce, Reading 254-35

The years between 1964, when I went to the Edgar Cayce Foundation, and 1974, when I met Chuck, were eventful ones. I traveled; I married and divorced and got to know the son of that relationship; I worked at many jobs and I started a successful antique business.[1] I also continued taking courses on hypnosis, personal development, applied psychology, mind development, mind science, psychic development, and continued guiding regressions for friends and acquaintances.

But I was unhappy inside. My life, I often thought, resembled a wave that I rode precariously on a slippery surfboard. I wanted more control of my life. I wanted to grow up. My studies helped. So did Patricia, whom I met in 1974 and with whom I had a loving relationship for four years — four years that coincided with a period of enormous personal and professional growth for me. I call these the "Adventure Years," after a house I bought in 1974 when Patricia and I returned from our transcontinental odyssey. In retrospect, I see that the Adventure Years had two main facets: the experience of home sharing and the development of my professional life as a hypnotist. Each contributed in its own way to my personal growth.

The house, which I bought from my parents, is in Ashby, Massachusetts, a quaint little town on the New Hampshire border. Patricia and I set about renovating it, using century-old board siding from a big barn to panel some of the rooms. (It had 11 rooms, not counting the two baths, a solarium, and a four-story tower.) We used the barn and part of the house for the antique business and rattled around in the rest.

But we didn't rattle around for long. Because we were frequently in Europe on antique buying trips, we found housesitters. Many came; few left. In addition, we held "open invitation" weekends for friends and acquaintances who wanted to explore new regions of consciousness. Some of these people stayed, too. Soon the house was filled with a large, shifting, human population, plus 18 cats and dogs and — in the fields — a horse named "Fred."

We named the house "Adventure Into Time," and called it "The Adventure." It was an apt name. We who lived there were seekers. All came for reasons of their own, the teachers as well as the novices. But most who came to stay or study were embarked on personal adventures into new knowledge and understanding.

LEARNING AND TEACHING AT THE ADVENTURE

Although we never planned for it to become a teaching center, it quickly evolved into one. With new people came new ideas and perspectives. Our community offered classes on self-hypnosis, therapeutic massage, yoga, astrology, and whole health cuisine conducted by people who were, or are now, professionals in their fields. Everyone, visitor or resident, contributed to the whole. Some came with music, others to read palms, cards, or auras. Psychics used their abilities to flash on past lives. (One of them asserted that many in our community had been together at least once before in another lifetime in medieval Europe, and that the souls of many American Indians had visited our tribe, or lodge.) Two professional astrologers lived at The Adventure and other astrologers came who had studied ways of detecting past lives in individual horoscopes.

Working and living in a close community with these varied and wonderful people became quite an adventure in itself — one of the most significant learning experiences of my entire career — for I gained much in my ability to relate to people. The Adventure was a nurturing environment for the free expression of our spiritual natures. Yet, even as our consciousness was being raised we occasionally had to endure the outbursts of ego and anger which are the almost unavoidable by-products of home sharing.

No one ever labeled our daily living "group therapy" but that is what it truly was. Daily encounter enabled us to understand and accept each other, but more importantly, to understand and accept ourselves. Here is where I learned that the best help is, as Edgar Cayce said, self-help. We strived to be "open-hearted" as well as open-minded and as a result our growth was fuller and deeper. While knowledge is learned by mind, wisdom is accomplished in the heart.

My own chief interest, or course, was exploring the past. I also started experimenting with guiding people into the future, but I soon realized that, for me, this was a less productive avenue. The subsconscious mind has access to stored material from the present and the past; the future is not so readily available, as it comprises only probabilities based on past and present. Besides, the patterns of past lives also reveal the directions future lives are going.

The sheer number of people passing through gave me an opportunity to conduct countless past-life regressions and to fine tune my skills as a hypnotist. Before long, I filled two cartons with tapes of sessions.

THE PROVIDENCE HYPNOSIS CENTER

Meanwhile, the question of my professional life occasionally arose. I was happy and successful in the antique business. Still, I told Patricia one day that if I were ever to change vocations, I would like to work full time in the field of hypnosis. It was one of those speculative conversations that ordinarily lead no farther.

Then, not long afterwards, I received a phone call from Robert Bow, the director of the Providence Hypnosis Center in Providence, Rhode Island. Would I like to come to work for him, with a view toward purchasing the center in the near future? I would. Bow had been a guest at one of our open-invitation weekends and had seen me do a demonstration of group hypnosis. He evidently liked my style, and followed up with his astonishing phone call.

I went to work at the center in October, 1975, and in 1976 became the director. I worked hard to build up the clinic and we soon became one of the largest in New England, with four therapists besides myself. We specialized in helping people lose weight and stop smoking cigarettes. We later offered a number of other personal development programs and courses on hypnosis and self-hypnosis.

I also found time to write booklets about self-hypnosis that were published through the center. In 1977, with a colleague there, I coauthored my first book.[2]

I was invited to speak at the local medical center and at schools, colleges, and civic organizations. I attended professional development workshops and conferences and conventions of other professional hypnotists. Later, I was a speaker at meetings of these same organizations. I enjoyed the local speaking engagements. Most of the time I simply spoke of hypnosis and its therapeutic uses. Sometimes, however, the occasion was more dramatic.

One of these evolved from a talk at a high school psychology class. Though the topic was hypnosis, the question of past-life regression quickly arose. The students and teacher were eager for a demonstration. I was reluctant to agree. Although I had had audiences, this would be the first time I would perform a regression in a classroom setting. Moreover, I didn't (and still don't) like doing this kind of soul work in a class or demonstration setting; it is too much like stage hypnosis. Finally, I was concerned about the atmosphere. A regression experience is characterized by high degrees of emotion and openness. These must be respected; in particular, the audience must not mock the subject. Could I create the right mood and setting for a high school audience? Something in the climate of the group reassured me and I agreed to come back the following week to perform the regression.

The teacher volunteered to be the subject. Under hypnosis, he quickly experienced touching episodes with two sons from a past life. The class was enthralled as he revealed secrets of his heart and rekindled the sparks of past love. After awakening, the teacher held his hands to his face and sobbed in a full, sincere, and spontaneous release of joyous emotion. I feared the students would mock his tears, but they were most considerate, mature, and understanding.

Working as a hypnotist at PHC was totally valuable. Hypnosis became an everyday tool, not an occasional one. The greatest asset was that I learned to work with all kinds of people in all kinds of circumstances. For instance, before going to the center, I probably would have been intimidated when a high-ranking state policeman in full uniform walked in, asking me to hypnotize him so he could quit smoking. Not now. Though I very much wanted him to succeed (for the prestige, if nothing else, for he was on special duty as the governor's chauffeur and bodyguard) I had learned a valuable truth: the most you can do is the best you can. In this case, it wasn't enough; he was in too much of a hurry and didn't give himself a chance, for all my rooting for him.

SEEKING PERSONAL GROWTH

As I've mentioned, at the beginning of the Adventure Years, I was at a very precarious place in life, especially in regards to my personal relationships. I had recently been divorced, and though my relationship with Pat was warm and rewarding, I was aware of some deeper immaturity in myself. Selling antiques is a fine business; so is working in the field of hypnosis. But I dimly realized then — as I strongly realize now — that personal growth, especially through marriage or relationships, is *the* paramount life issue for me.

In the Adventure Years, I began in a serious way to develop the process of change that I continue to use: I reprogram my present and work to explore and understand my past, including my past lives.

Because my knowledge and experience is in the field of hypnosis, it seemed obvious to me to use what I knew. Rather than go to a hypnosis clinic or center, I decided to work with self-hypnosis tapes. I used (and use) two kinds, the commercial ones and those I make for myself. The commercial tapes are pre-recorded and are sold in bookstores, pharmacies, and in the mail; they are used to reprogram a certain aspect of personality or behavior or to reach a certain goal. In the early 1960s, I used commercial tapes on personality development. But I also quickly realized I could make my own tapes for very specific individual projects and goals. I made my first tape to cure fingernail biting. (As you see, not everything I work on is "serious" — although my fingernail biting was a serious, advanced case.) Since then, I have made tapes to help me feel more at ease when speaking in public, to help me relax, to help me listen better to others, to find a good love relationship, and for many other reasons.

Using these, I began to reprogram myself, shedding some of the silliness of youth. I could not change the world, I realized, but I *could* change myself and *my* world. I believed my immaturity was rooted in past lives; therefore, I believed I could soothe the scars on my soul by delving into my own past lives. I had seen the healing process as I worked with others.[3] I believed the process could work for me and that insight from my own past contributed to my soul growth in the present.

Here is an example of how knowledge of my past lives helps me in the present. As I've said, one of the nagging problems of my life has been my difficulty with intimate relationships.

In the mid-1960s I was living in a remote part of Spain where I went to escape the bitter New England winter.

Ironically, the house where I lived was made of stone and was unheated, as are most in that part of Spain; I was not much warmer that winter than I would have been at home. In addition, I was full of sadness over a failed relationship and the loss of a son (from the relationship) who had gone with his mother. I brooded over other unsatisfactory relationships, too, for I saw the beginnings of my pattern of difficulties.

For several days, off and on, I prayed and meditated, hoping for insight into the origins of my problems.

One day, I sat drearily in my room, sick with the flu and a high fever. In my fevered state, a waking dream, or vision, came with very strong images and powerful feelings of sadness and tragedy. I was in a past life, in France, and I was abandoning a wife and our three children, two who had been born and one I didn't yet realize had been conceived. By the standards of the day, it was a good life — I had work; we had food. It was a normal peasant's life. And I was leaving that good life to go on one of the Crusades. In that vision, I saw that I left my wife for the magic, the joy, the glamour, and the glory of the Crusade — and for the lure of riches. My comrades and I were going out to fight the infidel for Christ, and we thought it was going to be great fun. We were fools! They called the Crusade *holy;* for me it was hell. We marched, and we marched, and we marched. When I got to Jerusalem, to the very sight of the Holy City, I died on the side of the road. I died of disease and exhaustion. My body fell into the ditch. The Crusader army kept marching.

That was the vision. It provided me with physical and emotional release. I cried; it seemed as though I cried for hours. When I finally dried my eyes, I was filled with peace and self-acceptance. I was grateful that my prayer for insight had been answered. In my mind, I sent my French wife my profound regret for abandoning her and our children.

I did not really know what to do with the information I now had. But at the time, it was enough that I had information that shed light on my state of mind; that my pain had been relieved; that I experienced calm and self-acceptance. Nor did I feel a need to do anything. I simply resumed my life. When I recovered from the fever, I traveled throughout Spain buying antiques in the tiny mountain towns (I was apprenticing with a dealer who taught me the trade), living almost as a native. After six months I returned to New England, working in the apple orchard (as I had in high school), traveling, working at other odd jobs — experiencing life.

But my vision stayed with me. In retrospect, it is a key episode in my life. Later, at The Adventure, (and transcribed below) I was able to confirm its truth when I was the subject of a series of guided past-life regressions. The hypnotist/guide in the following exchange is George Parker, who opens the dialogue.

HENRY
Summer, 1974
Ashby, Massachusetts

Okay, tell me about it.
It is me. It is in Jerusalem, the Holy Land. We ravaged a city. We burned a city like a heathen. We raped and we plundered. We killed. We destroyed everything. We burned their bodies. We burned their homes. It was a horrible place — a horrible thing.
Jerusalem?
Near there. In the land of Jerusalem.
Do you remember capturing Jerusalem?
I was killed soon after.
What was your name?
I died. I died disheartened, disgusted, rejected by my friends, condemned by the enemy. I died very bitter. I know what I have done, having sinned in the name of God, having destroyed in the name of Christ, having killed in the name of religion. My name is John.
From what country did you come?
From Europe.
Do you remember where?
No. I don't care. I know what I have done.

73

You learned a lesson from this life?
A very difficult and very bitter lesson.
Do you know what it is?
Not to go off to war.
What did you lose here?
War is not beautiful. I lost a family. I lost friends. I lost a home. I lost a life.
Is that all? Is there anything more of this life?
Is that ALL! I lost everything and I gained nothing! I went out seeking adventure and I found death.
When you left —
I went off to glory, found tears and sadness. I went off to the marching of bands and the blaring of bugles. Then I heard the wail of children dying, the stench of cities burning. Had a — [tape unclear] — ugly destruction. Clouds of death overwhelming us. We were destroying just to destroy. No reason, just to destroy. Oh, what waste! What loss! When will it ever end? When will it ever cease? It goes on today. It will go on tomorrow. Pillage and destruction. Rape and ravish. It goes on.

In a later session (Aug. 2, 1976, in Ashby), I reviewed the Crusades era again. Louis Acker[4] is the hypnotist/guide.

....I do see a green field, a dusty dirt road, myself in a suit of armor with a long lance, very well-dressed, a purple plume — a reddish-purple plume, a little dog beside me, a very nice horse — well-groomed — going off, going to the crusades in a lot of splendor and a lot of glory.

I felt this image before. I haven't seen it this vividly. The horse is white and brown, has even black on it. It's Middle Ages. There is a castle and a small town way off in the distance.

I left a wife and two, three children — two and a third one coming, there's three children — to go off. I didn't have to. I chose to. I wanted to go for the glory and the adventure and all I found was sadness and death and defeat. There was no glory and less adventure. There was privation, there was hunger, there was thirst, there was betrayal of friends, there were empty dreams and emptier promises, empty dreams and sad nights — a very unhappy time, a very sad lesson. The lesson being that sometimes we have something very good, something that we need and want so very much and we always feel like there's more. It's sad, but the grass is always greener, I suppose. What it's telling me now is to know what I have, to appreciate it, to be very content and very pleased with it. Granted, there can always be more, but there can always be much less.

In my present life, I have had two marriages, two children of my own (and others through marriage), and yet have been denied the companionship of my own children. Difficulty with relationships, the loss of wives and children — I believe I experience these now because in that former life I left a wife and children. I believe, from my heart and soul, that my present life situation is the payment due on that previous life, the balance that I owe for deserting a loving wife and family.

Even more perturbing is this question: Do I have an embedded cyclic pattern of leaving loved ones for crusades (in various forms) or is it my karma to endure (or be thankful for) the losses of family and relationships in my present life? Personally, I see karma as a self-chosen fate. It's like a credit card; the bill comes in and we must pay it, probably with interest. But we incurred the bill; in purchasing the item we have made a contract to pay it. Lives are like that; you pay the bill. You can pay it off all at once at any time you want or you can pay it in small payments over several lifetimes.

This is the great question of lives and the cyclic pattern of lives: How much can we change and write a new script and how much must we act out verbatim on the eternal stage of life? Investigating the hidden workings of the mind has brought answers that satisfy me. Past-life work can ease the mind in the present life and sometimes give information on which to base the new script. For instance, my vision in Spain eased my mind and spirit. While I didn't feel then that it was prophetic, it came to seem so, and the regressions at The Adventure confirmed the Crusade story. While I could do nothing about the recent past — the two marriages were over and the children gone — I could perhaps rewrite the script. I became more careful about my "crusades" and transformed the problematic patterns of my past lives. I give more thought to loving relationships, and I do not end them carelessly, but give them all I have.

LEARNING FROM MY PAST LIVES
    At this point, I understood karma as a "what ye sow, that shall ye reap" phenomenon; knew there were prices; knew there was choice in the sense that for every action there is an equal and opposite reaction. Later, through other hypnotic experiments, I was to gain more insight into the larger picture of lives; karma; the ways we change our scripts; and the use of forgiveness as one of the important healing processes. That understanding all began at The Adventure. So did my understanding of the cyclic character of lives. Two of my own past-life experiences illustrate this. Before I tell you about them, I feel a preface is in order for those of you who are new to the knowledge of past-life experiences — because the lives I am about to relate to you were both lives as females. You may have been under the impression, that once of one sex, always of one sex. And since I am presently a male, you might be surprised that I would not be self-conscious about stating that I have been a female. But, as I will explain later, we have all experienced past lives in the opposite sex to make us more whole human beings in our present lives.
    In the first of these lives, I was a wealthy, influential female prostitute in ancient Greece. I had an attractive body, a beautiful house, servants, and a clientele of wealthy politicians and generals, the elite of the country. Using my connections with them, I jockeyed myself into a position of wealth. Calculating and bitchy, I got what I wanted for myself and my friends. Every possession a person could have in life at that time and place was mine. I was even buried with great ceremony and state honors.
    Most unexpectedly, a contrasting life flashed vividly before me one night in Providence. I saw a vision that night while I was watching TV. I had had a long day at the hypnosis center and was relaxing, tuning out the conscious world. My

mind was in a relaxed, alpha state, but I was not looking for any past-life memory. (Psychic flashes can come on their own, uninvited and sometimes unwanted.) In this life, I was a younger girl. I was destitute and homeless, sleeping in the cold and windy corner of an innkeeper's mule shelter on the steppes of China. The only people who came through were the mule traders. After they finished using my body, they threw down coins on the dirty straw floor — coins of almost no value, more in mockery than in payment. I died of disease and malnutrition at the age of 13. With no ceremony whatsoever, my body was thrown into the pigpen. The body decayed and was eaten by the pigs.

How do these two diametrically opposed lifetimes relate to themselves and to my present life? Both of these lives were female, and I know I have had other female lives. With these two lives, I began to understand what Carl Jung meant when he spoke and wrote about the combination of masculine and feminine in all of us; the soul is androgynous. These lives shed new light on my sexual identity. The body is *far* less signifcant than our society thinks. Past lives in the opposite sex also give us *present* insight into the opposite sex. I'm sure that having lived as a female has allowed me to better understand women and helped me to grow as a person in my relationships with others. Thus, I believe the story of my two prostitute lives is one of balance. On one side of the scale is the pretty but calculating and avaricious Grecian. On the other, the poor, starving, beaten victim. Centuries later, as I see them both in my mind's eye, I like the Chinese girl best; she paid the balance without ever complaining. As gruesome as these two lives sound, they were a valid part of my soul's evolution. Granted, they were from a caterpillar stage of my growth, but without going through a caterpillar stage, how could I ever hope to be transformed into a butterfly?

To me, the interest of these tales is not in their gruesome experiences, but in using the past-life information to gain loving guidance for a more healthy use of my sexual energy in the present. An action in one life does not *cause* an action in another. In another life we choose (maybe subconsciously) an opposite. The Grecian prostitute abused power more than she misused sex; I paid my bill in my Chinese life. But I do not need to reexperience a life of prostitution and manipulation.

In these years of research and experience, I saw few set rules concerning past lives. People always seemed to have choices. There seemed not to be a moralistic rule of "right" or "wrong," nor did I observe any rule that said people must experience abuse in order to balance abuse. Patterns, I concluded, can be changed; hurts can be healed (or at least kissed). By the time of the Adventure Years I was beginning to view life as an unlimited school, with the different grades as different lifetimes. When we study and learn we pass our tests and we progress; when we neglect our studies and fail our tests, we take those tests over and over again. But in this school of life we are our own teacher, and we grade our own tests. Fortunately, "Earth school" is usually a merciful institution.

Psychic flashes, in myself and others, can awaken past and present experiences of life. Often simply telling another person of an experience, whether the telling is done consciously or under hypnosis, can give new perspectives and relief and allow additional information to come forward. When emotional attachments have been released, the person can generally see and accept a clearer picture of the information.

I believe it is a matter of letting go and continuing on in the human adventure. For instance, the vision in which I experienced myself as a Crusader — and a deserter of my family — is still strong in my mind's eye and my soul's memory bank. If I allowed myself to dwell on it I could dredge up the same feelings of terrible pain at my folly. But I must let go of my pain and move on. The experience of the process stays with us for use again and again as such awarenesses come to us in the exploration of ourselves, as we travel deeper within.

Endnotes:

[1]To me, antiques have always been closely linked with my past-life hypnosis work. Both deal with the past, one through the subconscious mind and the other through artifacts. The antiques are real, solid, living history I can hold and feel and see and smell. They are tangible history. I love each piece, but can also detach myself to sell them to others who love them. It is a win-win-win business. People are happy to sell their "old junk," and I am happy to buy it; other folks are pleased to buy it from me. Now, in 1988, I am so busy that I am retired from antiques and concentrate on speaking and writing as well as guiding regressions and channeling.

[2]Henry Bolduc and George Parker, *How to Unlock the Power of Your Mind With Hypnosis and Explore the Riddle of Reincarnation* (Ashby, MA: Adventure Into Time Publishers, 1977). Out of print.

[3]The work of professionals like Irene Hickman, an osteopath who also uses hypnosis for therapy, supports my belief in the healing potential of past-life experience. Hickman often uses hypnosis to help patients regress to a time of conflict or trauma. She has said that, "Whenever an emotionally loaded memory was revealed, and the incident relived..., there was a reported definite feeling of release and relief of tension, a lessening of symptoms of the illness, or a movement toward a resolving of personal relationships." Irene Hickman, *Mind Probe Hypnosis* (Kirksville, MO: Hickman Systems [4 Woodland Lane 63501], 1983).

[4]Louis Acker is co-author with Frances Sakoian of *The Astrologers Handbook*, one of the best selling books on astrology.

Chapter Five

HEALING THE PAST

Build thee more stately mansions,
O my soul.... Leave thy low-vaulted past!
Oliver Wendell Holmes
Autocrat of the Breakfast Table

THE ADVENTURE YEARS WERE OVER
By 1978, it was time to remake my life. I say that because
I was living in a group house, driving thousands of miles to
buy and sell antiques, commuting to and from Providence,
managing the hypnosis center, writing a book, and ending a
relationship. It was too much, and I had to slow down. I tried
to do it gradually, taking a townhouse in Providence in 1977
to ease the strain of commuting. But it became apparent that
I needed a complete break.

At a time when most people are feathering their nests, I
cleared mine out completely. In the course of a few months, I
sold the house, the antiques, the center, and finished the
sales effort for the book. Patricia and I parted amicably, and in
April of 1978 I went away for two months. I flew to England,
took a bus to Greece, traveled overland by bus via
Baluchistan (a region in South Asia near the borders of
Pakistan, Iran, and Afghanistan) to New Delhi, and then flew
home.

When I returned, Patricia and I parted for good. "Go south," my meditation told me. What did I know of *south*? Only the Edgar Cayce Foundation. So, packing all my belongings in my car, I headed again for Virginia Beach. There, I stayed with friends and attended lectures and did research on the Cayce transcripts in the library. I went to the meditation room and prayed for direction. I cried there also. My meditations said, "Henry, you are always going so fast that nothing good can ever catch up with you," so I decided I would plant myself at the beach until something good came and try to prepare myself for a new love relationship, hoping to be worthy.

One evening in summer a young woman came and sat beside me at a lecture. I saw her again the next day and for a few days after that. She left, then returned. Her name is Ann; we have been together now for ten years, marrying in 1981.

With her two children, we lived in Virginia Beach the fall, winter, and spring of 1978-79. There, at the A.R.E., I also met Geraldine, who was employed in the library. She recognized me from my picture on the jacket of the book I had done with George Parker, and we fell into conversation. At her request, I agreed to work with her on a past-life regression.

That was the start of a busy period. My regression work started slowly — one a night, a few nights a week, then every night and eventually, weekends. People brought their friends and their friends' friends. So many people wanted regression work!

I also started work on a book about how to make your own self-help cassette tapes. It was to occupy me — what with writing and rewriting and testing and evaluating — for the next five years.[1]

This was not what I had planned for retirement! A move to Dallas was afoot — Ann had to tie up loose ends of her life there. I resolved that there I would again simplify my life — I would give classes in self-hypnosis, but I would not take on more regression work, it snowballed too fast. That resolution

81

didn't last long, of course; for all my complaining, I love the work. In retrospect, I'm not sorry I worked so hard, for this period, between 1979 and about 1983, turned out to be the period in which I firmly consolidated the skills and knowledge I had been building.

To get back to Geraldine. Often people say, "Oh, gee, past lives are so interesting; I just want to go have a regression! I can't wait! This is going to be so much fun!" But not all regressions are fun and exciting. True, most are simple memories of normal life experiences. But some people find they are poorly prepared for some memories and revelations.

But Geraldine was serious and knowledgeable about regression work and hoped that past-life exploration might help solve a present-day problem, bad headaches and recurring nightmares. She recalls:

From the time I was quite young, I had a recurring nightmare. It was always the same. I was riding a big brown horse, sitting sidesaddle. I wore a pale pink, almost lavendar, hoop-skirted dress. I was tearing down the road and my long black hair had come unbound and was flying out behind me. The Spanish moss hanging in a long line of gigantic oak trees was hitting me in the face. I could see the lights far ahead shining in the window of a large plantation house. It was almost dark. I had this terrible sense of something wrong; something terrible had happened and I was speeding toward it.

For years, the dream ended with Geraldine's frantic efforts to reach the house. After her present-life husband died, the dream ended as she was running up the porch steps of the mansion. Geraldine would often wake up crying, distressed and fearful, but never understanding why or what the dream meant.

This nightmare had also presented itself to her conscious mind more than once in daylight while she was driving a car, especially if she was heading south. She says, "I was *there*. It was real. For a few minutes I was 'gone,' so to speak." It was clearly a hazardous situation. Her husband

and children were aware of her blackouts and used to them. Nevertheless, she felt she was causing a problem, and not knowing the cause was the worst thing. "You think you're going bonkers," she explained. Yet somehow she knew "It was on my soul and my soul remembered."

I agreed to work with Geraldine in the hope that a past-life regression might shed light on the source of her headaches and nightmares. We hoped for a therapeutic result — that is, that if her trouble had its roots in a past life, recall and acceptance would relieve her pain, or at the very least help her to understand it. Here is what happened.

GERALDINE
March 27, 1979
Virginia Beach, Virginia

....And now look around you and you will be able to tell what you see, what you sense, and what you feel. It will be very easy for you to speak. Your mouth will be pleasantly moist — always remaining at this same level of awareness — at one with yourself, at one with the creative forces — and at one with your own higher intelligence. Take your time now. Take all the time you want and tell me what you are feeling, what you are sensing, what you are seeing and experiencing.

A party. And the ladies have on hoop skirts, big wide skirts, and their hair is parted in the middle and fastened back with flowers and ribbons. The men have on long swallowtail coats and oh, they`re so polite and nice. And they're hovering around the girls like bees.

We're eating off of little plates that you hold in your hand like a dainty napkin. It's out on the lawn ... sitting on the grass. And our skirts are all around us, like flowers. It's a beautiful day. Everyone's so happy.

Look around you. Tell me who you see. Tell me the people you see. Is there anybody special?

Yes. There's one tall man with red hair. He's staring ... must be at me 'cause I have that long black hair. And he's bending over me asking me if I'd like to have a cool drink. I say, "Yes, I'd like

83

some lemonade," and he goes to get it. I turn around and watch him and think how graceful he looks. He's so tall.

And then what happens?

He brings me back the drink and he sits down beside me on the grass and we talk. And he tells me he'll soon be going back to — up north. And I tell him I hope he doesn't stay very long. I hope he comes back. And he says, "Oh, I will." And then he laughs.

Where will he be going up north?

Syracuse.

What will he be doing?

I think he's a banker

Go now to the next important event. What is the next most important event now in this life? What happens next? Take your time. [Geraldine's expression becomes very sad.] Tell me what it is. You will be detached from it. Just tell me what's happening.

Well, I'm on a horse and I'm riding down the road — something terrible!

Detach yourself from it and just tell me very calmly, very relaxed, very collected. Now what's happening?

I'm going toward the porch — and I'm riding on this big brown horse, sidesaddle. And I get to the porch and they tell me he's gone. And all the slaves are crying and I'm crying, and I say, "Oh, God, I'm too late." I know I'm too late, but I kneel down beside him and I say, "Love, don't go, don't go." But he don't come back.

And then what happened?

And then they put him in the box and I've got on a long black dress and a black thing on my head and they put flowers on him. They take him out and bury him under the magnolias.

Okay. Give him your blessings, send him your love and just let the memory fade now. Go forward and tell me the next major event. Let that memory go now.

[Geraldine vividly recalled this important event very emotionally, for there was such stress involved with this porch scene she had dreamed of so many times. Her mind was still blocking out the sequence of events and exactly what was happening. She was very tearful in this situation so I did not press

84

for more information in this first session. I did want to spend a little more time viewing this particular life, so I asked her to go forward in time to the next major event.]

And continue forward. What is the next major event now in your life?

Well, the war is over. And I'm all alone. And the big house is empty because all the slaves are gone — there's just a couple of faithful ones that stayed.

Continue forward — to the time of your death. What is happening? What do you see around you?

I'm lying in my fourposter and my hair is white and they've put a little cap on my hair. And my Mammy's still with me. She didn't go with the rest of them. She stayed with me. And she says, "Now, don't you fret, love," and she puts cold cloths on my head 'cause my head's so hot and she says I've got the fever. And I don't mind dying 'cause I know I'll go out there under the magnolias where he is.

How old were you when you died?

Oh, I think I'm about 68.

And where is the town where you are living? What is the name of the place?

It's near New Orleans.

And do they put you out under the magnolias where he is?

Yes.

Do they put a stone to mark your grave?

Yes.

What does the stone say? Read to me what is on the stone. You're just observing now.

It says, "Devoted wife and faithful friend, Sarah." Just "Sarah."

Is his stone there also?

"John."

Does it say anymore?

No.

Is there a date?

1846 for John.

What is happening now? What are you doing now?

85

Everything is sort of misty.
Okay. Very good. Thank you.

[Geraldine experienced a great emotional release after reviewing this life and allowed her tears to flow. Suggestions were given at the end of this first session that she would gain a better perspective and understanding of the life. Suggestions were also given to prepare for the next session.]

And look back at those people, at all the people there, and bless them and send them your love. And as you send love into their eyes and into their hearts, they begin to fade. Let them fade now, sending them your blessings.

As they fade, slowly start returning to the present.

You will retain in your conscious mind only that which is important and beneficial for you to retain at this time. The other memories, let them go now. You will be detached from the pain and sadness for that is past.

You are back in the present, where you have so much to be joyful for, so much to be thankful for. You have learned a great deal, you have gained a lot of perspective and understanding of yourself and of your world. You are one with creative forces, one with your higher self, the god-self, that stands above you and guides you and directs you. You are better understanding the purpose of this life. And this understanding is helping you now. It is guiding you and assisting you. And for that you give thanks.

Ask yourself now what it is that you may do that will help you in this present life to learn and grow and what steps you can take that will guide you into your next life. Answer the question only within yourself, planting the seed that it may grow.

Let the White Light surround you and protect you and encompass your heart and soul — and bless you. You are now in the present and in a little while, when you awake, you will feel very good. You will feel better than before. You will be wide awake, refreshed and happy.

I will count from one to five and at the count of five, you can open your eyes, be wide awake, and feeling fine — feeling better than before. I will count now: one ... two ... coming up slowly, releasing the burdens of the past ... coming up slowly ... three ... four ... and five. Open your eyes. Now just stay right there — don't jump up. That was amazing.

Geraldine said, "I've been crying."
I know, but that's very normal and very common — physically a good releasing. It's good emotion and there [are] things — sometimes buried within us — that need to be released and tears are a great blessing. Tears purify the soul and cleanse you. [Tears can be a vital part of the unlocking of the storehouses of the soul.]

I scheduled the second session for Geraldine approximately a month later to allow her ample time at the subconscious level to prepare for this next session. Again I began the session by looking for pleasant, happy experiences. I did not wish to start directly with an emotional or difficult situation. This second session began, as did every session, with entering alpha and present-life regression. This excerpt picks up after that point.

GERALDINE
April 17, 1979
Virginia Beach, Virginia

When you are ready, begin telling me what is happening.
I'm about eight years old and they are brushing my hair in curls all around. And my hair is black and shiny like always. And they're taking their fingers and rolling my hair in curls around the fingers and making them fall around my head. Putting on my long pantaloons and my chemise shirt and my petticoats and a blue silk dress with ruffles and a bow in the back. And Papa brings me in a little gold locket and puts it around my neck and says, "That's for my girl."

I'm going to a party. And I take Mother's hand and she takes me out to the carriage. Then Papa puts me in and says, "Now you all be careful, 'cause that's my girl." And Mammy's with me, and

87

the coachman. Caleb is the coachman and they've got two horses hitched up to the carriage. And he cracks the whip and off we go.

And now what happens? Take your time. Go very slowly. Relate to me what is happening now.

I'm going down the road ... going down to the house ... quite a piece. And the house is big and it's got wisteria hanging over the porch. The children are all out in the yard, picking up acorns and chasing each other. They stop the carriage and I get out and the minute I get out, somebody starts chasing me. The boys are being real mean. One of them untied my sash.

It's Mary's party. And her Momma calls us into the dining room and there's a long table with candles. They've got a great big cake. And they tell her to blow out the candles and she has to take two or three puffs on it. It's only about seven candles, but she can't blow 'em out. And anyway, they cut the cake and her Momma says, "Now be careful, 'cause we baked prizes in the cake." I've got a little ring in mine. I put it on my finger and it just goes about half way up my little finger 'cause it's so little. But I think it's real cute.

She gets a lot of presents. We all just sit around and watch her open up the presents. And then her mother takes us out back on the lawn again... it's pretty overwhelming in the house. And we play blind man's bluff and hide and go seek 'til about four in the afternoon. And then Caleb comes back after me. We go home. Had a good time.

That's very good. Thank you.

[As the regression proceeds and as the episodes unfold, the story takes form and texture. Her life becomes more vivid as experiences are related. I ask Geraldine for the next event of major importance.]

Okay. Now go to when you were a little older, to the next event of major importance, and you will find out that the more you tell me about it, the more clear this life becomes, the more vivid, the more easily you can relive these experiences. Take your time now and you will understand — you will learn and grow through this experience. Now, when you are ready, just begin telling me what is happening.

It's a garden party and they've strung Japanese lanterns all

through the trees with candles in them. They look like fireflies —
beautiful. And they have two or three people playing guitars.
They have a violin and they have a flat floor we can dance on.
Have tables set around under the trees.

How old are you, about?

About 17. And my hair — I've got it back — it's long and
I've got it sort of swirled on the back of my neck and have a big
magnolia pinned right where it goes together in back. And I've got
on a white dress. And I have a fan I hold up before my face.

Now what do your friends call you? What is your name?

Sarah.

*Do they always call you "Sarah," or do you have a nickname?
Is there a special name that somebody called you?*

Just "Sarah." [Expression of sadness]

*And why are you sad, Sarah? This is a party. Is there
anything that is making you sad?*

I'm watching for someone. He hasn't come yet. Somebody's
always asking me to dance and I'm dancing but I keep watching.

What are you watching for? Can you tell me?

I'm watching for John.

Does he come?

He hasn't come yet and I wonder what in the world's a-keeping
him.

Let's just wait and see if he comes.

Well, I keep dancing and I don't want anybody to know I'm a-
looking for him 'cause they'd be sure and tell him. I think I hear
him. Yes, it's his horse and he comes up to me and I say, "What
in the world! Where have you been?" And he says he.... [Here
Sarah stopped talking and appeared to be listening to an inner
voice.]

*What did he have to do? Listen carefully and you can hear him
say it. What does he say?*

Something about his horse. He started to ride one horse and
the shoe was loose on the foot and he couldn't take that one; he had
to take his dad's. And his dad's horse is so mean that you have to
watch the tang [thing?]; he's gonna throw you if he's gonna carry
you. But he got there in one piece anyhow. He's a good dancer.
And they play a waltz. I like that. So I tell him, "It's all right,

but next time, better start a little early."

And what is happening now?

Everybody's going home and the servants are picking up all the debris on the lawn. And John and I are out back in the grove where there's a swing, a-swinging. And he swings me real high and it must be getting late 'cause Momma comes out and calls me and says, "Sarah, you better come in; it's getting late." So he walks me up to the door and she stands there on the porch 'til I close the door. I think she's afraid he'll try and kiss me good night. But he goes on home.

Okay. Very good. Now continue to the next major event. The next event of importance to you. Take your time. It will be very easy for you to speak and relate what is happening. Feel the emotions and the experience and when you are ready, just begin telling me what is happening.

I'm in my bedroom and I'm putting on my dress — and a long white veil on my head. It's my wedding day. And Momma's fussing around fixing my hair. And she says, "You're not gonna be my baby any longer." And I say, "Yes, Momma, I'll always be your baby." And she says, "Well, at least you're not going far away," 'cause John don't live very far away. I'm kinda worried 'cause seems like a big step we're taking. But I guess it'll be all right 'cause I've known him for a long time. And Daddy comes and says, "It's time to go downstairs." I can hear the music playing. Someone's playing the piano. I walk down the stairs and I have to be real careful 'cause I have a long train and Momma takes it up over her arms so I won't fall. And a lot of people are in the parlor — all my friends and all our relations — never knew I had so many relations. They all show up for weddings and funerals. John comes in and I know everything's gonna be all right.

And what is happening now? What are you doing now?

We're on the lawn and they have tables spread out on the lawn and we're standing in a line and everybody's coming along kissing us and they say they hope we'll be happy. And everybody goes to the table and they have all kinds of refreshments. Then Mammy comes and gets me and I go up to my room and put on my traveling costume; I've got a green velvet dress and a little green hat.

And now what's happening?

I get in the coach and — I'm trying to think where we're going.

It will come; just relax. It will come to you. Ask John and he will tell you. What does he say?

He says "Savannah," 'cause he's got some relatives up there and we're going to visit. We're going to his aunt and uncle's in Savannah.

How is the trip?

Pretty rough. The roads are awful rough. We sit real close together and when the coach bounces, we laugh. 'Cause some of the bridges are nothing but logs stretched over; have to be real careful that the wheels don't go off.

Okay. Continue.

But it's fun really, 'cause it's the first time we've been away from everybody really. Feels sorta funny not to have all the people around.

Okay. Very good. Now continue back — continue on to the next event of major importance. Take your time; go very slowly. You understand and you know and you learn and grow from this experience. Now tell me what is happening. What are you doing?

Well, I'm in the house. Sorta nice to have your own house. It's big. Oh, I don't really have to do very much; just sew and always have a lot of company. Someone's always coming to visit 'cause I've got a lot of relatives and he has, too. There's always someone visiting, to talk to. And I like to sew and embroider, so we spend a lot of time sewing. And we have musicals in the evening and play the piano and sing and say poetry. And the days just drift along.

How old are you?

24. I'm about 24.

And what does your husband do for work? What's his work; what is his profession?

Well, mainly he just oversees everything. He's got an overseer but he rides out every morning and inspects everything.

And what year is this? Do you know the year? It will come to you; just relax. Listen and you will hear it. What is the year?

It's about 1834, I think.

91

And what is the town or area where you are living? Is there a name for this town or this part of the country?

It's on the Mississippi, but it's not really a town. We have a plantation out in the country. It's not really a town — it just — everybody's got a big plantation with a lot of farming land around.

Does the plantation have a name? What's it called?

Something "Oaks"– it's got this big line of oaks going up to the door. "Oak Alley" – that's the name of the way you get into it.

Very good. Thank you. Now, are you in a territory or in a state?

Louisiana.

Thank you. Very good.

[Because Geraldine was responding so well, this seemed a good time to continue with more serious work. As you will see, she was guided to that critical time that had always been a block. In this session she was able to relate the experience and understand it. She was thereby released from the emotions, guilt and self-blame linked to this memory. Geraldine's story continued with the pain from her past. She reexperienced the pain stored in her soul's memory and is about to break through and go beyond the pain. She is now ready to crack the shell and get to the heart of the experience.]

Now just relax. Feel yourself moving ahead. Listen carefully because this is very important. Moving ahead now to just before the time when your husband passes away — to just a few days before the time that your husband dies. Remain detached and stand above yourself, looking down at the events, the scenes, and the people.

Just look upon it without reliving, without feeling, without sensing, but just knowing. Uninvolved, detached, just looking. Now, I'd like you to tell me what is happening. Just looking down and seeing the events — what is happening now? Tell me what is happening.

It's not good. John's not feeling a bit good. And he looks real sick and I keep asking him what's the matter with him. He keeps saying he's all right, but he doesn't look good.

Has he been to a doctor? Has he seen a doctor?

No, he won't go. He says he don't have any faith in that doctor — he's a quack, anyhow. But I wish he'd go see someone.

Where is his pain? Does he talk about it? Where does he have discomfort?

He won't talk about it, but I think it's in his chest.

And what do you do?

Well, I fuss around him. He gets mad at me 'cause I keep asking him to sit down, and take it easy and lie down. He keeps telling me not to fuss. But I'm worried and Mammy's worried, too. She says, "There's something wrong with that man but you can't get him to stop going. He just gets on that horse every morning and goes out to those fields. He won't quit."

This is very important. Again, be very detached, and just look upon this event as if you were standing above yourself, looking down at the scene. Now go to the time of his death when you first hear or when you first sense his death. This will not disturb you. You are standing above yourself now. Relate this as if it is happening without the feeling, without the sadness, and without the emotion. Just relate the events, that you may grow, that you may learn through this experience.

Now tell me everything that is happening. Tell me your thoughts, your feelings, and the events. Tell me what is happening. For as you tell me, you free yourself from this burden. What are you doing? What is going on? What is happening?

It's morning and I get up and John looks so pale and I say, "How are you feeling?" And he says, "Oh, tolerable." And he asks, "What are you gonna do today?" And I say, "Well, I have to ride over to Mary's and return that piece of embroidery she left over here the other day." I don't know whether to leave him or not 'cause he looks so puny but he says, "Oh, go on and stop fussing." So I have 'em saddle the horse and I ride over to Mary's house. When I get there, her brother's a-visiting. We get to talking, having a good time, and I look out and say, "My Lord, it's almost dark! And I better be getting home. John will be worried."

And then what happened? What are your feelings and your thoughts? What is happening?

I'm riding down the road.

Tell me about — tell me what is happening.

And I see Jacob riding up the road on a mule. Oh, he's just a-tearing. I say, "What in the world is the matter, Jacob?" He says, "Oh, Miss Sarah, something awful's done happened." [Geraldine's face contorts, her body shakes with intense emotion, and tears flow freely.]

Detach — just the facts. And what do you say?

"My God, Jacob, what is it?" He says, "I cain't tell it." And I say, "Well, tell me, man, what is it?" He says, "Master done shot himself — he shot himself in the head." And I say, "Oh, God, Jacob, I can't stand it!" I fly down the road, run up on the porch — oh, no! He's lying on the couch and blood is all over his face. I said, "Oh, God, what in the world did you do a thing like that for?"

Detached, now — just standing above yourself, just looking.

Maybe he was so sick and tired he just couldn't stand it any longer. I will never know why — why he did it. Why did he do it?

You will know now. You will know why. Because I am going to count from ten to one and you can go to your Higher Self — that part of you that knows and understands all things — and ask why. Ten, nine, eight, seven, six, five, four, three, two, one. Now ask yourself and ask him and you will know why this had to be; nothing more and nothing less.

Oh, it hurts so much. It hurts so bad. I'll never know. Is it my fault or what?

What does he say to you? What does he tell you? Listen very carefully and you will hear him speak to you. What does he say?

It wasn't my fault really. It was just the pain; he couldn't stand the pain. He hurt so bad.

What are your thoughts?

Just sad — sad that it happened this way. He wasn't very old. We had a lot of good years ahead of us.

And now what do you do?

Everybody comes and tells me they're so sorry. They put him in the box. Oh, I guess that's the end of everything for me.

And then what?

Bury him out in the magnolia grove. And then everybody leaves and I'm all alone in that big old house. Just me and the servants. Momma comes and stays with me a few days. But she says I'll just have to face it and learn to live with it, 'cause she can't stay there forever 'cause she's got to take care of Papa. He's not well either. So she goes away and leaves me there by myself and I'll just have to learn to stand it.

Now listen very carefully, because this is very important. Before he died, look into his eyes that morning. Send love to his eyes and send your blessings and your forgiveness. Pour all the love you can into his eyes. And then, he fades. The more love you send him, the more he fades away.

And you let this memory go now. You let it go. And he is gone now, and you bless him and you forgive him, for you understand him now. You understand the reasons and the whys.

You release him, for this is not your fault. This happened — nothing more and nothing less. You let this memory go, sending love and happiness and compassion and understanding. Let him go now.

The purpose of past-life work is to understand, to learn, and to grow. I sometimes call it "healing the past." I knew that Geraldine/Sarah had experienced healing from both sessions. Again she burst with fluent tears. She had no recall of the sessions so I did not offer her the tapes. However, there was one more step for her to take. Here is her story of the last experience.

After a time I asked Henry if I could listen to the regression tapes. Every time I listened to them or tried to talk about it I was overcome with grief. I felt I had to face this experience and get over it. [Now that she had the name of the plantation she began looking through books in search of it. She indeed found a picture of an Oak Alley Plantation located in Louisiana.] One of my friends heard the tapes and said she would take me to New Orleans and we would look for the house. Two other friends came with us.

All the way down it seemed like I was going home, the South looked so familiar. We went to the Oak Alley Plantation near Vacherie, LA. We went around the house with a tour group. When I got upstairs on the veranda, I turned and looked back down the road and I started to cry. I couldn't help myself. I ran around the corner and leaned my head on the side of the house and cried it out.

A nice gentleman tapped me on the shoulder and asked if there was anything he could do. I told him it was too late, it was all over. And I knew it was. I dried my eyes and rejoined my friends.

I asked the guide many questions about the plantation. I told her what I knew and she confirmed what I said. I knew where everything had been and what it had looked like in the 1800s.

"When did they cut the Spanish moss out of the trees?" I asked.

She answered, "About 12 years ago the moss reached the ground and the lady who owned the house at the time said it looked too gloomy and she had it all cut out."

"Are the graves still over in the magnolia grove back of the house?" I asked.

"No," she said, "that property was sold and the graves were moved over to the parish church yard."

I felt like I had been to a funeral. It took me several days to get over it.

Geraldine has since reported that she has not been bothered in any way with the recurrent nightmare. By keeping an open mind, her sessions and after-session experiences enabled her to understand and to free herself of the guilt and trauma associated with that life. There has been absolutely no recurrence of the nightmares. The memory is healed.

Endnotes:

[1] Henry Bolduc, *Self-Hypnosis: Creating Your Own Destiny* (Virginia Beach, VA: A.R.E. Press, 1985).

Illustration #4
Oak Alley, built in 1836 on the west bank of the Mississippi River. The mansion is set at the end of an alley of 28 giant oaks trees. Vacherie, Louisiana.

Chapter Six

OPENING NEW DOORS

Time present and time past,
Are both perhaps present in time future,
And time future contained in time past.
T. S. Eliot, *Burnt Norton*

Until now this book has mainly been about my years of research into past-life regression. The Bridey Murphy book stimulated my interest. Experiments with Cal and many others over the years taught me how to use hypnosis to initiate regressions. My experience with Chuck convinced me once and for all that past-life regression — or time travel, a phrase I coined to cover any journey in time, either to the past or the future — is a reality; and my own voyages into the past were sources of enormous personal growth. Gradually, through these and other experiences, I came to see the therapeutic value of time travel, as the transcripts of Geraldine's sessions show.

I'd like to pause now in my narrative to reflect on some of the things I have learned about hypnosis and past-life regression. This chapter and the next deal with these topics.

Why travel to a past life? "Because it's there," as the mountaineer said when asked why he wanted to climb Mount Everest. Because I believe in the reality of past lives (and believe that we all have many), I want to explore them. I want to explore the process of time travel — simply to experience the experience. But also, I am a soul explorer on a life quest, a learning quest. I seek personality integration, spiritual development and just plain fun. The people I work with share some or all of my motives for traveling in time. Some hope for relief of a problem; some seek spiritual enlightenment. Let me discuss these things more fully, as well as offer some suggestions for the beginning time traveler or guide.

HAVING FUN WITH TIME TRAVEL

To me, past-life work is like dancing in eons of time. The Bible says that the Holy Spirit will "bring all things to your remembrance" (John 14:26). This is what my work is all about. If I choose, I can walk into the misty, echoing ruins, witness ancient happenings, tune in to primeval beginnings. I grow to realize that each lifetime is but a step in an eternal dance, and I am one of the dancers. Fun? Yes! Enjoyment is a valid reason to do this work. During my school years I noticed that teachers who made their classes and subjects fun were the ones who enjoyed their work the most. I observed that as students we learned and remembered far more from those teachers. Education can be fun; life can be fun; spiritual development can be fun; work can be fun. If my work stopped being fun I would quickly find something else to do.

I am not saying this work is a laugh a minute — no way. In fact, I witness more tears than laughs. But the tears of remembrance wash away the crude shadows and stains of the past, and people then speak of great relief. That is rewarding, and that is accomplishment, and that is fun.

Of course, there are sessions in which a person laughs and laughs. There is great release in laughter also; there is a whole spectrum of human experience in these time travel sessions.

Closely allied to the fun of time travel is the pleasure of experiencing the experience. Why do people travel to England when they can go to the library and get a book, free of charge, that shows almost everything they will see and tells more than they will ever learn? Because they want to *experience* it, to be part of it, feel and smell and taste it. And we all want to experience it firsthand, whether it be a present or a past life.

SPIRITUAL DEVELOPMENT

Past-life study gives an overview of the soul's journey and purpose: spiritual development. Most especially, journeys through time gain clarity or an overview of life eternal and universal. Spiritual development is the most important reason for undertaking time travel, but it is not necessarily everyone's first choice. A far larger number try it out of curiosity. Still, that curiosity may lead to a fuller understanding of the continuity of lives.

Spiritual development is personal and different with every person. The goal is to learn, to improve, expand, and unfold into a more whole, healthy, and happy person. Spiritual development is what *Earth school* is all about. But as children in school we seldom think of our reasons for being there; and even less about our purposes and ideals. We are there because we *have* to be there to learn our lessons.

PERSONALITY INTEGRATION

My work is practical, not theoretical. I see that delving into past lives sometimes eases the pain a person experiences in the present. For instance, Geraldine (whose story is in Chapter 5) was relieved of nightmares and headaches after her sessions. I don't know *why* it works, although I believe we are on the verge of great discoveries about the mind's and soul's memory; as we *do* more we will learn more. (For those who wish to pursue the theoretical and practical foundations of regression therapy, a reading list is included in the Appendix.)

I am not a psychotherapist and I never call myself one, practice as one, or offer my coworkers in time travel assurances that therapeutic goals will be met. (I do not call them "clients" because I do not accept payment for the regression work we do.)

Once, in a reading, I was told that my role as a regression guide is to be a "door opener." Can't you just see it on a business card?

Henry Bolduc, D.O.
Door Opener

But that's really what my work is. When I agree to work with a person on a past-life regression, I am helping open the doors of the subconscious. I want to help people learn about themselves; I want to learn about the processes of past-life regression; I want to cover new ground and explore new territory and I want to set up a program that can be duplicated by others.

Time travel is a tool for better understanding one's inner self, for obtaining greater insight into soul origins, life purposes, and skills. With great self-knowledge, the past can be used to relieve present-day problems and to build a brighter, more rewarding future.

Although triggered by present-life circumstances (parents, school, friends, television), human neuroses and character disorders are usually rooted in the soil of times past. Budding, they grow again in the present. Past-life therapy is not a gimmick nor a quick or painless process. In past-life therapy, patients may experience once again the terrible hurts, the loss, death, and pain of times past. The work is not always easy and tears flow in abundance. But these are the tears that wash and cleanse the soul; therapy without tears is like bathing without water. But the most painful lessons of the past are usually the ones that teach us most in the present, and growing through these lessons is what brings true wisdom. For wisdom is but having learned to grow from our myriad incarnations.

Past-life therapy helps people to be more balanced and responsible, to gain emotional and spiritual maturity and a sense of their true worth. In some cases, the recall and

101

therapy is so vibrant that it is like a total and complete spiritual release, followed by profound peace.

Although many people experience great revelations in past-life exploration, there is no guarantee that everyone will. In fact, some stored memories can be very difficult to accept or even to understand. A person with major psychological problems may wish to clean up some present-life situations before delving into other lives, and disturbed people especially may wish to undergo traditional psychotherapy. Past-life therapy is a good tool, but first comes the desire and determination to get well no matter what method is used.

There is another reason for pursuing past-life regression than erasing and healing the problems of the past: great benefit comes also from reliving joyous experiences — the times of great love and accomplishment. I help people focus on positive patterns of fulfillment, the triumphs of their soul.

As for myself, integrating my present and my past has not always been easy. First I have tried to get the essence of each life condensed or distilled into its most important nuggets. I search for the reasons for each life and seek its most important lessons. I then try to form this into a whole picture — to bring all the varied parts and experiences together to get an overview. I study how the past fits into my present and where my present is reflected in my past. I then look for ways to build a better future. Many revelations have come from this process. The biggest one is that what I dislike in others is often a part of myself (past or present) I am unhappy with. As I grow more tolerant and appreciative of others, I recognize parts of them as parts of myself; I see myself reflected in other people. Most of my problems are thus self-created, whether in a past life or the present one.

A personal example of growth is that I have been able to combat a childhood sense of inferiority and self-doubt. I had learned to compensate for this by masking my feelings with arrogance. Then, after being regressed, I saw that those extremes were rooted in my past. By using self-hypnosis tapes, I was able to create a more healthy self-confidence. I have learned to laugh at my follies and the really dumb things

I have done (and do). I have improved my attitudes, learned to understand my emotions better, and discovered reasons for living more fully by seeing my many lives as a whole and growing experience. In turn, I become more whole.

HYPNOSIS AS A TOOL

Hypnosis makes past-life recall easier by bypassing the critical conscious mind to give access to the subconscious memory banks. It is not the only tool used to reclaim memories of past lives; others are dreams, meditation, study, imagination, travel, and drugs. I believe hypnosis is the quickest and most direct. Drugs are unstable and uncontrollable. The other approaches are valid and time-tested, but very slow. Shirley MacLaine, the actress, reported using acupuncture successfully to stimulate past-life recall.[1]

All recall is based on accessing short-term or long-term memory files. Present-life memories are often recalled both consciously and subconsciously. Most present-life memories are readily available in the conscious or short-term memory (except early childhood and repressed traumatic memories which are buried in the subconscious). The conscious mind questions, filters, weighs, and analyzes information. Past-life memories, on the other hand, are usually only recalled subconsciously. There is little conscious confirmation or rejection. The subconscious stores long-term memory and information. It does not confirm or evaluate.

Hypno-regression procedures access different types of memory throughout the experience. At first, some people may have only "cerebral memory," but soon can access "emotional memory," "physical memory," and "soul memory."

Cerebral Memory —	facts/data
	names/dates
Emotional Memory —	love/hate
	joy/sorrow
	tears/laughter

103

Physical Memory — accidents/pain
birth/death

Soul Memory — understanding/acceptance
and assimilation of life's lessons.

Those who respond to life predominately from the cerebral may have less vibrant experience than people with more intuition or feeling for life. Others may overly analyze, criticize or filter their information flow. The "feeling" person can have easy, free-flowing experiences but may need to develop soul perspective. The goal for everyone is to experience, in fullness, all types of memory for self-discovery and self-betterment.

Past-life events and experiences that are not well-understood have a way of appearing as either miraculous or sinister. In truth, they are simply events and experiences that need to be further explored and better studied. Facts are simply that — facts; there is no judgment. In my early experience, for example, I was perturbed to discover I had been a prostitute, but now that revelation just amuses me.

PAST-LIFE PROOF

But is the information gathered from past-life narrations true? I believe so, but who knows?

I wonder sometimes at the intellectual arrogance of those who scoff at the idea of past lives. The idea that the Earth revolved around the sun, instead of being the center of the universe, was considered heretical (by the Christian Church) and idiotic (by scientists) as recently as the 17th century, when Galileo espoused it; yet now it is the foundation on which all astronomy is built. Not until later could scientists prove the original idea, propounded by Copernicus in the 16th century, was correct. Is it any less possible that the existence of past lives — in which Eastern cultures have long believed — could someday be similarly proved?

My friend Eileen, of whom you will read in later chapters, likes to tell a story that illustrates this point. Some scientists are climbing a mountain to find out what God and creation are all about. They struggle over all obstacles, they learn all the scientific rules and unlearn them. They are about to conquer the highest peak and yell out their victory. And as they pull themselves over the last rock, there we all are, meditating.

So until proof arrives, past-life feelings, like love, are hard to prove or even measure. Who can prove love or God or even life? Long ago I stopped trying to prove anything. I have also stopped worrying about seeming discrepancies of dates or years or names or places. What did you have for dinner only one week ago? Where were you when you were five — and can you really prove it? Many case histories have acknowledged discrepancies or inaccuracies. For example, here is a tape excerpt from a regression session with a friend.

SHARON
Nov. 19, 1979
Dallas, Texas

What are you doing?
We are standing on the steps. I'm patting down my dress. We are waiting for the men to come back from the hunt.
Tell me more, please. What is happening?
Some are riding up and getting off their horses and coming up. The king has come up and he will — he's giving his wife, the queen, a kiss. We're turning back to go up the steps. And they are going off to his chambers. We are going to ours, where we will wait 'til supper.
And now what happens?
I've got — I keep checking my left arm. There's a handkerchief in my left sleeve. It's a nervous habit I have. And I'm looking for something to look in to see myself. I'm looking for a piece of glass, and I seem to have found it. I'm just fixing my hair to make sure it's tucked in. I'm walking down the hall, past the guard and I'm going and turning around and sitting on a bench in my room until I am summoned again. I see myself writing. I see light coming in from a window. I'm writing to someone — I'm writing to someone named "George." I can look

105

out the window — and see the lake and there are trees. It's a very nice room. It's nice and airy and open. It's got a very big bed — centered. And there are long high windows on either side. I'm sitting at my desk on the left side of the bed. This is my room.

What are you called? What is your name?

My name is Eloise.

Do you have a family name?

The name in the castle is Hanover — I — that's not my name.

That's okay. We'll come back to it another time. Where is the place? Do you know the country?

Yes. We are in London.

And do you know what date this is, what year?

1640.

And who is the king that rode in?

It's Henry.

And how well do you know him?

I know that he is king. I know that he is husband to the queen, Catherine.

How close are you with Catherine?

I am one of her ladies. We tend to her.

Do you like her?

Yes. She is quite nice. I am treated very well.

What are your duties?

I help her pick her clothes — cut flowers — fix her hair. Sometimes I read to her.

What do you read to her? Is there anything that stands out, that you enjoyed reading?

The Bible.

Is that her favorite?

Yes. She likes the Book of James.

Okay. Thank you. Now continue on ahead — to the next event of major importance. Continuing on now, when you are a little older, to another event — a major event in your life. See it, sense it, relive it, and then when you are ready, begin telling me what is happening, what you are doing.

We have just come in from a carriage ride and I'm taking off my coat. The ladies are knocking the snow off my hair and I am walking in by the fire to warm my hands. It's quite cold out there.

We have a lovely house — it's the Lancaster house. You can look up and there are windows from floor to ceiling. It's very warm in here; it's very nice. And George has come in and he is standing beside me. We are both getting warm from the fire. It *is* cold. We have just come from a visit to the king and queen, who —

Tell me.

Well, it's not Catherine anymore; it's Anne. He seems to be changing daily. But — he *is* the king. We're getting ready for dinner. Oh, and the children are coming down. Oh, we're going to have pheasant tonight and we're all at the table now and we're holding hands to say grace.

Who says the grace?

George does.

Do you remember what he says? What does he say?

Well, "Bless this food, O Lord, and be glad that we're all here together tonight. Praise be His name." It's nice.

Yes, it is. Thank you. Tell me about dinner. You said it was pheasant?

Yes, pheasant and corn and some potatoes and gravy and wine.

And as always, Michael and Seth are sitting there chattering away. It's nice. This is a nice time of day for us; we're all together.

Okay. Thank you.

Now, any historian could pick this material apart. The most obvious "mistake" is that in 1640, the King of England was not named "Henry." The king then was Charles I, the second Stuart king. Henry VIII, to whom Sharon seems to refer (because of the references to Catherine and Anne, the first and second wives of Henry VIII) reigned much earlier, from 1509 to 1547.

On the other hand, there is an interesting historical usage of which Sharon presumably knew nothing: her mention of corn. We all thought it was a mistake because corn, or maize, is native to the Americas; it wasn't known in Europe until the 17th century. But she was *not* mistaken. The British and many Europeans still use the word "corn" to refer to the most widely-grown cereal crop in any given district — so wheat, rye, oats, or barley could all be referred to as "corn." The information we all thought was wrong turned out to be right for that time and place.

Do the discrepancies matter? Sharon may have had information overlap from her two or more lifetimes in England. Moreover, the flow, the message, the emotion, and the sincerity are real, at least to Sharon, and that is all that counts. If it helps her or entertains her, what has she lost? — a few hours of her time.

Hoping to prove past lives to a closed-minded individual is a Catch-22, a no-win situation. When recalled information is not substantiated by history, it is discounted or rejected. If the recalled information is confirmed in a book, then the cynic will smugly say that the subject read it as a small child and consciously forgot reading it.

Follow-up research and investigation can verify or disprove any historical information. (Though I sometimes wonder about history. History is only as unbiased as the people who write it, and the victors write the history.)

The personal validity of the information is proof for most people. For others, the experience is, in itself, sufficient and revitalizing. People who brush aside regression experiences by saying that they are just imagination have probably not truly experienced them. For others, there can never be proof.

Past lives do not necessarily need to be literal to be helpful; allegorical past lives can be equally enlightening. Truly, the overview and the potential for learning is enough in itself. Although *I* accept most of this work as valid or "really real," some people accept it only symbolically or allegorically, as archetypes, metaphor, or a collective unconscious. This is fine; people can receive benefit and betterment no matter what they label it.

Sometimes in a session a past or present-life memory can be disjointed. Sometimes information comes and there is not time to follow up on it, or the follow-up questions are not asked. For example, I would love to know more about Louana and the principles of Pyramadis from Chuck's sessions in Chapter 3. Sometimes the full picture becomes clear only after several sessions.

I encourage people with whom I work not to be distracted by attempts at verification, but to continue on the path of honest, open-minded exploration. Each of us tells a story with our lives — one different from all other stories — our own unique history. Results do not even require belief. Open-minded inquiry is all that is necessary. Several people with whom I have worked did not believe in past lives. Nonetheless, through the experience of time travel, they achieved positive results and insight. Not all information proves to be applicable and a person may wonder if he or she is just making up details of the life. Often a person thinks it's his or her imagination. Shirley MacLaine wonders at length about this in *Dancing in the Light.*[2]

The human mind is an unlimited storehouse of knowledge. The answers are already there. All that is required is to ask the right questions and evaluate the answers. The mind resonates with the excitement of discovery. Time travel is perhaps one of today's greatest adventures.

Endnotes:

[1]Shirley MacLaine, *Dancing in the Light* (New York: Bantam Books, 1985).
[2]Ibid.

Chapter Seven

ADVENTURE INTO TIME

During deep meditation it is possible to dispel time, to see simultaneously all the past, present, and future, and then everything is good, everything is perfect, everything is Brahman. Therefore, it seems to me that everything that exists is good — death as well as life, sin as well as holiness, wisdom as well as folly.

Hermann Hesse
Siddartha

A beginner in past-life work is likely to focus on the personalities or the prominent figures of a time. He or she wonders, "Was I someone famous or important?" Well, yes; some of us *had* to have been. But the odds are against it. Sharon, who was lady-in-waiting to a queen (Chapter 6), is the only person I, myself, have worked with who was near the great and powerful.

The experienced time traveler focuses on the lessons to be learned from past lives and seeks to apply that knowledge in the present. The important question about other lives is not proving who we were, but rather evaluating what we did and how we helped others.

If you wish to look at your past lives, first ask yourself why. You may find things in your past that are not necessarily pleasant or easy to accept. Some people are sidetracked by reliving the past over and over like a rerun on television. The present is where growth is experienced.

TRIGGERS TO SOUL MEMORY

For those people who are ready, there are some good beginning steps to take. You do not have to seek a full past-life regression immediately.

Begin the journey inward with a prayer for protection and direction; start with a search of your motives, your reasons for wanting to do this work. Then, practice relaxation techniques such as those in yoga; there are many books and teachers to help you find desirable methods for you. When you are in a relaxed, meditative state, try this exercise. Practice "daydreaming" by recalling a special episode from the past — a vacation, a talk with a friend, a day in summer. Everyone has such an event, a wonderful, magic, never-forgotten day. Go into your mind and relive that special day. Remember the details and the feelings; recall the other people who may have been there. Describe what you and others are wearing ... and saying. Bring this memory into the present; think of it as happening right now. Do this exercise with other events. Later, choose sad events also; recall even a tragic time. Let the gears of your memory — your image storage and retrieval system — begin to turn.

At first, do your daydreaming as you meditate. Later you can do it in a waking state when you have a few minutes to wait — when driving to work (if you are not the driver!), waiting for an appointment, standing in line at the bank. Not only is it enjoyable to review episodes in your life, but you will also learn more about how your mind functions.

You can also take some of the courses that are available for spiritual development; there are many, offered by many institutions. You can also buy or make self-help, self-hypnosis tapes.[1] If you would like to make a tape using my format, I have included the full transcript called "Accessing Your Soul's Memory" in the Appendix. In it, I take you through the Blue Mist approach which is explained later in this chapter.

Study your dreams and daydreams and keep careful journals about what you experience. Keep a notebook and pen or pencil near your bed. On awakening take a few minutes to jot down your dreams. Some dreams have hints and insights into the past in this life and other lives. Dreams do not prove the existence of past lives, but many people find them a useful door into the subconscious. There are books on the interpretation of dreams, but you are the best judge of their meaning, and you are likely to see patterns of meaning very quickly. A recurring dream (a few times or more a year) is especially significant.

Travel is a good way of triggering memory. Any place in the world can bring forward impressions or memories. Some people say they are drawn to places in which they lived in a past lifetime; sometimes this hunch is confirmed later in regression sessions. Or they travel to a place, only to sense they are having a very familiar experience; the place itself reawakened the memory. Where you want or do not want to travel may be a clue that you have been there before; where you have lived before may subconsciously pull or repel you now.

Many people I know yearn to go to some particular place for no apparent or logical reason. Now, if a person has a strong desire to go to Ireland and that person is very proud of her Irish ancestry and her family always talked in glowing terms about the Emerald Isle, that yearning is pretty explainable. But — perhaps — that person has chosen Irish parents for the close tie-in with a soul memory.

Then there are the places a person *never* wants to go. After high school in 1964, I dated a young woman who refused to eat at any Chinese restaurant, though I love Chinese food and often coaxed her to go to one with me. She *hated* Chinese food, she said. Before we broke up (not over the choice of restaurants), she asked for a regression session. It was the only time we worked together. The one lifetime she explored was a very unhappy, poor, miserable time in (you guessed it) the Orient. Of course, there is no profound conclusion here that people with pleasant past lives in the Orient now love Chinese food, or vice versa. You will recall I had a short and tragic life in China on a barren trade route yet I presently enjoy spring rolls and lychees more than anything else I can think of to eat.

There are many other triggers to soul memory besides traveling. For instance, sometimes in a feverish state, past-life insights come through, as they did for me when I was living in Spain about 20 years ago.

My own past lifetimes have flashed as sudden revelations, as insights, as dreams, and as daydreams. They have come at most unusual times and places. They were not always the result of hypnotic regressions, but came spontaneously. I didn't ask to experience my life as a poverty-stricken girl in China; I was in a state of reverie, watching a television program (it wasn't even about China), and the memory came very powerfully. At the end of the vision or memory, I could immediately contrast it with my lifetime in Greece as a rich and powerful prostitute and see how, in some way, one life was a payment for another.

Astrology can give insight into past lives. I learned this at The Adventure, where two astrologers looked at cyclic life patterns brought forward from the past. Possible future direction was clearly shown from past patterns. Palm, card, Tarot, and crystal ball readings can trigger past-life memories in sensitive or psychic people.

The bottom line is that searching into soul memory is a personal experience and a personal adventure. The regression guide or facilitator can be of help because of his or her experience and knowledge as a guide, but you are the person doing the real work. Furthermore, according to Edgar Cayce, you are the best judge of your personal experiences.

Probably the best way to prepare for a session with a guide is *not* to prepare. Simply go in without expectations, without wanting to explore anything specifically. Leave judgments and assumptions outside the door. Use your first session to get to know the guide and become familiar with the procedures. The guide may suggest homework and exercises. Learning to pay attention and listen carefully to one another is the best preparation for success later.

Assuming, then, that you wish to experience a past life through a hypnotic regression — or that you are interested in guiding a regression — here is what you might expect in my sessions. Other researchers and guides use similar techniques and procedures.

THE GROUP REGRESSION SESSION
When working with a group, whether it is large or small, I first answer questions. There are always good questions — not usually about the technical aspects of the process, but rather about general concerns. "How do we know if this information is real?" is a typical question. I suggest participants concentrate on the experience and evaluate the information and feelings later.

Almost everyone in a group will participate freely. If someone decides not to, I ask that he remain quiet so as not to distract the others. Those who watch (often other professionals who wish to see how I work) are often as interested as those who take part.

In a group, I use my standard hypnosis procedure. This has been an evolving procedure over the years and incorporates the best of what I have learned.

Sometimes during a session an individual may start to cough and clear his or her throat. In the past this behavior was thought to show resistance to the process. Now we have found that the person is so very relaxed that the nasal passages drip a little; it is a sign that the session is going well for that person. The behavior is likely to stop shortly; if it does not, the individual may wish to leave the group until the coughing stops.

Sometimes a participant will cry, loudly and openly. I have never witnessed (nor heard of) a reaction more distressing. My job here is not to intervene, but to enable the person to release the information or experience through hypnotic suggestion. I then give wake-up and return suggestions to bring the individual back to consciousness.

After the session I give people plenty of time to reorient themselves. This time can be likened to awakening in the morning; folks need a few minutes to gather themselves together.

After that I give people a chance to share their experiences. No one ever seems to want to start, but once one person opens up the rest quickly follow. Time limits usually allow only a few people to share, but I encourage everyone to write down or tape record their experiences.

Many people find writing or taping their memories, feelings, and impressions brings forward more information and greater clarity of recollection. The sooner notes are written or recorded the better, as some memories fade quickly.

OUTCOMES OF THE GROUP SESSIONS

People tell me they get a lot from group work. Certainly most seem to enjoy themselves. Only rarely does a participant fail to experience something. Once, for example, I said to the audience, "Look down at your feet and see what you are wearing." One man did so — literally. He opened his eyes to look and became so disoriented he could not continue the session. I suggested he work with tape recordings of the session to see if he could recapture other memories. (I now word the suggestion, "Mentally, look down at your feet....")

Group exercises and small, private group sessions are helpful in introducing people to time travel. They are also useful in my own research because people willingly share their experiences afterwards.

In a group session, it is not possible for a dialogue to take place between the guide and any individual. Nor are group sessions a substitute for professional regression work on a

115

one-to-one basis. A group excursion is like a field trip into the mind — an experience in which students try to confirm laboratory data and/or explore new learning. As such, group sessions are good preparation for individual sessions at a later time and a good introduction to the field of recall and accessing stored memory.

INDIVIDUAL REGRESSION SESSIONS

In individual sessions I try to most effectively guide each person by wording suggestions according to their unique temperament and needs. I can only accomplish this by listening acutely and observing closely all that the subject says and does. You will see examples of this later in my work with Eileen. A very nervous person, for example, may need deep breathing exercises before we begin. On the other hand, an easy going person or a person with whom I have worked many times requires less time to enter his or her natural level of relaxation. This approach — sometimes called the "naturalistic" approach — was pioneered by Dr. Milton H. Erickson[2] and usually brings quick and deep results. Throughout the session the hypnotist uses what is received from the subject and rewords or reframes it in terms the subject relates to, incorporating stories, parables, and visual examples from everyday life.

As a guide and facilitator, my job is to see that the entire process is orchestrated. I make sure the subject is cared for: soft lighting, a comfortable chair or recliner, a light blanket to cover the body (because the metabolism slows down), a quiet, private setting without disturbance from phones or doorbells. This all builds trust and protects the subject from distraction; it is particularly important during the first stage of hypnosis. Next, I help any visitors to place their chairs and get quieted. (I encourage the time traveler to invite a spouse or a friend to sit in on the session.) I always double check the cassette tapes and recording equipment. Because the throat muscles are completely relaxed, many people speak in a very low voice during a regression. I have found I need to sit close by and to use a good external lapel or tie clip microphone with the recording equipment.

But all of these are mechanical procedures; the truly important part of my work is helping the person to simply experience the experience. That is not a cute play on words; some people are simply too anxious for dramatic results or too self-doubting or self-critical to just let go and do it. I tell them the only real problem is in too much self-analysis. We are not trying to prove anything but just to experience the experience.

Most people are a little nervous at their first session, which is normal. Progressive relaxation and hypnosis quickly relax them. These days I am able to show first-timers a VHS video cassette of myself working with a new subject. In the video I explain all procedures and answer all questions, which seems to de-mystify the experience. The viewer witnesses a full regression and can see the benefit that the man experiencing the regression achieves. This allays much of the apprehension before the session even begins.

The best subjects come with an honest and open attitude. My own first sessions were a life changing, positive experience that I will always remember. I try to make it that way for others. My principal role is that of questioner, guide, and facilitator. My function is to act as a spiritual partner, counselor, and stabilizer. My most important allies are patience, mutual trust, and an open mind. My major qualification as a guide is to be an experienced hypnotist. I have undergone years of apprenticeship and study. I am sensitive to the needs of the subject and the group, and this is balanced with the strength and knowledge to take charge for the entire session. Like a teacher in a classroom, I accept my role of being in charge.

THE HYPNOSIS PROCESS

When everything is ready I begin the hypnosis process. The human brain has four levels of activity, each having a particular cycle per second rate of electrical activity. Most

117

researchers call the normal everyday waking state *beta*. *Alpha* is a transitional phase somewhere between waking and sleeping. We all experience this state as we go into regular nighttime sleep and again later as we awaken in the morning. *Theta* occurs in deep hypnosis, intense meditation, and during the early stages of nighttime sleep. *Delta*, perhaps the least understood, is the deepest sleep or unconsciousness.

Most people experience the hypnotic state when they are in alpha, and many sessions fluctuate between the levels of alpha and theta. Most people pass through alpha so quickly every morning and evening that they hardly realize it, let alone utilize it. It is, however, the door to the subconscious and is sometimes called "waking hypnosis." In a way, alpha hypnosis massages the mind and relieves mental stress. As a session continues, many people automatically enter theta as more and more trust develops. Theta is deep hypnosis and is usually accompanied by clear, strong recall and accessing of deeply-stored memory.

The entire process for time travel, or hypnotic, past-life age regression, has five distinct stages, although each stage progresses naturally into the next. They are: hypnosis (one's natural level of deep relaxation); present-life regression; prenatal regression; past-life regression (the Blue Mist); and the return to present life and awakening.

As a person enters the hypnotic state, the natural level of relaxation, he or she is automatically guided into the second stage, present-life regression. Present-life regression is simply recalling, mentally viewing, or remembering events or impressions from the present life — something we do almost every day of our lives. Hypnosis simply starts the gears of the mind turning, as in an audio or visual playback, and opens the door to clear recall. At this point the time traveler is asked to relate what comes to him or her, no matter how it comes through, and to state the impressions he or she receives without analyzing, censoring, questioning, or passing judgment. Some people relate a flood of information with little questioning required, but most people prefer the active dialogue of questions and answers.

During this stage, different senses come into focus. As new levels of perception and awareness are reached, some people may see an image, others hear a memory, some feel an experience, and others sense an impression. Occasionally someone begins by "smelling" a recollection — a smell actually comes to the senses which reminds the person of an experience or initiates it, and the recollection follows — and there are even people who mentally read inner records from their own *book of life*. I have found that responses of different people vary widely, even from session to session.

Time travel is usually easy and enjoyable. Beginning sessions usually look at happy, pleasant experiences, and during subsequent sessions, more in-depth exploration can be experienced. I also begin therapeutic sessions by requesting pleasant memory stores and files. Soul disorders and stressful material will surely erupt soon enough, without rushing it.

After a present-life regression, the subject may explore the third stage: the birth and pre-birth experience. This "rebirthing" can be intense, so I usually pass through this step without lingering though many pscyhologists and past-life facilitators explore this time in great detail.

Prenatal regression is a term given to exploring the formative months before birth and has shown that the unborn child has perceptions and reacts to stimuli from the outer world. The perceptions of the forming child are somehow also connected to the mother's thoughts. I recall a case where a prenatal-regression subject realized that she was an unwanted baby. (This fact was later confirmed by a parent.) This realization was so strong and the subject cried so much that she could not continue her session at that time.

THE BLUE MIST APPROACH

Past-life regression is the fourth stage. The procedure I

have developed to help the subject reach it is called the "Blue Mist Approach." This terminology is not intended to sound mystical. I call it the "Blue Mist" because that's how most people in this stage perceive it.

Previously, I used the approach that Morey Bernstein used in the Bridey Murphy book. Later I used an awareness technique called the "Christos Experience," in which the subject is asked to imagine getting larger, then smaller, floating safely above the body, floating safely above a building, and then returning and standing upon the Earth in a different time and place.

I designed the Blue Mist Approach while working with regression subjects in Virginia Beach. It was inspired by the near-death experiences of clinically dead patients and by what my subjects described specifically as the transition state between lives. Different regression facilitators have adapted it to fit their individual styles. The approach goes like this.

....Continue back to when you are two — and then one. You find that you can even go to the time of your birth. And you can go beyond this time. Going now to that very warm, very safe, and very secure place where nothing can harm you — where you feel so very good — so protected. This is a good time — a forming and growing time.

And you find you can go beyond this even — going now into the Blue Mist. And the Blue Mist protects you. This is a time of trust and a time of understanding. This is a time of rest, of ancient echoes and quiet movement. A time you only thought you had misplaced.

Look into the deep recesses of your own mind. Open your memory banks to the remembrances of your innermost feelings, for through the avenue of the heart, all things are revealed to you. Embrace the feeling — reach deep within.

You are happy here. Yet part of you longs for movement — and you look out toward the horizon or as if looking through a long tunnel — and you see a light. You begin going, flowing, moving toward the light. You merge and converge within the light. The light surrounds you and protects you. You feel the life energies flowing throughout your being.

As you mentally look down at your feet — describe what you see on your feet. What do you have on your feet?

The more you tell me, the more clear and vivid it all becomes.

At this time, I usually wait, giving the person the necessary time to respond before continuing to ask questions about the description of the clothing and the body. As in present-life work, this can be give and take of questions and answers, or it can be a monologue delivered by the subject. Some people require little questioning to pour out a veritable fountain of information. Either way, past patterns and hidden clues emerge from the deep recesses of the subconscious.

EXPERIENCING TIME TRAVEL

There are at least two different ways of experiencing past-life time travel, *reviewing* and *reliving*. In the first, the subject is a detached observer. Many memories and impressions are recalled and related from the viewpoint of a spectator of the scene rather than as a participant. It is almost as if the person is looking through a family photo album and commenting on some of his or her favorite pictures. Reliving can be more intense and dramatic and is not always desirable in an early session because of the intensity; this level is a deeper soul memory. Many sessions are actually a combination of the two, with an ebb and flow of involvement and detachment, or reviewing and reliving. If you will look back over the transcripts of sessions in this book, you will see how often subjects change from one state to the next and where I tend to guide them back into the reviewing stage.

One lifetime or several can be explored in a single session. A detached view of the death experience is also valuable near the end of the session. Death is simply another stage of growth and most people with whom I have worked are amazed to discover that their awareness does not end with death. In fact, many people achieve their greatest personal insight through reviewing their former death experiences and the many passages from life to life.

I have discovered that most memories are recorded and stored as images, emotions, emblems, and symbols. Often a person will describe, at length, his or her feelings about just one image. The more emotion involved with an image, the more vivid it becomes. But because the mind more easily stores and retrieves images, names and dates may be difficult to remember. This is not a credibility gap but merely the lack of a stored image or emotion for a particular name or date. Emotion-filled scenes and memories are usually much easier for most people to remember and relate; some memories are relived as emotion only. Experiences differ from person to person, session to session. Some people even speak in languages they do not know in their present lives.

When I talk about time travel and regression it may seem that the work centers in the mind or in the head. This is not usually so; most soul work centers on what people call the "heart." The heart encompasses the emotions, the attitudes, the will, and the feeling part of a person. *This* is where real past-life therapy is — at the feeling level. We begin by going through the mind, but the accomplishment is in the feelings, the soul or spirit. The mind stores dates; the heart stores sorrow, anger, fear, and joy, hope, and love.

RETURNING TO THE PRESENT

The fifth stage is returning to the present and waking. Closing the mental, emotional, and spiritual door to a past-life memory is as important as opening it. A person's subconscious usually has the final say as to which memories are to be consciously retained and brought back, and which are to be refiled for future reference. Just because the subconscious mind can understand the lessons of a past life does not guarantee that the subject's conscious mind can also deal with it in the present. Most information *can* be assimilated in the present but some is best refiled and stored for future processing.

This type of healing suggestion can be used near the end of the session.

Now see in your mind's eye all the people you recognized in this life (or lives). Look into their eyes. Now, send love from your eyes into their eyes — and they begin to fade. Bless them. Release them and let them fade. Let them go.

You will retain in your conscious mind only that information which is beneficial and helpful for you to retain at this time.

These suggestions are a gentle yet definite way of closing the door to the past while allowing the subject's subconscious the choice of what to remember.

Two of the biggest lessons I have learned in this work are the closing of the door to soul's memory and the careful return to the waking state. The transition back to everyday, beta level awareness (the normal waking state) should be smooth, whole, and complete; otherwise, people can come back temporarily disoriented. I call it "spiritual jet lag." The considerate guide or facilitator does not cut corners or rush the wake-up process. In fact, this can be a special time for the subject's full spiritual comprehension and digestion of information.

Returning to the present and wake-up suggestions similar to this approach can be used.

... Returning through the Blue Mist — going to that warm and safe and very secure place... returning to the present and feeling the life energies throughout your being. Your conscious mind may forget to remember[3] all that you accomplished here today. You are in the present, the date today is _____ and the place is _____. I will count from one to ten; at the

count of ten you can be wide awake, clearheaded, refreshed and relaxed.

One, coming back now. Two, stepping firmly into the present in fullness of strength. Three, coming up slowly. Four, feel total normalization at every level of your being. Five, feel the circulation returning to the extremities. Six, awakening to your full potential. Seven, perfect equilibrium. Eight, reenergized. Nine, revitalized. And ten, wide awake and feeling great.

As the person awakens, because of the suggestion or their own subconscious regulators, there may be little or no conscious recall of the session, or only certain parts may be recalled. Most commonly, the person recalls the entire session and can add more details and information not mentioned during the actual experience.

PAST-LIFE INSIGHT

Subsequent sessions can complete the narrative by giving insight into the patterns that link past to present. Past-life insight doesn't usually come in one big flash. Information comes as pieces of a puzzle. As the pieces come to me, I size them up, hold them up to the light, and turn them one way and another until they all fit in and the overall picture becomes clear.

In regression work I always listen carefully to what each person is telling me. A story may sound strange or disjointed at first because memory is not always sequential. However, by the time a session is completed, the individual pieces usually form a clear picture. Listening carefully reminds me of the tombstone that says, "I told you I was sick." As I trust people's information, I listen to their truths no matter where they come from, or how, when, or even why. Whatever occurs in a time-travel session is a legitimate part of the process of self-discovery. At crisis times or with traumatic events in present or past times, some people need to tell their story over and over and over

The keys to a soul's memory are trust and patience. Trust cannot be created artificially. Above all, it takes *time*. It grows from the foundation up, just as a house is built. The foundation is the most important (and often seems the most time-consuming) part.

Trust in the process builds as both people work on the foundation projects. A foundation project is any project in which the hypnotist and client work together on preliminary exercises. An example would be a session whose only purpose is for the client to experience hypnosis; the object is for the client to learn the procedures. I prefer a couple of sessions for preliminary work before we begin an advanced project such as psychic development or exploring the chakra system. (I'll be explaining this term later in Chapter 10. See the illustration in that chapter.) Similarly, in my book on self-hypnosis I recommend that people tackle the easiest, most entertaining procedures first.

If I have learned one lesson, it is the need for patience. In this age of fast food and faster living, people are accustomed to quick and easy — the dollar buys everything, fast. But wisdom cannot be bought. Some people, it seems, want their soul's evolution revealed to them, in full, in a few hours. The mind does not work like that. Knowledge comes as the person is ready and able to accept it.

Not everyone is able to digest the food of memory; it must be eaten slowly and carefully. Except for the unusual and unexpected session (the one with Chuck, Chapter 3, for instance), I do not work with past-life subjects until we have completed the proper preliminary foundation sessions. If I detect impatience in the early sessions, I will usually go even more slowly. This is not intended to be annoying, but rather to allow the subject to prepare more fully for what is usually a major life experience. For those who insist on *instant* enlightenment, I usually suggest 40 days and 40 nights of fasting in the desert.

Endnotes:

[1] The Association for Research and Enlightenment (A.R.E.) and Atlantic University offer year-round courses in psychic and soul development. They also offer courses in many parts of the U.S. as well as home study courses. For information write A.R.E., P.O. Box 595, Virginia Beach, VA 23451.

Another excellent course is Silva Mind Control. For an introduction, read *The Silva Mind Control Method*, by Jose Silva (New York: Pocket Books, 1978).

Two magazines, *New Age Journal*, 342 Western Ave., Brighton, MA 02135, and *Body, Mind & Spirit*, Box 701, Providence, RI 02901, publish regular calendars of events for people seeking soul development.

Other publications can be found in bookstores, natural food stores, libraries, and pharmacies.

The same kinds of places sell self-help hypnosis tapes. The commercial tapes are usually very good, but it is far superior to make your own tapes. If you wish to read my book on making self-help tapes, *Self-Hypnosis: Creating Your Own Destiny*, it is available from A.R.E. Press, Box 595, Virginia Beach, VA, 23451, and at bookstores. The price is $8.95.

The four cycles I recommend as preparation for age regression are "Developing Psychic Ability" (p. 138), "Beyond Tomorrow" (p. 146), "Friends and Soul Mates" (p. 152), and "Chakra Attunement" (p. 156).

[2] Milton H. Erickson, M.D.(1901—1980), was a pioneer in the development of modern hypnosis and psychotherapy.

Erickson developed a nonauthoritarian, indirect approach to suggestion, demonstrating that patients could use their own unconscious minds to solve their own problems. In the 1930s, when he began his work in hypnosis, it was regarded as a dark and fearful art. He was one of the first to demonstrate, experimentally, that hypnosis is a safe procedure.

126

He was an authority on the use of naturalistic induction techniques, hypnotic utilization, metaphorical and subconscious communication, and the use of behavioral tasks in order to effect change, according to one description of his work.

Erickson spent his formative years in rural Wisconsin. At 17, he was paralyzed by poliomyelitis. He recovered largely through his own efforts, developing techniques for relaxation, use of sense memory, and observation that later became the foundation for his work as a hypnotherapist.

He received his medical degree from the University of Wisconsin. After years of experience as a clinical therapist in mental hospitals, he went into private practice in Phoenix, Arizona, remaining a private therapist there until his death.

He was president of the American Society of Clinical Hypnosis and a Life Fellow of the Americian Psychiatric Association and the American Psychopathological Association. He was the founder and editor of the *American Journal of Clinical Hypnosis,* and is the coauthor of *Hypnotic Realities, Hypnotherapy, Time Distortion in Hypnosis,* and *Practical Application of Medical and Dental Hypnosis.*

I have learned much about his work from *The Collected Papers of Milton H. Erickson on Hypnosis,* a four-volume work edited by Ernest L. Rossi (New York: Irvington Publishers Inc., V. 1, 1983).

[3]This reads oddly, but it is a very advanced suggestion, derived from Erickson.

Chapter Eight

MEETING THE ETERNALS

All that speak are one and we are of the eternal.
The Eternals

Ann and I left Dallas in 1980 and moved to Independence, a tiny town in Virginia's Blue Ridge Mountains where we began construction on an underground house Ann helped design. Without realizing it, I had also turned a major corner in my life's direction.

As a way of becoming better acquainted in the community, Ann suggested I teach a short course on self-hypnosis at the local library. A good idea; I scheduled it one night a week for four weeks. Our town has fewer than 1,000 people so I expected that perhaps a dozen would attend. The first night more than 100 people showed up, during a storm, no less, and the rest of the sessions were just as crowded. Thanks to the class, I met my neighbors, who included a local psychic with whom I later worked; people from the state mental health department, who invited me to speak occasionally at their programs; and members of the local and state police forces, whom I was privileged to assist in a few special cases requiring hypnosis.

I also met Daniel Clay Pugh. He wanted to get a job at a hypnosis center to help people with tobacco and weight problems. Would I teach him to be a hypnotist? Impressed with his sincerity, I agreed to do so, although I had not taken individual students for some time.

In 1983, for six months, Daniel and I met once a week on Tuesday evenings. I gave him lots of homework and he did more than I required. For instance, he used self-hypnosis tapes, which either he made or I made for him, at least once and often twice or three times a day. He was already getting interesting and prophetic dreams that he recorded in a dream log. To help him interpret his dreams and psychic flashes (or daydreams), he frequently used a tape entitled, "Developing Psychic Ability." It was not intended to help make him a channeler, but it did, in fact, prepare him for what was to come.

Daniel also practiced hypnosis techniques on me and on a local dentist who came to some of the classes. He was an apt student and became a very good hypnotist, quickly acquiring the skills he would need for weight and tobacco control. In June, 1983, I thought he was ready to practice at a clinic. As he was walking out the door (and, I thought, out of my life), he turned to ask, almost as an afterthought, "Did you ever try to duplicate the kind of reading that Cayce did?" No, I had not. But I was willing to try. Instead of going out of my life, Daniel Clay was really introducing the next phase of my learning and spiritual development — channeling.

For those of you who are new to this field, channeling is the process by which a person becomes a "vessel" or "channel" for his or her own Higher Self to come through or for the spirit and voice of an entity or entities from another dimension. The voice represents a superconscious, a collective unconscious, or a universal mind. In Biblical times a channeler was known as a "prophet" or "prophetess."

In a hypnotic state, a vessel opens to a different reality, or an altered consciousness. Like a material vessel, a container which holds water that can be shared with many who are thirsty, a psychic or spiritual vessel holds spiritual nourishment which flows through and is communicated through this altered consciousness. The information or guidance does not originate with the vessel (or the guide) but is simply channeled from a higher source which has been variously called "higher beings," "ascended masters," the "Akashic Records," and the "collective unconscious," etc. — but these are all one in accessing the same source. In regression, on the other hand, a person is seeking past-life information through his or her own subconscious mind.

Channeling is not to be confused with mediumship. In some small manner and form, mediumship may have been the forerunner of channeling. But channeling is definitely of the New Age and recognizes little or no resemblance to its ancient ancestor. Mediumship is a process wherein a person can inadvertently open his or her body to possession. Channeling is a process wherein a person seeks high levels of awareness while seeking inner truth. A vessel is thus a messenger of soul guidance, opening to innermost Light and sharing these eternal truths with those who ask.

Edgar Cayce, the American psychic, visited the Akashic Records (soul records) while in a self-induced trance. While there, he "read" from the life scrolls of people who had asked for counsel. The topics of the readings ranged from diagnoses of health problems to explanations of the astrological influences playing on individual lives and relationships; he interpreted dreams and even gave financial advice. It was readings of this type that Daniel wanted to emulate.

Cayce had fascinated me from my very first introduction to his work in the Bridey Murphy book. When Daniel suggested we follow the trail Cayce had blazed so many years before, I was enthusiastic. The thought of trying to duplicate the Cayce methods, as I had once duplicated the Bridey Murphy experiment, excited me.

I had scheduled a business trip to Virginia Beach. Ann and I drove down and while I worked, Ann went to the A.R.E. library to search the 14,000-plus Cayce readings. And she made a great discovery. With the help of the librarians, she found Reading 294-19, the process Cayce had used to gain access to information after he was in a trance. We returned home prepared for a new experiment using Cayce's own procedures.

Simple hypnosis would not guarantee success, I found. After entering a trance, Cayce went through a series of levels of consciousness to reach the place where he could read from the soul record, or Book of Life, of an individual. When Cayce was ready, his guide (usually his wife, Gertrude Evans Cayce), gave him the suggestion to begin the reading. If the proper suggestions were not given at the right time, he would drift into normal sleep and there would be no reading. I certainly didn't want that to happen with Daniel. I would follow the Cayce process as closely as possible.

THE CAYCE LEVELS

As a first step, I simply read the Cayce material below while Daniel, who had proved to be an excellent subject for hypnosis as well as a student of it, was in a trance. The only change I made was to change Cayce's "I" to "you." (It is important to note that after each session I read the steps in reverse. Returning through the levels was vital in enabling Daniel to become safely oriented in the present.) I said:

You see yourself as a tiny dot out of your physical body, which lies inert before you. You find yourself oppressed by darkness and there is a feeling of terrific loneliness.

Suddenly you are conscious of a white beam of light. As this tiny dot, you move upward following the light, knowing that you must follow it or be lost. As you move along this path of light, you gradually become conscious of various levels upon which there is movement.

Upon the first levels there are vague, horrible shapes, grotesque forms such as one sees in nightmares. Passing on, there begin to appear on either side misshapen forms of human beings with some part of the body magnified. Again there is a change, and you become conscious of gray-hooded forms moving downward. Gradually these become lighter in color.

Then the direction changes and these forms move

131

upward and the color of the robes grows rapidly lighter. Next, there begin to appear on either side vague outlines of houses, walls, trees, etc., but everything is motionless.

As you pass on, there is more light and movement in what appear to be normal cities and towns.

With the growth of movement, you become conscious of sounds, at first indistinct rumblings, then music, laughter, and singing of birds.

There is more and more light, the colors become very beautiful, and there is the sound of wonderful music. The houses are left behind; ahead there is only a blending of sound and color.

Quite suddenly you come upon a Hall of Records. It is a hall without walls, without ceiling, but you are conscious of seeing an old man who hands you a large book, a record of the individual for whom you seek information.

Strange things started to happen. Daniel began shaking violently, almost like a person in an epileptic seizure. I had seen this kind of energy release before. Convulsive paroxysms often accompany the sudden unblocking of dormant psychic channels in the same way that a volcano can roar to life in one instant. Profound changes were taking place beneath the surface, and Daniel was shaking in response.[1] Then he began to speak. At first, his words were scattered and disjointed. He spoke about the crisis in the Middle East, the bloodshed in Lebanon, and the unresolved tensions between Israel and Syria. His words contained Biblical references to the strife in these stormy crossroads of the world.

We did not record this first session because we were not sure anything would result from it. But something was coming through, and we tried again with a recorder a week later, following exactly the steps of the first session. Again I witnessed a startling eruption — Daniel's psychic channels, or chakras, were bursting like floodgates. And again Daniel seemed consumed by the events of the troubled planet. Much of what he said, however, was incoherent, which is typical in beginning channeling. As he voyaged through the layered seas of his subconscious, his voice changed dramatically. When he awoke he had no conscious recall of what he had said.

Gradually, as we repeated the procedure in the following weeks, he spoke more coherently and his exaggerated body movements abated as he accepted the energy that flowed through him.

MEETING THE ETERNALS

As Daniel tapped a different level of consciousness, the sources (what could be termed the "Universal Consciousness" coming through Daniel) explained that more than one entity was speaking. The voice always referred to itself in the plural; that is, it said, "We are eternal"; "we are" so and so. For simplicity's sake, Daniel, Ann and I and our circle of friends began to call the source "The Eternal" or "The Eternals." We could not say, "Daniel said ..." when referring to something The Eternal told us, for it was not Daniel's message. In the same way, Cayce Foundation people say, "The readings say ....," and not, "Cayce says ...."

In these early days we learned how to work with The Eternals. We learned a new vocabulary. For example, The Eternals rarely called Daniel by name. He was almost always called "the Vessel." I was called "the Guide," which is an accurate description of the hypnotist at work. We accepted new concepts; the word "karma" and the theories about its meaning were replaced with "balance and counterbalance," and the word "reincarnation" became "progressions."

Gradually, our meetings assumed several forms. In some, The Eternals gave personal readings for participants. Some sessions were experimental. For instance, some of our first sessions involved readings in which Daniel seemed to develop telepathic skills. We had called a few friends — people we thought would like to be part of this continuing experiment — and asked permission to request readings for them. Everyone consented. Each person was given a specific time to be at home, resting or meditating, so as to make a better link with the inner mind and the source. At the prearranged time, Daniel picked up the receiver at his end of the psychic line. Two of our early participants reported that they "felt" Daniel plugging in and also sensed when contact was broken, about an hour later.

Some of our sessions we called "work sessions." These were meetings in which we asked The Eternals for guidance on how to conduct the work. For instance, we discussed ways to make the sessions accessible to a wider public. How should we describe our work? I asked, "Exactly what is the service offered?"

The Eternals answered: "You are counselors, guided by God, given power by God to see into the deep recesses of your own subconscious minds.... This service is the soul guidance."[2]

Later, The Eternals advised us to form a community of seekers, an organization that would handle personal readings for our group and others. This we did, calling it "Ageless Expressions."[3]

THE TEACHINGS

The Eternals then asked us to form a group to meet once a week. We called these meetings "Teachings," to distinguish them from the sessions in which personal readings were given.

They said: "We ask that one day a week you set aside one time specifically for us, the Eternal, that we might teach. We will give you the Teachings that we have given through the ages, that they may be written again. These shall be compiled and put together for there shall be many who will seek it for the Light that we will give through you."

The text of the rest of this chapter and of the next few chapters is based on the dialogues that took place in the Teachings. We invited people from the community to listen, to learn, to ask questions, and to seek the counsel of The Eternals. Participants ranged in age from about 20 to 60, with an equal number of men and women. Many were professionals; we had mental health workers, teachers, lawyers, construction workers. Some came once and did not return. Many who came out of curiosity returned week after week, attending all 10 Teachings.

My back room was too small for the numbers attending, so I brought the recliner and recording equipment into our large combination living/dining room. I dimmed the lights. Everyone was silent as I guided Daniel through the hypnosis exercises and then the Cayce levels. Then, soon, a very different energy began speaking — speaking with great authority, but always with warmth and humor.

One never knew exactly what to expect. Although the Vessel did stand up and even walk a little within the circle, he always had his eyes closed. Even for me, as someone familiar with psychic events, it was eerie to have someone speaking directly to me, touching my innermost soul, with eyes closed — and seeing more clearly than if they were open.

Most sessions lasted about two hours. Afterwards we all discussed the information that had come through. Ironically, only Daniel felt out of place. He had no recollection of what had been said and felt odd and a bit estranged from the group. He once explained to me, "I must admit one feels a bit like a fool when he awakens from a slumber and is greeted by friends who claim he has just uttered words of profound wisdom. Talking in your sleep ain't half bad, if someone tells you you muttered nonsense, but words of wisdom?

"Anyway, what am I doing talking about karma, reincarnation, and Atlantis? Much of this goes against my upbringing. Yet, what the soul sees with eyes unseen cannot be denied."

Our gatherings were full of love and humor; often the whole group laughed joyously together. The love shared was a beautiful experience to enjoy and to behold. I well remember how we eagerly awaited each Tuesday evening to get back together again, and how we sat enthralled by events. The sharing was far more than just questions and answers. There was constant movement and hand motion as the Vessel demonstrated chakra centers, balls of energy, and the like.

Most people in the group were novices, with no previous knowledge of the psychic field. The Eternals were always patient with us and our clumsy gropings into these new realms.

The Teachings were a holy and precious experience. I suspect if I elaborated on their holiness, I would be accused of being a religious devotee of a ghost guru. So I have carefully tried to keep the tone of this book factual and to present our material as an experiment or a new type of research. But it really was a profound and life changing leap into a new age. For those of us who participated, this chapter represents the beginning of a new adventure.

TOPICS FROM THE TEACHINGS

The Teachings covered a wide range of topics. Questions came from many people at many times. In this and the following chapters, the material is arranged not chronologically, but by subject matter, so readers can easily find what interests them.

The Eternals began at the beginning.

"You have your choice of topics to be discussed. At times we shall introduce our own topics, but only if they are overlooked.

"We shall be careful, if we make indications that would be called 'prophetic'; in that case, when transcribing, do not alter tenses though they may seem to be in need of correction.

"You have nothing to fear by bringing others, as long as they know to what they are coming. Their questions will be helpful to you. You may travel in this light. Now shall we proceed?"

Who Is Communicating?

We all wondered about the obvious question of who or what was communicating and why. One member of the group asked,

How do you identify yourself? Are you saying that you are

136

just pure energy, or do you have a personality?

We are eternal, we are the force of life itself. We are what has been called the "Holy Spirit," the "power of God." We are Elohim, Krishna, Yahweh, Christ. We are the total consciousness. We are the supermind of the All Powerful.

We exist in you. We exist in the Vessel. We exist in the trees, and in the walls. We come into the Vessel and speak as is befitting. Sometimes we speak and tell the knowledge that we know, and sometimes we come through the Vessel and show pictures, and he speaks from what he sees.

Sometimes we speak in audible terms, and it is received and then respoken. Sometimes the vibratory force itself flows through and is then translated. Sometimes we give the view omnipotent; sometimes we give the view of another, around. Sometimes we impress ideas; it is just what is fitting to the situation.

Are you saying that spiritual entities are with us during these teachings? Do they come to participate?

They come to participate, they come to speak. We are one; all are one. And yet, we are many.... Therefore, we have called ourselves "the Eternal," for we were, and we are tomorrow, even as we are today.

Is that what you were speaking of when you said that there were others around this gathering?

There are others.... There are others in and about you, communicating with you. There are those, a host of those, around each. There are those who are here to watch and oversee, and there are those that are here to speak. And yet all that speak are one, and we are of the Eternal.

The Voice of Vishnu

There is a famous Eastern religious tract. The subtitle is "The Breath of the Eternals." Is there any connection to your being called "The Eternal?" The other question is, what is meant by the Breath?

Ee-I-a-voice-of-Vishnu, the voice of the most eternal and ancient. If we be the voice of Vishnu, how is it that we are not the breath of the eternal? Does not the breath bring life? Does not the eternal bring life?

Does the whole text that you are referring to contain information where it came from, the Voice of Vishnu?

Yes, and even so you shall call this that you have placed before yourselves here, when compiled, *The Voice of Vishnu.* That which you have seen in dreams shall come as the "Visions of Vishnu."[4]

What Happens During Channeling?

We were all trying to understand what was happening during the channeling. A man asked,

Do you have any trouble expressing yourself through this Vessel? Do you have to go through the brain to do it? Can you just come into the body as you are and express yourself any way you want? Is there any problem expressing yourself?

We are in the body. We are in all bodies. We are in everything continually.

Now, in effect, expressing oneself plainly, there is trouble at times. We function through the subconscious mind. There is a state at which the subconscious mind reaches a consciousness with all subconscious minds, so to speak. All minds are one, and they come together. But when we speak, we can pull out new words, for they are floating in the other conscious minds. It is simplest to use what is already stored within the Vessel in one sense or another.

When you are not speaking through this Vessel, on what level is the "we" of "you"?

Now you speak of something different. The "we" is eternal. That which was spoken of, I am, we are, that which is, but we are in you. We are in the trees. We are in the walls of this house. We are in the Vessel. We are in everything that exists. Yes, we are in your car. We are in the flea collar on the dog down the road. We are in the shingles, we are in the rain that falls. You are asking what exists in the eternal essence. We are everything. We are the level that you seek.

How is it that you, The Eternals, share the Vessel with the physical person, Daniel? How does that work?

[The Eternals explained that parts of Daniel's present life and parts of his past lives prepared him for this work. Then they went on with what follows.]

We share the Vessel with everyone, and in essence, this is what we are speaking of as accepting. You accept this and it grows, and it flows totally through you.

This Vessel requires the crutch [hypnosis], ... but this will be removed when the time is proper. And there shall be those of you who will work with the same crutch, and it shall be removed when the time is proper.

You are all the chosen, the appointed, the elect, and the ordained. It is your responsibility to choose the path of Light. It is your privilege to bring Light. And your ability and your divine right, your heritage, to bring good to yourself and to all those around you, physically, mentally, and spiritually.

Working Within the Self

Gradually we realized that the Teachings encouraged us to work within ourselves. The Eternals said,

First, you must clean yourself. You must remove your faults. You must accept yourself. You must bring Light to yourself or Light to your own little corner of the world, or Light to the few people you can reach. You must remove the dirt, the speck, the problems, the large massive glob blocking your own willingness to reach the inner self; the eye, so to speak, where the energy flows, the eye.

Broadening the Scope of Information

As the Teachings progressed, we grew to know each other better and talked about what to ask in the sessions. We wanted to broaden the scope of the information. We asked,

How can we bring more Light, more understanding, to humanity?

Now, if you wish to bring Light, truly to bring Light, there is a great deal that can be done. First, these Teachings, they shall not go on for a great length of time. They will end after what is of

139

value has been covered. Should you bring the fifth chapter, the sixth chapter, the seventh chapter of Matthew, and study it and base the questions from there so that we may work from a spiritual sense, we may quickly cover great ground. There is very much covered in this area. There is also the little book of John. Now this is simple, and it would be an easy way to go. Yet, if you do not desire, if you desire to steer clear of such things, if you desire to use other types of scriptures, say the Vedic or the Talmud, whatever you would please, it is acceptable. Or, you may use none, but base your questions as you will, and then pick and choose as you write that which you must place back together. For you will find yourself with a volume of Teachings that you will then be ready to distribute.

This is for the enlightenment of those who will accept it. This is done through every age. This is done through almost every lifetime of man. And a few accept. Many don't. There is usually great ridicule. It has been done with many before. It has been done with Joseph Smith. It has been done with Edgar Cayce. It has been done with Buddha and with Jesus Christ. And it has been done with people whose names have passed to obscurity, and people couldn't care less about them.

It really doesn't matter, the greatness, so that you shed Light in your little corner. But if you desire to shed Light in a great way, or if you are willing to truly help mankind, then we would tell you.

Vibratory Forces and Opening

Many of us asked questions about our own fields. A psychologist in the group said,

I'd like to talk about the vibratory forces. I've been doing some reading in the new physics and quantum physics, talking about frequency realms. I notice your rhythms are different tonight, and I wonder if that's something you would like to comment on.

Different? How be it that they are different? Would you choose to have it worn out?

[During this exchange the Vessel rocked back and forth in the recliner chair. He had done so frequently in earlier sessions, but the behavior had become much less frequent. "Have some pity for the chair," a woman said, and we all laughed. The Eternals then went on to talk about vibratory forces.]

It's an adaptation. You will see the same thing when others open up. You will find that when you first open to the vibratory forces, when your first light strikes, it strikes the body like this [demonstrating by rocking]. And then again, you adjust and you become accustomed. Eventually it accustoms your line and continually comes into better vibration. Each time the vibration is with you, it raises the force of energy around you.

The purer and powerful energy that flows about your own body, that of white, of gold, and of the green, raises each and every time. Every time you heal a person, you become a bit purer. Every time you reach a level of consciousness through meditation, you become purer. Each step builds strength.

This Vessel was shocked open, and received tremors and shocks and quakes. And by these shocks and quakes, were the eyes opened. Not only was the one [chakra center] opened, but the energy that flows through, flowed down, and removed all clogging that the energy might flow more freely. Therefore, it is possible to see the energy flowing without problem, the energy where you wish it to be.

If there is energy about, and it is usable, then make yourself into a magnet and allow it to flow through you. For where the river flows, there is water. And in your belly is a river of water, and it brings life and healing. Therefore it is your heritage to heal, and it is your heritage to prophesy, and to see, and to open, and to look upon all that is. It is your ability and your divine heritage, and your right, in sonship and as of God ... to set yourself free that you might soar.

Each and every time that you raise yourself, every molecule, every atom of fat, protein, bone, sinew, blood in your body is raised one vibratory rate higher. Then the vibration coming through is not such a shock.

No, this is not something out of an Alfred Hitchcock movie,

and this is not a fanatic religious idea. For there is more than one of you in this room right now that can both see and heal. But they say not, for fear of the rest.

What chakras of the Vessel were opened?

Each and every door opens. To open and to see, you must open every other. Afraid? It's like a line with stoppers in it, and in order to have the fluid flow out of the top of the line, you must remove every stopper in the line.

Will these stoppers close back on him? Or will they remain open always?

You cannot close that which has been opened.

Is there need of protection in this condition?

Not as much as one would generally think. But to open the chakras, first you must think pure thoughts. But beware.... For a man of pure evil, meditating, will open his chakras, or his power, and receive this heritage to do all the evil he desires. Therefore, the light and the law of the Lord in meditating [mediating?] his law, day and night, that you might not be among those in the outer darkness. Your philosophical viewpoint will not accept this, and you have no way to believe it. And if you do not believe, how can we show you?

Is Channeling "Real"?

Daniel himself wondered how much information was channeled and how much was a product of his own mind. In other words — and this is a question that always arises — are "real" entities speaking? Or are they, at best, a projection from the mind of the vessel or, at worst, a hoax?

We pressed for clarity, and were told that the question will always exist and will always remain. The Eternals said, "There is no way of doing away with the question without doing away with the individual, and this is not a desirable solution."

The Eternals told us that all material is pure from source, but is internalized and then projected outward. For instance, someone said,

I have noticed that the Teachings through the Vessel are

couched in very religious terms. The books we've been guided to are the great religious works. I've been told that the Vessel is a religious man and comes from a religious background. If —

And you want to know the validity of this. How can it come through without being tainted?

I want to know if the Vessel were a molecular biologist, would his words to us be the same?

No, but they would have the same meaning and the same truth. Does it matter whether you say "God," "Vibratory Force," "Krishna," "Christ," "small particle," "molecule," "atom"? Does it matter whether you say "Elohim," "Joshua," or "Yahweh"? Or whether you say the "God of Truth" and the "God of Light"? Does it really matter what terms you use to describe what you describe? "It was a big, bright, yellow car" is the same thing as saying "It was kind of [a] greenish color, maybe sort of like yellow, and it was a Cadillac." That's still big, and it's still yellow, and it's still a vehicle or a car, an automobile. So what does it matter?

Physical Manifestations in the Channeling

Not only was the Vessel constantly moving his hands to illustrate his statements, but he also often made movements to align his own energy field so as to be a better receiver. A woman asked,

Tell us of the motion you make with your hand, when you cross [it] from left shoulder to third eye to right shoulder ... and then back again?

There is an energy that needs to be balanced. The energy flows from the chakras downward. By balancing in this way, from right to left, it causes it [the energy] to flow more evenly through the three chakras to the top. By the evener flow of energy, it is possible to allow the Vessel to remain more stable, not to vibrate as much as has been done in the past. As the Vessel becomes more open, this is less needed. If the Vessel was completely opened, it would not be needed at all. And yet, so, by some, it is needed even more. Therefore, they open not three but four chakras in this way.

That seems to be very much like the sign of the cross by

Greek Orthodox and Roman Catholics. What is the similarity, or is there any connection [with] the basic part of that movement?

You transfer the energy from side to side, from top to bottom. Even they have realized this innately.

I have heard that ... the voice of the spirits ... often come[s] through the left ear of the human. Is there any validity to this, or is this just something someone has said?

When one hears in the audio sense, they hear. But it is not a voice. For if you look to your right or to your left, then you say, "Did you hear that? Did you?" Everyone will look at you as if you were nuts and say, "What? What did you hear?" And you say, "Oh, nothing. I guess I was just imagining things." But when you hear a clear and audible voice, it comes from within. It comes through the inner ear or even the inner eye. But it is as loud and as audible as any other voice. It is as real, and should be heard and listened to. Not necessarily the left ear or the right ear, it's simply there. Even as, when you receive by sight, it's simply pictures, or shapes, or motions, or outlines, or colors.

If you have your eyes closed, they are. If they're open, they may be completely real, and your reality may be temporarily completely blocked out. Or you may see through them and see both at the same time. Or they may only appear as a shadow. Or you may only receive a glimpse. Even so, you feel the same way. Through each of the senses you can receive. You can smell that which is not, and yet to you it is. There are always messages coming. And if you open your eye to see, you will hear and see and feel when you desire.

A Parting Thought

Each Teaching (and each personal reading) ended with a blessing. Though the actual blessings have been omitted for reasons of space, the following excerpt is similar, and seems a good thought with which to end this chapter. The Eternals said,

We have come not to bring evil, death, nor condemnation, but to bring Light and life that you might have life abundantly. I am with you always, even so. Knock and it shall be opened, ask and it

Illustration #5
A regression session in my home. Daniel Clay is channeling The Eternals.

shall be answered. The door is set before you and that which you have opened, no man can close.

If you have ears to hear, hear; and if your eyes will see, see. The seals are broken, one seal, two seals, three seals, four seals, five seals, six seals, and yet there is a crack rent in the seventh. The time is at hand, the time is close at hand.

Take not thought for tomorrow, for today is evil — evil in abundance — and tomorrow will take care of itself. You have no power to change one thing. Therefore, change what you can — yourselves, and yourselves only.

Endnotes:

[1]My first experience with this phenomenon occurred in Massachusetts, at The Adventure.

Bob Whitehead, a friend I was guiding into a past life, shook so hard it seemed a real possibility that he would levitate. He seemed able to continue his journey into the past, but his wife, who was present, insisted I take him out of hypnosis. Afterwards, he seemed pleased, high, and exuberant, and talked enthusiastically about the wonderful things he saw in what seemed to be a technically advanced civilization.

The next time I encountered the shaking was when George Parker had been participating in a number of psychic gatherings. One night after the session he was overcome with convulsive shaking. Frightened, he left his bedroom and came into the living room, where eventually people in the house gathered round him to be with him in support and prayer. The shaking did not stop for several hours, after which George went back to bed, slept soundly, and awakened feeling fine. During the episode, several people said that his shaking was a psychic unblocking, a spiritual opening of his internal channels.

Since these two episodes, I have witnessed what seems to be the same thing with others who were just becoming open to their full psychic potential. It almost always signals

146

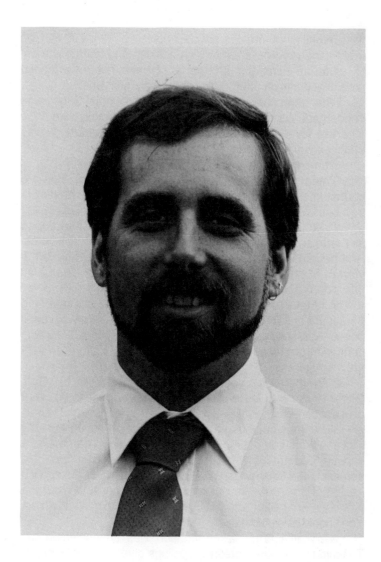

Illustration #6
Daniel Clay

the unfolding of greater psychic powers. While it can be frightening to witness a major unblocking and the adjustment to different vibrations of energy, I have not experienced problems during or afterwards, and I rarely intervene.

When the shaking began to occur with Daniel Clay, I was concerned, but still confident that I could bring him to a different level of consciousness. As it happened, it was unnecessary; the shaking abated spontaneously.

[2]The entire answer is as follows.

"The service offered is guidance or counseling. You are counselors. We tell you this inasmuch as it is much safer to be a counselor than to claim yourself to be anything else.

"Psychics have not respect. Prophets are looked upon as madmen. Seers are tainted. And oracles are Ouiji Boards. And people who dabble are witches or Satanists, and in the view of all those who are round about. And yet, the same as this is done daily in the name of God.

"And for this reason, those who do it in the name of God persecute and destroy everyone else, that they may have full power. Or, because they do not understand the evil and the confusion of the world.... Fools, they destroy that which they are themselves.

"Yet, therefore, you are counselors, guided by God. Given power by God to see into the deep recesses of your own subconscious minds.

"Now, inasmuch as I have told you this, I have not really told you what you seek. For you wish for me to name it as a service, and not tell you what that service is. Therefore, this service is the soul guidance. That is the name of the service itself, not the name you assume of an organization, but the name we are calling what you are doing, what it is known as. You should give guidance."

[3]Very little personal information was channeled in the Teachings. Yet the personal readings given by The Eternals were so valuable we wanted to share them. On the advice of The Eternals, we formed an organization, Ageless Expressions, now located in Troutdale, Virginia.

People who join the organization pay a membership fee

($65 at this writing). This fee entitles them to a full reading (physical, mental, and spiritual); the information given usually includes health advice, emotional support, and spiritual guidance.

Daniel Clay Pugh, who channels The Eternals, and his wife run the organization (she is also his guide). Most people send their questions in the mail, although some come to Virginia. Readings are scheduled for a time when the questioner is at home and able to relax quietly alone. The Eternals' message is taped and sent to the member.

While readings take first priority, Ageless Expressions also is developing publications. One now available is "The Visions of Vishnu," written by Daniel Clay from his dreams and visions. Much of the material is prophetic in nature.

For further information about readings or publications, write Ageless Expressions, P.O. Box 100, Troutdale, VA, 24378.

[4]This directive is the reason this section of the book is called *The Voice of Vishnu*.

Months before Daniel became the Vessel and began transmitting the Teachings of The Eternals, he had experienced a succession of vivid dreams. Even though he had difficulty understanding them, let alone accepting them, he kept a careful record of the dreams. It was as if The Eternals were trying to speak through Daniel, through whatever channel was available. Once we started our sessions in hypnosis, the dreams suddenly stopped.

Chapter Nine

PROGRESSION, BALANCE AND COUNTERBALANCE

So in the soul mind is that which weighs, as it were,
the benefits as well as sorrows, also what
the entity has gained by soul experience.
Edgar Cayce Reading 5125-1

This chapter introduces The Eternals' ideas of progression, balance, and counterbalance. Progressions — and — balance and counterbalance are two distinct concepts. As I understand it, "progressions" is used to mean that we progress from one lifetime to the next and the next. I had never known a single word to explain this concept before. Edgar Cayce and Kahlil Gibran (who lived and died within a few years of each other) both used the words "continuity of life." (That was the best and most poetic expression I had heard until The Eternals said, "Down through the shadows of millions of yesterdays flow the waters of a life everlasting.")

With "progressions," The Eternals gave us a single, succinct word to explain a major concept. "Reincarnation" is the word generally used, but many people think that reincarnation means returning as an animal also. The Eternals make it very clear that we do *not* return as animals.

150

FROM THE TEACHINGS
Progression
Some people in the group had no knowledge of nor experience in the psychic field. But one person was especially curious about ancient Egypt and the pyramids. It was because of his questions that we first discussed reincarnation and probed to understand the concept.

As you progress in this life, you shall certainly progress from here and the way you die. How do you progress afterwards?
Birth and rebirth, and birth and birth again. Yet you do not have to have a body to progress. For the body itself is merely physical, and you are more. You are God. You are a spiritual being. You are eternal, and you do not need this body; but you would progress in exactly the same way. The consciousness progresses. There is no better way to describe it, for it cannot be in the physical itself. It must be seen and felt.

As people, entities, move through progressions, progression upon progression, do they ever move away from truth and knowledge? In other words, are there downward progressions as well as upward progressions?
A blunt answer would be "yes." However, a football player on the field must often take several steps backwards to avoid being tackled, and yet he proceeds toward the goal. You must realize that often a step down is simply gaining a sturdier base to step up on. If you see a ladder has a weak rung, you will step down and size the situation up before you step forward two rungs.

There is really no such thing as failure, for failure does not exist. You simply are moving about, obtaining that which you obtain, in your own way, which is your way, your good way.

Do not fear being set back, because being set back is actually a move forward also. You can perceive this in your own senses of perceiving reality.... There is no such thing except for what you make for yourself. And who would make an evil reality for their own self?

One questioner had read that everyone on earth had to

pass through seven rings of soul evolution or seven progressions. He asked,

In respect to the seven progressions, where are you now?
Who?
Whoever is doing the Teachings now. Whoever is coming through you.
You're asking a series of questions. First, we are all one. And I, and you, and we are the same.

Now, you speak of seven rings, or progressions, but that is not correct. Seven is a very small number. You do not progress, so to speak, through set floors or levels, or rings, or through seven worlds separate. Your progression is an infinitesimal and minute thing. It continues individually, and yet it continues together. You are the pieces of a jigsaw puzzle that shall be placed back together. You have fallen apart. You have been taken away from your original and individual state, your holiness, the one vibration which you were originally. And yet it shall come again, and it shall be many more times apart and together. For there is the creation and the re-creation, and the re-creation, and the re-creation, and always the re-creation.

[And at another time the Eternals said:]
We can speak through the Vessel. We can speak until one is blue in the face. And yet, we cannot force you to accept a thing. You must learn on your own; everyone must. That is of your own choosing.

Now you speak of where everyone here is in their progressions. We shall speak of the Vessel, for that is allowed, and we shall speak of you, for you have brought the question forward. We shall not speak of anyone else, for it is improper for us to do this, or to reveal their inner thoughts.

Now, in progression, or in life, there is a circle which is traveled. When you reach the end you have, in essence, reached the beginning. And you must simply start over again. We are not telling you that you are going to pick up this same body again at some later date, and have to travel with it again, and with its same infirmities. This is not what we're saying. We're saying your life ends and starts, ends and starts, and you shall constantly travel this cycle.

[And again, in another session:]

Don't look so much to see where another sits, or where you yourself sit. For it has been written that in my Father's house are many mansions. In life, there are many levels of consciousness. It is your choosing, where that you look, whether you look through the eyes of the physical, or whether you feel with the mind, or look through the eyes of the spiritual. It is of your choosing. And this, in essence, determines where you are, or at what part of your progression you are. You can, relatively well, right now, skip the rest of your progressive cycle and be in the last stages of the final cycle ... or you could set yourself back. You do this by accepting a reality other than that which you have now accepted.

Doesn't that just speed you around to the end and then back to the beginning again?

Yes. If that's the way you want to look at it, yes. Without life, there is no purpose. It does place you back to where you start again, but you will start at a higher level each time.

How do we raise our present vibration to a fuller, more positive, spiritual vibration? [Author's note: "Vibration" means "level of energy flow," "level of consciousness," or "awareness."]

In order to bring about a raising of the frequency, or an attunement to, the greater vibration, look deeper into yourself. You must forgive yourself or, as we say, cancel all debts, so that there is no balance nor counterbalance to be imposed on yourself. [Author's note: "Imposed" is an odd word. I think the idea is that no outside force (God) is imposing a punishment, nor is there any inner self-judgment.]

Look deep into the recess of your mind — for within you are all things. You are all that exists and all that exists is within you. You are God and God is you. Therefore, if you will search, and really accept and believe in your own self, then you have all power at your hands.

When a child is conceived and comes into the physical being, how does the vibratory force of a previous progression come to be in that special child?

Between three months after conception, and one month after birth, a force, so to speak, vibratory, can enter in any empty vessel. A vessel is formed out of need or desire, either on the part of a vibratory force, or on the part or desire of those who create or carry the life, that they might have creation. For there are two ways to create. It can be created externally or internally. You [pointing] can create life, or these sitting over here [pointing] can create the same life within you, if they desire it to be so.

Could you clarify the idea that we progress up to a point and then return to the bottom, yet enter at a higher plane. And also, when we have finished our progressions do we join you as Eternals, or is that something separate?

The point of confusion lies in the symbolism that was used. It was not to be explained all at once. Let us explain in full.

It was a cycle, as was said before, that you go around and then you come back to the point at which you begin, for your first estate was that estate which was with the force of God, or was with the creative force, and you left that estate, or you left that place of perfection, and you worked again back to that place. Now, this being the case, it would be a cycle, as was said, and each time that cycle is completed, you go higher and higher. But this was not all. You see, this was all that could be absorbed by those that were present.

Now it was also mentioned in passing, inasmuch as could be said, that you returned to the one creative force that you have left. Now it was said that this cycle was repeated again and again, and one asks does that mean we simply return to have to repeat the cycle, and the answer given was "yes." And this is true, and this was all that that one who inquired could absorb, but there is yet more. Yes, it is true that you're only going through a cycle, and it is true that you are eternal; but if you were in a perfect state once for a time, then it is possible that you will be in that estate again, even for a time eternal. Therefore, there can be an end to this cycle. When you reach that state of consciousness which is known by some as "Christ," or by some as "Krishna," or by some as the "supersoul" or "oversoul"; when you reach that state, then you are at the level where you may actually stay, seeing all and knowing all.

154

It is a cycle, but that cycle can be broken; and you enter the creative force, for you are of the same force we are of. All things in the beginning were of the same force. You break away, yet you are still the same force. Let us put it like this: If you were a tree, if you were hit by lightning and splintered, the wood that came from that tree, sum total, would still make the same tree; and yet, it is not the tree so you are not the original creative force. But if you bring all of these splinters back together, it is still the original tree.

Is the earth the only place for progressions to take place?

I think your question is more, Must you depend only on the solid, that which we are in now? No. But if your question is, Should we depend on other worlds such as Mars, for example, or Neptune? that answer also is "no."

Extraterrestrial life ... is science fiction, is the best way to put it; is an unreal fantasy, a fairy tale. However, all worlds are not solid. And there is world on top of world here. You may work within the energy flow, so to speak. The next body that is around this body can also do the same toward progression. This seems to have brought more confusion than light.

I suppose what I'm wondering is, is the earth the only place where progressions take place; or are there other places in the universe where there are people progressing?

Don't look to other places in the universe. It is here, but there is more than one plane of progression. It is here. It is in this same area that you call "earth solid," "terra firma," "solid land."

And yet in this same area are sources of energy which exist in what you would consider a non-solid state. When a person's body dies, the energy does not always die. The source does not always return. They can stay and work as they wish to progress.

There are others that are progressed to the state already, to the state beyond solid. And from there they work. And yet there are even states that are less solid to that. For they perceive — should we say,... those in what you would perceive as a non-solid state — perceive life as a solid to themselves. And yet, they know there is another state higher, which they perceive to be non-solid. And again, in turn, is so, and again after that.

The Astral Plane

Is it true that the progression above physical reality is called the "astral plane"?

[Author's note: This is a wonderful example of The Eternals answering a question literally. The questioner was asking if a dimension outside our physical world was on an "astral plane" (these were words he had read in a book). Because he did not state his question clearly, he was asking what this other dimension was *called*. In other words, the question should read, "Is the progression above physical reality the astral plane?" And that is the question The Eternals answer.]

Astral plane, call it what you will, — it is really immaterial. If you choose to call it "astral plane," then astral plane it is. You're asking what it is called. This is a question to say in the English language. Those who choose to call it the "astral plane" will do so. Those who choose to call it "specters" or "ghosts" will do so. Those who choose to call it an "energy plane" may do so.

Can living people go back and forth between the spirit plane, or must one be dead?

Why do people always want to die to claim their heritage? Look to two of the greatest masters who have lived, to him known as "Jesus" and to him known as "Krishna." (We would say "Krishna" and "Christ," for "Jesus" and "Christ" are not interchangeable words.) These two masters had the power, they had the knowledge, the belief, and the faith that they were able to walk through walls. Therefore, death was not death to them. But they were still alive. And therefore they walked on the water. The same is with the prophets of old. It is by this power that they were able to make the iron axes float. It is by this power that they were able to see into the minds of the others.... At least part of you must be able to reach out into that other plane. This is not normal, this is your heritage, this is your right. You are a living god. And you have the right to claim all power. You have the right to create. But you say to yourself, "I can't do that! I cannot do that because I am human." You can't do it because you don't allow yourself to.

How does one do this?

With total belief. But when we say "total belief," it must be made clear what *belief* really is. Belief is powerful, but it must be total; for the least doubt, the least shadow of fear, the least thought of apprehension in the corner of the mind is total disbelief. Therefore, I tell you, we tell you, that the path is straight and narrow and that there is nothing to stop you, but you are stumbling over your own feet. There is nothing in your way. You light a light and you point it in your own eyes and blind yourself.

Are the Akashic Records on the astral or energy plane?

This is a more important question. This is a question that has been dealt with fairly often. For the prophets themselves have guarded it, and unscrupulously so, quite frequently. What you are referring to — the permanent records of life, the permanent records that are kept of every act and deed, of all history and of all thought, of all medicine and technology, of all advancements, are kept in your own consciousness. The consciousness of every individual. Therefore, if you look deep within, you will see all that exists, that has existed, and will exist. This is hidden in the recesses of your own mind. You must be willing to accept yourself and to look deep within your own mind, and then you will see and understand and perceive this. Everyone here present is desiring to see, and this group is not brought together by chance; and everyone here is on the threshold and the verge. For it is opening, and opening, and must be opened.

DANIEL'S DOUBTS

Daniel, who came from a Christian background, had a hard time accepting the information that was coming through him about lifetimes as steps in soul evolution. Edgar Cayce stumbled at this very same spot on his own path. Neither he, nor later Daniel, could see how the concept of soul evolution fit their beliefs, for modern Christian orthodoxy rejects the idea of reincarnation. As The Eternals observed, Daniel "does not want to accept that life can be a continual thing, not destroyed." However, first Cayce and then Daniel came to accept soul evolution as enhancing and expanding their understanding of Christianity.

Cayce objected so strongly to the multiple-life information channeled through him that he stopped giving readings when the past lives concept was first mentioned. It took a long time for friends and family to convince him that the readings that contained past-life material benefited people.

Daniel also had serious doubts about continuing our work. But he was willing to learn and willing to look at new ideas. He delved into Cayce's story and saw that Cayce had resolved the conflict. One of the books that helped him was a biography of Cayce, *There Is a River*, by Thomas Sugrue. Also, Daniel says, "Believe it or not, my study of the Bible helped. The Bible and 'religion' do not say the same thing on all issues. Also, the visions and dreams had changed my outlook on life. Seeing people helped and healed was positive, and the Bible does say, in Exodus, that only God heals. Last but not least, once you break through and feel the oneness of the universe, life changes profoundly. It's a feeling beyond all words or description, but it is unforgettable."

Gradually, Daniel was able to accept the statements of The Eternals. He said once, "You're getting me more and more to the possibility that there could be something to this." But he also wondered why he was doing this work in the first place. Granted, he had asked to do it. But the readings and Teachings took a great deal of time away from his wife and three little boys.

Both he and I, we were told, were doing this work to balance the scales of earlier lifetimes, when we could have helped humanity but did not. In Daniel's case, The Eternals said, the circumstances of his upbringing (five of the 10 men in his grandfather's generation were ministers of the Gospel) brought about a condition —

....where the person was constantly seeking, and seeking again, for the truth, much of which was not to be found where expected, and much of which has not been found. But it brought up the condition of searching.... And with the searching and the accepting of the faults [i.e., self-acceptance], then they can look into themselves. And this is what has been accomplished, although it is not what can be admitted [by Daniel].

You see, if it could be admitted, this [the channeling] could be done at all times, and not just in this state, which is theta [a very deep hypnotic state]. Now the process of growth can be instantaneous. Because we say that it took time in this Vessel, do not feel that it must always be instant, or that is must always be time consuming.

In the progressions past, this Vessel lived in a monastery — not the Vessel itself, but the energy force — in the China area. And he was studying in the arts of defense and aggressiveness. At the same time, they studied the recesses of their minds. Then, at birth, there was chosen a point where the continual study might be accepted and progressed upon. And this study has been progressed and progressed to the point that this one has believed dreams that have come through, and has accepted many things in the waking.... And by this being done, just the sheer acceptance is what has allowed it. As we have said, everyone here sits on that threshold. It is the divine right, the privilege, and the heritage of everyone.

Balance and Counterbalance from the Teachings

"Balance and counterbalance" was another new term. I understand this phrase to mean "the weighing of our actions." I picture in my mind a big scale with our deeds — both good and bad — placed on one side. On the other side we put new actions and deeds. The good deeds are like credits or interest in an invisible bankbook. The bad deeds need to be erased by better actions. In Eastern philosophy the word to explain this is *karma*, meaning "action and reaction." The Christian and Jewish traditions explain the same ideas as "An eye for an eye" and "As you sow, so shall you reap."

I understand the concept [of balance and counterbalance], but are there more subtleties to it? Is there a deeper significance that we could understand of this phenomenal concept?

Life is a giant scale. And anything that is put in to weight one side shall be directly weighted against the other side. Yet this may be done on an individual or national or even a world basis.

Could you explain the Law of Karma or balance and counterbalance and how that relates [to the Biblical idea of] the Law of Grace?

You have done the deed and it is weighted. Yet this deed must be un-weighted, or counterbalanced, so that you have balance and counterbalance. If you accept yourself freely and you understand all, and you can look, then you are within the Law of Grace. For you accept yourself. When you accept yourself, you set yourself above and beyond that which would bind you. And no longer are you bound, but a free being, a free man, freed from all of your past bonds. No need to balance and counterbalance. Looking within, when you accept all that you have done, and hold nothing against yourself, then your conscience does not condemn you. Then you are not condemned. And he who is not condemned is free indeed, for they are free from all and free in all.

So our conscience holds our karma?

And you set yourself free when you have a clear conscience. Therefore, if you have freed yourself, and you bring not more evil upon yourself, you are free.

When the soul enters the fetal body or newborn infant, is there a significance in the matching of vessel and vibratory force?

Balance and counterbalance. That sums it all up. That puts it in a whole. That gives it in a nutshell. Balance, balance, balance and counterbalance. This is set by what your balance is and what the balance is around you, and how that one may counterbalance it, that what that force has done in the past and what must be counterbalanced. And by what the heavenly bodies, themselves, say must come about. And yet, they are of the least influence. For the balance and the counterbalance, and that which is within, the soul drive, that spirit essence, is more powerful.

Do people get sick because of ... karma?

This concept — not everyone knows the division on reincarnation, so to speak, or birth and rebirth. You are not coming back as an animal. You are not coming back because you did not do well, as an earthworm, to get run over by a choo-choo train. You are energy flow.

Now, in essence, a karmic reality, having to do with a cripple — if you have taken delight in an evil in your past progression that has done serious harm to another, or if you have caused serious harm and delighted in it, this could cause a karmic result that must be balanced. Now there are several ways to balance this problem. One, it could be balanced in the same lifetime, either by being maimed or injured much in the same way, or by suffering in some other way related; because of this, you commit a sin and then you suffer in the flesh for it.

You commit adultery and you are a male, you suffer mentally, you may suffer physically from venereal disease. This might be the counterbalance. And yet there might be no balance in this lifetime, the balance might be in the next lifetime when you're born crippled, or where you're born deformed. And yet this is again not to say that you are stuck there, for you can progress onward to a better state. And even in one lifetime, you may be healed. All you must do is accept the reality that you are whole. [Author's Note: This question and answer show how a seemingly trivial question can trigger a profound response.]

Don't you choose to come into this world crippled, or whatever? Don't you choose your situation?

To choose a road, to choose a traveling way, is to know that that path must be balanced; that that path must be counterbalanced; that you or another must travel the other way.

So, in other words, it is not cruel that somebody comes into the world crippled, or we should not feel sorry for someone because they are crippled, because they knew that that was the best way for them to balance their debts.

This is possible, but you do not have to be balancing a debt to be born crippled, or not a debt of your own — you may be a good soul balancing the debt of another fool.

That doesn't sound fair.

If you are so kind as to accept it, then it is fair.

What power comes to cause one entity to pay for the debts of another entity?

Choice and free will.

Of which, the suffering entity or the one who escapes the pain?

You sound as if suffering is necessarily evil. This is not the case. First, one person may choose to be evil continually and

161

another choose to be good continually. And one may be good and counterbalance it with evil; and evil, and counterbalance it with good; and evil and evil, and then good and evil, and good and good. So long as it is balanced and counterbalanced, there is no problem, there is no worry.

One may choose to be evil and another good, in the same light that one may choose to be whole and another crippled. Now, crippled is not a natural state; full and total health is the natural state. And if you can accept this, and believe in this, then you shall remain in that natural state. You do what you do of your own choosing.

If you have a reason to balance or you desire to balance for another soul, should we say another life, or another entity, then you may do so of your own free will; but you are not forced. Yet this is working good for your own growth.

[The questioner thought that one might have to pay another's debt. Until this exchange, participants thought karma, or balance and counterbalance, was strictly within one's own karmic pattern. But The Eternals say that someone *can* choose — by "choice and free will" — to help pay someone else's debt, out of love, or for any other personal reason — depositing money in a friend's checking account, in the spiritual sense. To use a simple example, suppose a young man gets a speeding ticket. He has a debt against him, but no money. So his father can choose to pay the fine.

The exchange continues with the question of *who* makes the choice, the suffering entity or the one who escapes the pain? The Eternals immediately answered the bigger, unspoken, question of suffering. The young man gets a ticket for speeding; he is thought by others to be suffering a punishment. But it is not necessarily evil that he got the ticket. He could learn from it; it could be looked upon as a blessing. The Eternals then answer the spoken question. Yes, there are countless combinations of how one may balance for another person. Every person can choose to do good or evil – or both. Anyone may have a reason to choose to balance for another, but even this is working for his or her own growth. Personally, I don't think that a person can *make* someone pay his debt. I believe by even trying to force this he would create more debt.]

162

Does the vibratory force that is seeking a body choose a crippled or deformed body on purpose for its progression?

It can change the body to make it crippled or deformed for its purpose. But in the same light, it can choose one if it has been created that way by the force of the parents, so to speak, who had to balance their own debts.

Yet it must be realized that if you can rise above this, and accept yourself and all of your whims, and your errors, and do everything without malice, that you incur no debt. When all is done in purity, even that which comes to evil by accident, it is not held against you. Therefore, you should strive to be pure. You should strive to balance yourself and not worry about how others are balanced. Or what road they have chosen to walk.

What about the idea of helping one another?

It is not a question of should I help another. It is a duty to help all those about you whom you can help.

Is it interfering with their karma?

No, the balance and the counterbalance would be that you are part of. There is no such thing as interference when realities overlap. You would not even be in their reality if you were not to be there.

The Possibility of Evil

As we look in on ourselves, do we create the risk of opening ourselves to evil forces?

If you leave yourself empty, if you cleanse and purify yourself and do not accept the good vibration or what is termed as the "Holy Spirit," or do not accept the power of God or the full force to flow back through, then you have an empty vessel and you are in the most dangerous position. You would be better off if you had not started.

Is there anyone here tonight where that is a risk?

Everyone runs that risk, because you have the option of not accepting.

Does evil ever become a permanent reality for any entity?

If you choose it to be so. But yet, in time, it must be counterbalanced; if not by that entity, then by another entity choosing permanent good. All things are balanced. There is a

163

balance and a counterbalance; nothing exists except it is leveled.

Do people who are extremely evil remain eternally evil or do they eventually come back around and become good entities?

....You may balance your own self by counterbalancing, or it can be overridden. One may choose to be eternally good and one may choose to be eternally evil. And yet there shall come a time when all shall choose to be well and good. For how long would all choose to be evil and bring destruction upon themselves?

CONTACTING SPIRIT FRIENDS

When entities are between progressions, are they aware of the people that were in their past progression? Do they keep track of these people, friends and relatives?

It can be done, it does not *have* to be done. But this does not mean you should go out and start trying to contact your spirit friends. More evil can be conjured in this way than good. For there are also those souls upon the Fifth Heaven. Look at the evil ones on the Fifth Heaven, bound in chains — yes, we do speak in allegory — look at those bound in the Fifth Heaven in chains. Would they not love to contact you? Would they not love to own your body and to possess you, mind and spirit? Don't allow the openings for this.

Is that what happens with Satanic groups that do conjurings? Do they bring forth those entities?

An entity can be brought forth as real as you are, as strong and as potent as all the power of the universe. Yes.

Do people who have died keep track of their relatives on earth?

You are speaking of, Do they keep track of them, do they incarnate with the same people around them again, etc. They can, but they do not *have* to. They are free-will entities. And being spiritual, as they are in nature, you must remember that all are one to start with anyway. If I were a total spiritual being, then I would be with all of you. And being with all of you, I would naturally keep track of you because I would *be* you, and yet I would still be myself.

Can the dead body be contacted by use of a spirit medium?

Beware. You have been warned. We warn you again. It is one thing to contact consciousness, and to look for that which is or has been. Do *not* seek to contact those who are no longer among you in flesh. For those beings, withered and in chains, those perpetually foul beings would love to take hold of the mind. They would love to find vessels to be within.

It has been long since they dwelled upon the earth; even before the days of the deluge. They made the giants and they made those with webs in their fingers. The great men who did great deeds because of their great size — do not unleash these. Do not give them right, for by this cause comes much insanity — "possession," as you could call it, and "evil." This you do not desire.

Do not hold a seance. Do not go to a spirit medium. Do not invoke a spirit. There are "evil beings," if you would choose to use that term, vibratory forces without physical bodies that would find good expression and can take control. That is not needed.

Your answer was "yes." Do not go through a spirit medium.

It is natural to be concerned about friends or relatives who have passed on — to want to be assured that they are doing well in another dimension and to be reassured of their continued existence. But The Eternals caution that in seeking to contact a spirit on the other side we are apt to get more than we bargained for. Not only do seances have a reputation for fraud, but I always wondered what a recently departed soul would want to say, anyway. The experience of death does not in itself bestow any great wisdom upon anyone who did not already have it on the earth; information has to be weighed and evaluated whether the source is living in the flesh or in the spirit.

I have learned that it is best to sever the ties with our departed loved ones because in holding on to them we retard their progression as souls. If we have their good in mind, we will bless them and let them continue on their new journey.

In my extensive travels to other countries I have seen many unusual things related to psychic phenomena. In some places in the world misuse of mind power is the norm. We need to bear in mind that the spiritual world, like the

165

physical world, is governed by certain laws. Two that easily apply here are: *Seek and ye shall find* and *Like attracts like.* Thus, if it is our aim to contact the dark side, we will find it. And the greater danger is that once we have found it, more evil will surely and easily come because more will be attracted. The dark side does exist, but as Daniel says, we have a choice as to whether we give it our energy.

I think it would be far more sound to develop our own inner guidance and even to develop the ability to access the superconscious or Higher Mind. In whatever manner we spiritually seek — through meditation, through regression or channeling — our purpose should be to seek the Light. The channeling sessions I share with you in this book were always surrounded in great Light and prayer — each was a holy, charismatic and healing exercise. As we, as individuals, grow to the Light we surround ourselves with protection against the shadows and use the spiritual laws to our soul's benefit.

Chapter Ten

OPENING THE CONSCIOUSNESS

You must bring light to yourself.
The Eternals

I sometimes felt very strange in my work with Daniel. It was almost like landing on another planet and needing to know all about it. I felt like a person transplanted from the primitive life of the Amazon delta to the middle of a teeming American city; I was in culture shock, spiritually speaking. But the source speaking through Daniel made me and the other participants feel comfortable and answered all our questions patiently.

We needed that patience. We phrased and rephrased our questions in order to understand The Eternals' ideas, which were new to most of us. So, of all the topics in the Teachings, the one involving the opening of the consciousness was perhaps the most enlightening because The Eternals gave us practical steps for achieving it.

In my experience, channelers must go through a process of unblocking the psychic energy and opening to the spirit of the universe in order to be receptacles for the messages that come through them. But all of us can benefit. Later in my work, I incorporated information on opening into my hypnotic procedures and this made the process more dynamic;

subjects responded far better with specific exercises to open their energy centers and bring new light into their beings. I now use opening procedures when I guide channelers and often when I guide past-life regressions, too.

A spiritual opening, which is what The Eternals are talking about, is not a physical experience nor one that can be easily observed by others; it is an inner process at the soul level. It brings knowledge, wisdom, peace, and a sense of empathy with the joys and sorrows of others. It can help us heal ourselves and others by helping to unblock, or move energy around.

Opening the consciousness is the same as opening the "Eye," but the eye is not the physical one we see through. Rather, it is a single invisible eye located in about the center of the forehead. It relates to the "third eye" (familiar to us from Eastern thought) or the pituitary gland in the brain (in Western science). In Western science, the pineal has been the least understood of the endocrine glands — also called "ductless glands" or "neuro-hormonal energy centers." In Eastern thought, the third eye is one of several "centers" in what is called the "chakra system," corresponding roughly to the endocrine system. Westerners have become familiar with the idea of the chakra system, and while there are variations in the names of the centers and their exact locations, the number (seven) and general locations are agreed on.

OPENING THE CONSCIOUSNESS

Participants at the Teachings interpreted The Eternals' information on opening the consciousness in individual, personal ways. I, myself, understand opening to be similar to opening a new door, a new book, or even a new dimension of reality. During the process we get in touch with new learning, understanding, and growth. We open to inner light by unblocking bricks from the dark walls we have built around our consciousness.

Here is how The Eternals explained it to us.

What is the best way to open up our consciousness? To open up, what specific steps would help this group?

See the ball? [Making a motion with his hands, as if holding a ball.]

No.

What you think exists exists. What you do not believe does not exist. When you allow yourself to actually look inside deep, to simply believe that which you feel, then you shall be open. Look and see the gold ring? [Drawing a ring in the air.]

No.

You will see it only if you yourself make it. For if I make it, it is my ring; and if you make it, it is your ring. Place your hands upward in the air, and you will feel energy flow. First it will be a slight sensation. Now, some of this will be caused by the blood draining from the arms, so do not count entirely upon the physical.

Then you will feel cold or hot, because the heat itself is cold and this is the energy that moves through. This is the energy that comes outward. As we allow this energy to flow outward and in, the energy flows downward through the arms, out through the bottoms of the feet and outward of the palms, and inward of the palms and inward of the feet, and outward of the eye.

Now, if you will close your eyes and be in perfect peace, you will feel light. And that light will enter; and as it enters, it will enter into the forehead, over the forehead, and outward. And if you can see and feel this, *then you have opened the eye.*

It is your right and your heritage to open it. It is the divine heritage which you have to see. Do not close yourself in, for you and only you close yourself.

Now, at this time, when the eye opens, do not allow yourself to go outward, because this will cause a disorientation that you will not realize what it is. At first you will feel like you are spinning, that your are completely unhooked from your body. And you are. You have set yourself free. This is your right, your divine heritage. From this state we work. From this state we are, for we are eternal. You are eternal. We are you and you are us.

Why are some of us afraid to open up? Why do we hold back?

Because you must be willing to accept yourself totally: evil, good, fat, thin, tall, short, stupid, or brilliant. You must be able to accept every foible and whim that you have. If you cannot accept yourself in total and complete as you are, it is impossible to look inward. And if you cannot look in, you cannot look out. For if the glass is clear enough to see inward through it, then it is clear enough to see outward through it.

Can the process of opening cause physical problems? Can it make you ill for a time, physically, as you adjust to it?

It can cause illness if it is not accepted and allowed to flow. If it stagnates within the being, then there is discomfort. For how can energy sit in one place? Energy must move about. It has been said already, once, that the energy itself is powerful enough to knock one out completely unconscious — an immediate bolt. How be it if you open yourself and allow that energy to flow, and flow freely, then there is not a side effect?

Don't worry too much about what will be. Don't desire end results too hard. Allow it, and it will happen. Let go and let yourself — from your innermost recesses, guide — that you are not inhibited by the conscious mind. Allow that ball of flame, that ball of fire, allow that ball you have to radiate through your innermost being. For what good is it that one be baptized with fire if they allow the fire to burn down? For a toothpick smoldering will not heat a room.

Is there any sort of living, or lifestyle, that helps facilitate the opening of the eye — that prepares us for what is coming?

It depends individually on each individual. It depends on what has been done in life past. For obviously, if you spent much time in the monasteries during the 1600s preparing yourself — even if you live in the city and are greatly distracted today — it shall be much easier for you to reach out and grasp the truth than for one who has spent his whole life doing other things; of all of their lives they have spent in the city, around people, not being allowed to meditate, or concentrate, or think.

Peace is of the greatest essence. When you find peace with yourself, and accept yourself fully, it does not matter how you live. It matters that you have inner peace. And when you have inner peace, you shall have all things. For peace does not come without the opening; and neither does the opening come without peace. And yet many who live in peace would not go out and proclaim the opening, nor may they even recognize it at times. And many who are opened do not appreciate the peace that they dwell in.

Is this an endocrine process or is this just a spiritual process? Is there movement in the body in this process?

The shock can be strong enough to knock the body out. The shock will often lay a body flat. It depends on the openness, it depends on the trauma the shock gives to the body. For the chakras are already partially open; or if one or more of them are already open, then the shock is not as great as it would be otherwise. There are those who cannot receive at all, and those who can receive in part, and those who can receive in full. To receive in full is to open — to open — to open — open — open — open — and open — and open — totally and completely, that all might be released.

Does it relate to the endocrine system or the chakras? Is its path of opening through the chakras?

It must run through in order.

Beginning at the lower ones and coming up, or beginning at the higher chakras and coming down? Or does it matter?

To unclog — a total unclogging — we usually start upward, traveling downward, and back upward, at the same time. Even as you look in, you see out; and as you look out, you see in. So it is that they must be opened from both sides. For the energy flows not one way, but in both directions.

ENERGY FLOWS AND BLOCKS

You speak of the energy around each of us. Are there rays of energy that come from our abdomens?

You are a total creative energy force. The energy flows downward over the body, downward from here [motions from the top of the left side of the body] and down. The energy flows inward into the palms and outward from the palms; inward to the feet and outward from the feet. You're much like a radiator in a heating system to a house. The energy is constantly flowing around and around and around. But you pick up more and more energy, much as there is a fire in the boiler, so there is a total force of energy for you to tap, to draw upon.

Now, you may project yourself forward, upward, and outward.

171

You move upward [motioning with hands], upward, upward, again and again and again [moves over the chakras], and outward [hands held above the head]. This is a way to project. You can project pure and raw energy, or this was also commonly called "astral projection," if you wish to do so. The energy is complete, it is constantly circling about you, and yet in the far corner of this room is still energy moving about. There is nowhere there is not an energy flow moving. If there was no energy, there would be no life.

What causes chakras to be blocked?

Energy is meant to be flowing; it is meant to be a continuous moving thing. To try to hold that energy in is to cause a build-up, like a cork swelling, and then the energy cannot flow properly. In order to remove this, you take one who can heal, one with a green healing aura, and allow them to actually shock. The force will actually drive the force through.

Now, in the normal stagnation of only slight bits, the gentle strokes from the crown chakra down is enough to simply bring the energy back to flow. But this is not always the case. If there is truly a stagnation, a stagnation near death, the hand or a part of the body that expells it, a free moving energy circuit must be set up.

Take the healing vessel and realize that energy comes through, and out from the eye itself [hands held in front of the forehead]. This is the strongest point of healing. But also the energy flow can come down, you allow it and you allow the energy flow to travel complete this way [moves hands downward over the body]. And when contact is made, even with just the energy field, that close, when you touch the energy field itself, there is a shock and it will flow and the power will move downward through the healing vessel, and will be like ramming an electrical current of 220 volts straight into a fuse and it will blow, and the cork will shatter from the bottle, and the energy will begin to move.

Will meditation help one to discover things within himself?

Meditation is a doorway. But you cannot proceed through the doorway if you have fear. It is merely a way that you can travel to do this. You must look within yourself — deep within yourself — to see all things. And when you look within, all things shall proceed out, and you shall see all. Yet, if you cannot accept what

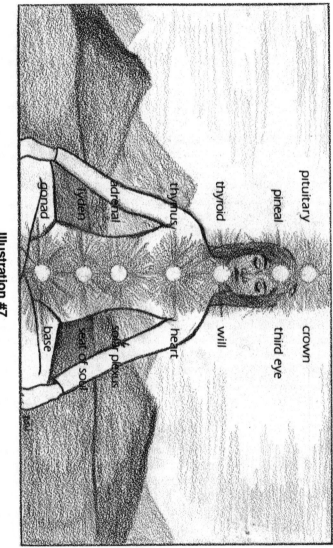

Illustration #7
Chakras with associated glands.

is within you, and if you cannot look at yourself without prejudice, then it is not possible for any doorway that you picked to open, which you need.

There are those people who would try to short-circuit this by taking drugs that would open the consciousness. In effect, this creates what would be called "Pandora's Box." By so doing, you open an awareness which you are not able to accept. You open a reality which you are not prepared for physically, mentally, or spiritually, and which, in essence, could turn upon you and destroy you. But yet, if you prepare yourself, and are ready, then no matter what method you use to open the door, then you shall proceed and learn as you would or come to know and accept.

What methods do you recommend for looking deep within oneself?

Now in this respect, we would say that the meditations are good. Any form of opening the awareness, the studies of the spiritual nature, looking at yourself in full, the studies of philosophies, any method of relaxation — that which you call "mind control," "hypnosis,""meditation," "yoga" — these are all routes which may be traveled. These are all roads, and all these roads converge at one intersection, so to speak. Yet some of the roads are easier to travel than the others. And life in itself is also this road. For even if you are unaware, and even if you do not try to develop ability or try to accept, you are still in balance and counterbalance; you are still constantly walking forward — always walking, always progressing, and always moving. One does not stand still. You must move or you are dead. That which is dead does not move. That which is alive moves.

Could hypnosis help open us up? Is that a useful path to look inward?

Yes. Hypnosis is a form of meditation; meditation is the key. Hypnosis gives you a talking guide in the full, physical, conscious level which you don't desire to leave. And since you don't desire to leave it, it gives you a guide with both feet on the ground, that you can depend on. And since you're not willing to depend on anything but have a little bit left to the physical world, then you must go the route of hypnosis. So, yes, it is good. And those here shall travel that way.

174

Illustration #8
Chakras

What are the first steps to open yourself up?

Look into the dream work; keep a record. Keep that record over a period of time that it might be compiled together. Look at it and see. Translate and transcribe the meanings to yourself. Write this down when you wake, if you remember your dream, which you shall; then write it while it is there. This is good exercise for the mind and it is a good step for the beginning. When you realize that this same consciousness works through the day as well as through the night, then you are open. It works whether you are relaxed or not. Being in a relaxed state allows people to realize, to slow down and to see the process — and not to confuse it with the physical world that is around them.

How does [this] continue to expand our consciousness?

Your consciousness is a mechanism that works 24 hours a day. The subconscious mind — that which functions and seems to be unreal — is the real reality.... It is your inner mind's workings. Now when you are aware that the dreams exist, when you begin a method of relaxation — this has been used in many different ways through the centuries but meditation, in essence, is what it is, no matter what you call it — whether you call it "hypnosis," "yoga," or "mind control."

Now if you find yourself with problems relaxing, first, expend your energy in strenuous exercise. If you do not find the trouble, you may go straight into a relaxed state. There accept every impression — they come as they will, in pictures vivid in color; they come in pictures, black and white; and in pictures not quite tangible. They come in sounds — a voice that will speak to you, loud or soft, roaring as thunder, or as the chirping of a small bird. They come in feelings, and they come in vibrations.

When you find that you have reached the point that they come in vibrations, you can simply say what is impressed upon you. The vibrations, themselves, are what you need. When the vibrations begin to flow freely, you will feel what others around you feel — you can feel their pain, you can feel their sorrow, you can feel their physical pain, and you can feel their joy. You will know what they need, and what they do not need. When they think, their voices will speak to you in your head.

When you have reached this state, all things become open. In the state of meditation, or in the state of relaxation — let's call it "relaxation" to avoid prejudice — when you become open to your subconscious, and to the consciousness of all that is around you, the colors of the universe shall flood into your soul. There shall be a bright red energy and it shall lift itself and magnify itself and become intense. It shall center and come together. And after you have seen the colors come together, and after you have seen the colors scrambled and reflected and refracted together into this red, they shall shoot up, forming quickly, quickly through the colors of the scope until they turn an intense blue, and then a white — a blue-white beyond speech — and this shall reach out, and then you are part of that vibration and you see all things. You know, and yet you do not have to know anything to know this.

What will be the hardest part in expanding our consciousness? It can't be an easy path.

The path is easy. The path is straight. The path is narrow. And few travel it because they are not willing to look within and accept their own faults, to accept their own sins, their own foibles, to accept their own idiosyncrasies, their own unpleasantness, their own evil as well as their own good, their beauty, their wonderfulness, the serenity that lies within them, their greatness, and their power. If a person was willing to accept — but you must note: very, very few are willing to accept themselves, or anyone else for that matter — this is the hard part, to overcome your own self. Once you overcome yourself, you have overcome all things.

The path is easy, but there is a great stumbling block in front of the path: it is those which travel the path who fall over their own feet.

What does that mean, that we stumble over our own feet?

You do it to your own self. You create your own doubts; they are of your own making. Without this doubt which you yourself create, there would be no problem. But your feet are attached to your own body and to fall over your own foot is your own fault — because you stick it in front of the other one, or you're too stupid to pick it up off the ground.

In the same way, man is too foolish to believe that he has the power that he has, and he is too stupid to accept his own heritage. He is too ignorant to remove the doubt from the corners of his

177

mind. Therefore, he is falling and stumbling on a smooth, straight road.

What about doubts and fears? When these come into your mind, how do you deal with them?

Why have a doubt or why have a fear? There is no such thing as that which you should be afraid of or doubt. These are of your own making, they are not external.

There is no such thing as fear, there is no such thing as doubt. There is no such thing as unhappiness, it is how you respond to the situation. You can be happy or you can be sad of your own making. There is no such thing as any emotion, so to speak, in this sense, for you make your own reaction. And you can react any way that you condition yourself to. Or shall we say, "If Pavlov would allow it, you could foam at the mouth"?

By what process are these doubts removed? Is it just a mental thing where we say, "I believe," and cancel out all doubts or is there a growth process for belief?

The problem is that if you say to yourself, "I believe, I believe and I have cancelled out all doubts" — you are saying it because you don't believe. That in itself proves that you don't believe or you would have no need to say it to start with. Belief has to be total, complete.

Children have belief. The smallest children have belief because it has not been taken away from them. You have conditioned yourself to believe in the reality that other people have accepted and set; the unreal reality that they have adopted you have also adopted. If you were as children, if you were as the babes that had come from the womb of the mother, then you would have total belief. You must be able to cancel all doubt and yet do so without having to say, "I cancel that doubt." Because to do so is to admit that you doubt. And to doubt is to have no belief. None.

DREAMS

What can we do to make that final step to open it, if we are all on the threshold? What is the answer to get beyond that threshold?

We have told you to keep track of your dreams, to form a log. This is the first step and the most vital step. Once this has been done for a term of time, progression will then become rapid.

Is the next step learning to control your dreams?

At night, no. In the day, no. But the next step is learning to accept those impressions of dream quality — day, night, morning, evening; awake, asleep, anything — those feelings come. For if a person stands beside you once you have been open, and they cut off their finger, you shall feel their pain. Therefore, you must be able to open and close at desire.

Should we strive to make our dreams more clear?

This will happen automatically once you begin to log them. Once you keep track, you will find they become clearer and clearer and clearer. And though there may be a period of six months that will all of a sudden be deleted for no reason at all — you may remember nothing — there will come a time there again where it will just open and flow.

While flowing, it is important that you keep track and each time it will become clearer. And when you realize and understand what is really happening and can apply it to your waking state, then you have it mastered. People lay down, they let go, and they accept without prejudice when they sleep. And yet when you are willing to do this in a waking state, then you have reached that point where you shall perceive.

Is there a dreaming self that can be developed, an awareness that can finally be developed to the point where it can move among what we perceive as the real world now so that we can, in effect, be in two places at the same time?

You are where you lay when you sleep. If you move the energy upward and it comes together, and you see the lights, and then you will feel yourself, you rise up from this point [motions up from the top of the head]. This is the energy you speak of, it is what some term "astral projection." It is what some would call being "carried in spirit." You rise from this point [hands held above the head], and at that instant there is a whole disorientation, it is as if the whole world spins. It is because you are not used to that sense of perception. This can be done also in a waking state, but this is what you are speaking of. Of the dreaming self, so to speak, it is real; it is not a false perception and dwells within you.

But when it is loose, when it is what you would consider floating, it is an altered state of reality from what you are now

179

accepting. Therefore, your whole world seems to reel, at least for the first few times that you do this. Once that you have realized that it is possible, and that it is acceptable and easy, then you can move out with assuredness, and you can span any distance in an instant, and to any spot at will.

Is your instruction to us to record our dreams and to try to improve our dreams an attempt to reduce that chaos, that disorientation at that stage or that point we speak of as "astral projection"?

No. It is to make you aware. Once you are aware, the chaos itself will automatically disappear because once you realize what you are really perceiving, you will realize it is not really the scrambled mess you thought it was. It is like a person who is looking in a frying pan full of eggs and they are scrambled. A person walks in who has never had anything but a fried egg and he says, "What's that mess?" But to you it is a scrambled egg; it is very intelligible. In the same sense to a person who has never projected before, when he projects he goes: "Ahhh! What is this?" And yet, when it has happened, they can accept and they know what it is and they say, "Oh, I am projecting."

AURAS

One of the benefits of opening the consciousness is to be able to perceive auras. An aura is an energy field that extends beyond the physical body. It can vary in size, shape, or color, though it is not normally seen by the naked eye. Some people in the conscious state can perceive the colors of an aura and some can do so after training. The colors seem to change with different moods and emotions. Sometimes, hotspots in a person's aura give clues to specific areas that need healing.

Could you explain what the various colors of the aura mean? Sometimes I see blues and purples and different colors around things and around people. What do these different colors mean? Sometimes they change....

Yes, it is energy and it is in a constant state of flux. This energy is also what was being asked of that [which] was being

Illustration #9
Aura

termed "astral plane." This energy is not a solid to you, yet can be perceived as a solid.

But do the different colors have a meaning? For example, do they signify different moods of a person?

....When you see which you would perceive as whites, you are seeing pure, strong, full energy in its true purity. Look at distilled water — a vibrant, pure white. [White indicates] a person with a very pure mind. Gold, gold-yellow is a reflection of intellect, of joy and extreme happiness, of intelligence. A blue is of happiness, peace, and tranquility. Going deeper into purples, you are mixing red and blue; it's a more energetic peace. Greens are what you shall see around a healer — one who can reach out and heal, one who can perform miracles, or span time. The same green energy is used for all [of this]. Black is bad, very depressed, if not death. Brown is earthen and depressed.

Spots or holes of black in the energy flow is often caused by alcoholism or excessive use of drugs. There are holes eaten into the energy and into the personality, holes eaten into the mind. Spots are also often seen over cancerous or troublesome areas. Red will often be reflected over any organ that is causing pain, or infection. Red, when surrounded by green, shows that the pain or the infection is there, but that it is being healed. The brighter, the more intense the green, the stronger the healing. The duller, the weaker, the slower the process. Pine green is a weak system trying to heal itself. Jade green, bright green, is a system healing or healed, or a system that can heal those around it.

It is frequent to see these colors mixed, for it is very seldom that one side of a personality shows, but that several at one time will show; that one type of energy flows at a time, and though a person might be a healer at one moment, they might not be at another. You may radiate total green at one minute, and the next minute radiate nothing but a pure gold. But it is not uncommon for a person to radiate two or three colors at the same time and usually there will be a blending of other colors closely knit together in between that.

How does one go about sharpening one's ability to perceive these colors?

If you were born an excellent [baseball] player and spent all your time sitting in the locker room, chewing tobacco and throwing darts at Miss January [laughter from the group] — Hmmm — [more laughter] — you would stand very little chance of ever making it to the batter's cage, let alone the batting box. This is the same truth with every gift, whether you be skilled in working with metal or carpentry or whether it is a gift of the spirit. It is the same. It is 99.9 per cent your effort, your work, and your desire.

The best baseball player in the world goes to a coach to have that developed more perfectly and more quickly. Who can coach us?

It is true that you can gain guidance and direction. Now, people gain guidance and direction much in the same way as a ballplayer would. One ballplayer might go to his father and be taught, another might go to another ballplayer, yet a third would go to a coach and a fourth would work it out on his own, slowly but surely; ... yet that fourth would probably be your famous ballplayer in the long run. He will be the one who, after he has overcome all difficulties, really knows what he is doing. Yet the refining from the coach will still help him. In the same way, you may go to another that is so gifted, as you would go to another ballplayer. You may go to one who purports to teach such knowledge — remember, this is usually a retired ballplayer or somebody who wasn't good enough to make it to begin with — or you may go to your father as a young child might, wanting to learn baseball, that original creative essence; or you may dig deep within your own subconscious, much as the player would teach his own self. And then when you have found and built, go to the coach and polish yourself slightly.

Chapter Eleven

FROM THE TEACHINGS

It is your heritage to heal, to prophesy, to see,
to open, and to look upon all that is.
The Eternals

Sometimes during Daniel and The Eternals' channeling we had to stop and take a few deep breaths; the amount of information coming made us feel overwhelmed. Even The Eternals commented on this. The source remarked that the energy was becoming heavy in the room; or, "the energy feels to be turning in on itself." Sometimes a joke or a demonstration from The Eternals relieved the sheer density of the atmosphere.

Each session provoked questions and the questions required answers and the answers provoked still more questions. Aside from the questions we asked aloud, we all had underlying questions. My wife Ann and I often discussed these, and she talked about the changes occurring in herself as a result of her wonderings. She said:

"When communications purporting to be from a psychic source started happening in my own house, I was interested and intrigued. At first, I wasn't sure who or what they were, what purpose they served, or more especially, if they would ring true for me. But suddenly it occurred to me that the questions were addressed to sources who were not limited by space and time with their knowledge, and this gave me pause. Asking the right questions seemed important because I wasn't sure how long these sessions would last.

"In retrospect, this seems an all too human response of mine because I can see now that this was a false fear. We were not given just knowledge, but wisdom on a much deeper level. My mental concepts definitely broadened, along with my horizons, which I now more clearly perceive as having no end."

I believe most participants in the Teachings felt much the same way. Here is a sampling of the questions they asked; you can judge for yourself the wisdom of The Eternals' answers.

FREE WILL

You said earlier this evening that everything is predestined. And you have also said that there is total free will. Could you explain this seeming contradiction?

Everything is predestined, that is true. If you take control, you set yourself at liberty from all things. If you have liberty, then how can that which you do be predestined? Yet you chose to be born where you are born. Therefore, you have predestined your life and even as much as given yourself the chance for that liberty. So the liberty in itself was predestined, and therefore all the choice you make from it.

That was a masterful use of words. It's very difficult, I'm sure, to explain. You're saying that perfect freedom can be preordained or predestined, so that every free choice that is made once the liberty is attained, was predestined just because the liberty was predestined?

To have total liberty you cannot have predestination. Because if you have total liberty, you can do anything that you choose. And yet, if you placed yourself in that situation to begin with, you have predestined yourself or prearranged for this to take place, already knowing that you could make either choice. You have arranged to make the choice that you desire to make. Therefore, in essence, it would suffice to say that everything is predestined, that there is no free will in that sense.

EXTRATERRESTRIALS
In the entire universe, are there other planets that have life forms similar to our own?

No, this is not entirely what was intended, but the person that brought this up seemed to think that they were going to go to another planet to work out their progressions. This is not to say that there is both life terrestrial and extraterrestrial, that there is even glory terrestrial and extraterrestrial; for when you receive your divine heritage, that which you are, that which you have a right to claim, when you receive full power, you have command of the whole universe, and if you had command over all, would you spend your time here? Wouldn't you travel as you wished?

Therefore, there is life and there is force and there is energy at this time all about the universe and all about the stars, and each star itself is a life and an energy and an entity. How come, if it were not so, that the prophet Daniel would say we shine, shine, shine as the stars? This was why it was written, for you, yourself, have the capability of taking any form you desire. It is only your own mind and the abstracts which you hold yourself into, it is only in the reality which you have desired to perceive, that has bound you to this earth physical.

But do not think you're going to go elsewhere to work out that which must be worked out [here]. The slave will not go to the quarters of the king to perform his hygienical tasks. Therefore, how will man go to the heavens and the stars to perform the inner cleansing? If it be that your abode is in heaven, then the spaceships shall be there before you are. If it be that you shall return to the sky, then the birds have heritage over you. If it be that you go to the ocean, if that is where your life is, then the fish go before you.

If it is that the kingdon of God is within you, then you shall have all the divine heritage before all else. Does this make this clear?

Somewhat, I — it is clear.

It isn't clear. It's not clear. Okay. R2-D2, E.T., and little weird worms with eyeballs are not living on Mars working out progressions. If all is energy forms, even yours, though you perceive yourself as solid, you are bound to this earth only inasmuch as you have bound yourselves. Yet because we have chosen this as the ground to work out, or to purify ourselves, this is the only place it may be done. For those who will accept, there is an eternal heritage, a divine heritage among all energy, among the stars, a glorious and a wonderful heritage, so to speak. But for those who will not accept, they cannot go beyond this realm, and there is no chance of leaving it. They are terrestrial, they are terra firma bound.

MEN AND WOMEN

I would like some input on the spiritual roles of men and women.

Is woman less than man? Man cannot be born unless he passes through the womb of woman. Christ was carried in the womb of a woman nine, yet ten months, before he was delivered to the world. If God saw fit to give his son to a woman (before he gave his son to the men of the world), then is not that woman placed first?

It has been said that there will be no marriage, no giving or taking of husband or wife in the kingdom — the kingdom that is within. All are equal and all serve a function. You are the same in spirit, be you male or be you female. You have the same rights and the same power. You have the same chance for glory both terrestrial and extraterrestrial. You have the same rights and the same heritage. Male cannot live without female nor can female live without male. If one cannot live without the other, then one is not superior to the other.

What about their roles and symbolism? There is a lot of symbolism in Eastern religion, talking about the Yin and Yang, the female and male principles. Also, in a lot of alchemy, they talk about androgynous persons. Why is that an ideal — to be androgynous?

The Yin and Yang of the Chinese people is the balance and counterbalance, is good and evil, dark and light. They have accepted it as the Yin and Yang to be called "female" and "male." Yet this was not the original intent. But it is the dark and the light, the truth and the nontruth. To be a person who is totally one within one's own self is to be spiritually full.

To set yourself aside, to purify yourself, to say, "This will make me holy if I do not have sexual intercourse"; to say, "My hymen is not broken"; or "My semen may not leave my body" does not make one better. For it does not matter if you indulge daily and are thankful for the gift you have been given or if you give praise by not doing. Each, in its own way, is bringing glory and it is the state of mind that you accept this with. Therefore, there is no gain and no loss in the state.

In a book called Secret of the Golden Flower, *I have read references to "the secret" being involved in some sexual process. I wonder if you could talk about this.*

You have two different modes of thought. The thought of the Westerners is that they should take their sexual drive and turn it inward. [But] it gives them no more power, no more potency. If this is what you seek, it is of no benefit.

On the other hand, if you are God and your body itself is the living temple, if you yourself are the son of God and the God, then to defile your body is to defile God himself, God herself. To do this is to bring about a defamation of that very God which you would worship. Therefore, out with sexual practice which is harmful to the being, as practiced in the Satanic cults and in some of the freer cults of witchcraft and in some of the cults of the nethergods of the mother Earth and of the moon. This is defiling that which was made in the image of and is of God itself.

It was written not to commit adultery. Now, if you commit adultery, you are lying. And all evil evolves from lies and lust. If you take any sexual practice and do it for self-gratification and you care not for the other person, then you do injury to that person. And if you bring a child into the world and that child has been conceived at an ill-conception, he shall suffer the evil also. And yet, this can be overcome by balance and counterbalance. To love, to give of yourself freely to another, to sacrifice yourself in this way, is proper.

BURIED CITIES

Have there been entire living cities deep inside the earth—not the cliff dwellings of the Southwest, but entire cities deep inside the earth?

There are even *now* entire cities in the very earth itself. You see, the government looks for the nuclear holocaust. They know what is coming. They have set themselves aside and have built entire cities with fountains, streams, lakes, ponds; yet they are buried ... this gives escape routes to our executives in Washington when the time of trouble comes. Oh, they think not of these poor people about here who shall be burned to pieces, but of themselves. In their little secret chambers they think no one knows of their places and where they dwell under the grounds.

....There are those in the desert. There are those on the very edges and outskirts of the metropolitan area of Washington itself — slightly to the south and slightly to the north. They build these thinking they can escape and leave the rest of the world to be burned to a sizzle. You see, they take this threat very seriously and they know there is no way to make a lasting peace and that the earth shall fry, fry, and die.

....These cities shall be bombarded and destroyed, burnt, crushed. And the remains of these shall look like Hiroshima, the center of Hiroshima.

THE CITY OF THE SPIRIT

....There is also that city where those that are spiritual dwell. It is not found by man, but by spirit alone.... The city is open and yet no one can proceed through except that they be in spirit, that they might travel through the earth itself. For the door is open and yet only to that which is spiritual. It is a city where the spirits are indwelling. It is the city where there are many learning centers and the facilities are great. And many go there for rest and seclusion. It is also in the deserts of the West of this country but only to be found in spirit.

....If you can lift yourself out of body, then you can travel to where you wish to go. And if you are out of body, you are in spirit and if you are in spirit, you can walk through the doors of the spiritual city and there attend your schooling, and there enjoy your leisure.

What is the name of this city? What is it called?

189

Ala-made Rish-nard, Ala-made Rish-nard, Ala-made Rish-nard, Ala-made Rish-nard [as in a chant].

Can these schools [in the spiritual city] be visited in dreams?

They can be and they are, quite frequently, and usually unknowingly.

Why is there a physical location for a school, for a city, of spiritual beings?

You have an earth. They have an earth. You're in the same place and yet you do not see them. Do you not think they would desire to have a home to live in? And yet, they create what they believe and what they desire so they may have all fullness of beauty as they wish. And among them they have consensus that they should have a place of rest and peace and learning. And this they have made.

Do the inhabitants of this city have physical bodies of any nature?

This is a physical body [pointing to his own hand]. Yes. This is the body they have [pointing to about two inches beyond his actual hand, as to the aura].

ASTRONOMY AND ASTROLOGY

At the beginning [of the session] you said we had the power within us and the right to override ... [planetary] influences. Wouldn't it be better for us to make the choices rather than for the planet to make the choices for us [i.e., to exercise our own free will without regard to the planets]? Wouldn't astrology then be a diversion, a distraction that shouldn't be emphasized?

This is why there have been so many commands and ordinances against it — even the holy rites of the Jews. These commands have also been taken by the Christians.

Should we follow that idea and disregard astrology?

Look within. Astrology is nothing to you. If you can see, you have more than you can find in the stars. If you are God and you are the Creator, and you have divine essence, how will you go to the stars and ask them, "What's going to happen on my date tomorrow night?" Are the stars going to tell you more than you can find by searching your own soul? It is impossible. Look within yourself and all things will be clear. But do not think this

190

makes astrology invalid.

What has validity in astrology, as it is practiced now, and what is merely a product of wishful thinking?

Astrology does not tell the future as some would desire it to. Astrology is a guide to personality characteristics or tendencies or traits, and yet can be overridden by the person. Astrology is not binding. It is a trend and a trend only. To put it in scientific terms (terms more acceptable to the scientific community), biorhythms follow a small clock. In turn, astrology is simply a larger form of biorhythms turned out on a greater time cycle, a larger clock. All of the superstitions that have come down with it through the millennia are nonsense. Yet as much good has been lost as has been gained in superstition, for much of the truth of it, at times, has been obscured; and yet there is always the light of hope.

ARMAGEDDON

Without question, The Eternals' view of the future was the most difficult, controversial, and upsetting to everyone in the groups. The Eternals painted a grim picture of the future. They said there will be cataclysm, devastation, and holocaust affecting the entire planet. Whole continents will disappear. Much of the destruction will be manmade. Great warring armies, led by figures of evil incarnate, will destroy the world; no one nation or people is to blame. Some of the destruction will also come from polar shifts and wavering.

Here are a few excerpts.

Is this the reason the world won't come together [in peace]? Because one or more of us has greed?

One of you has greed? One?

One or more.

The world is *filled* with greed. And those among you who say, "I do not have greed, I want nothing," don't think that the ego trip of placing yourself totally without greed is not also a form of lust and greed for its own sort of power? Not one among you has completely defeated greed. It is not something you can totally overcome because there is always the latent possibility. It sits there and because of your free will, it can blow up at any time. It's like a little egg in your skin, just waiting to hatch and infest you with worms. Greed is a rot and a leprosy and a death. And that is the reason for the destruction. The destruction comes quickly.

You mean the destruction of the world as we know it? Is that what you are talking about, or the destruction of the individual?

The destruction of the world, the end of this age. The time shall come to an end 60,000 years, and yet, 500 do pass. The time is short. [This was one of The Eternals' cryptic answers. We were told that "all time is sealed," meaning that some dates were not to be given.]

If we, as individuals or as a group, were to decide that there is to be [peace on earth], is that possible?

Yes, but — and we must stress this strongly — you speak in terms of "is it possible" in your realm of reality. It is possible in our realm or your realm of reality, or anybody's, so to speak. But you must have a group consensus to bring a "peace" that is to everyone, that is to all. A collective peace must be brought about by collective realities converging together for this. *That* is not to be reached in the near future. There must first be an unbalancing and a total upheaval. Once everything is scrambled, then it can be placed back together.... Things must fall apart. They must be completely destroyed before they can come together.

How can we best prepare for this scrambling?

The best way to prepare for it would be to be dead. It's going to be very unpleasant for those who are alive ... in the physical form. There will be melting of flesh. There will be horrible times. There will be great droughts caused by the radiation and by the screens or the ionosphere being destroyed. There shall be great heat from the sun scorching because of the atmosphere being in such a disarray.... And yet at the very end of this, at the very collapse of this, is when — your society — *shall become utopian.* Only by being completely destroyed can it be brought back together again.

Is all this to occur within our lifetimes?

Yes, it will be in the lifetime of some, but not all. Fortunately, some shall escape. But this is not of really great importance, for what is physical is of no importance. It is only a minor speck of reality. Look within yourself, this is important.

You say everything will be so destroyed that there's no point in preparing for it physically. Is there?

What good is it going to do you to build a bomb shelter if the earth decides to make a great quake and collapse it? What good is it going to do for you to make yourself an undersea getaway, if somebody is going to come along with a torpedo and blow it to pieces? In essence, there is nothing that can be done to prepare. Prepare your innermost self, and don't worry about the physical.

Will all the people on earth be destroyed?

No.... The things that will be destroyed first will be the large population areas. But there will be people surviving in every area. Some shall survive to rebuild when they have regained their strength.

Will they be mutated from what they are now?

No, life will be as it is. There shall be surviving and everything shall not be totally destroyed. And after a time of cleansing and purification, it shall all be rebuilt.

Should someone consciously have a child, knowing that this terrible time is coming?

If you fear the time, then you should not have a child. If you do not fear the time and you can teach your child not to fear, then there is no cause not to.... Yet if you can alter your consciousness and accept it as truth that you are divine, then you will walk upon the water that is shifting under your feet, you will walk upon the molten rock and you shall thrive. Therefore, there is no evil for those that know and receive of their heritage. And if it be your child that receives his heritage, then there is no evil. But for those who would look after the physical, it is chaos and utter destruction — a place of agony as will not be seen again nor past.

How long after all this turmoil will the peaceful times come, and will there be anybody present who will survive into those peaceful times?

Yes, there will be some who will live, and the time shall come immediately because consciousness shall be altered; and once the consciousness is altered, immediately everything changes to that state. There will be no delay. This is the reason that some of the Apostles chose to say that things would happen in the twinkling of an eye, in a moment. For once that consciousness is gained and believed, it is set in motion and it is instantaneous. There will be no gap, but there will be a rebuilding.... [It is as if people say] "Oh, my God, the world's blowing up. There must be something else. Wow! Look at all these horrible things happening. I must search for the truth quickly." With enough people thinking this way instantly, the consciousness shall be altered. With enough people wanting the truth, seeking the truth, it can be altered. The whole thing could be avoided if people would simply change their ways.... It can be, but it won't be.

Is there anything that can give people a sense of hope, instead of despair, fear, and anxiety?

There comes a new land and a new time.... There will be years of peace, a time of continual hope. And it will take many years to bury the bodies from the destruction at this time of peace. And the peace shall be lasting and will not leave. There will no more war come about after the peace has been.... For man shall find his place — his most holy place — among the lights.

RELIGION

People at the Teachings often questioned The Eternals on religious topics. For instance, there were many questions on the meaning of specific passages from the Christian scriptures or on Christian figures like Joan of Arc. There were questions on Mormonism, Judaism, and the Rosicrucians. There were also questions on the writings of Confucius, Castenada, and Gibran, who, while not concerned with sectarian religion, have written on spiritual, ethical, and moral issues.

These questions, I believe, reflect two concerns. First, for most at the Teachings, The Eternals' concepts were unfamiliar and new, and the doors to spiritual experience that seemed to be opening puzzled and sometimes troubled them. Second, if they were familiar with a religion (I use the word to mean an organized institution propagating certain beliefs), people tended to compare the teachings of The Eternals with those of the churches familiar to them. It is almost as if they were saying, "Is this right? Or this?" But The Eternals spoke ever of oneness and universality, of balance and counterbalance.

Thus, for instance, there was this exchange.

You mentioned Christ.... Is that one in particular, or are you centering on that one name?

We are many: of Vishnu and of Mohammed, and of Christ and of Elohim, Yahweh, and Yeshua, of those who guided the hands when the Talmud was written, of those who walked along and guided the words as Confucius constructed, of those who sent visions to Mohammed, and those who brought about the visions to Joseph Smith, to those who were among the Shakers.... We are many, and yet we are all.

How much of the teachings of Christ have been altered over the years in translation?

A great deal.

How much of them can we rely on and how do we tell what's proper and what's not?

You can rely on a great deal of them also. The changes have not been in the sections that contain the truth.... The underlying teachings — the teachings of truth, the teachings of light, the teachings of self-consciousness, the teachings of love, the teachings of the inner spirit, the teachings about the inner eye, the teachings about the spiritual world itself — all remain intact.

What has been done has been the creation of such things as would allow the churches to take over. The substitution of such things as sabbaths and Easter, the substitutions of ordained priesthoods.

[The Eternals expand on this idea in other exchanges. The gist of the remarks is that while the teachings of religion are correct in essence, they have been misinterpreted or "manipulated in such a way as to allow for authority figures to come in and take over the willing sheep."] The questioning goes on:

The vibratory force that was Jesus Christ ... has that same force been on Earth in other progressions?

Yes. All forces travel again and again.

Has that force ever taught again as it did in the form of Jesus Christ?

195

The consciousness of Krishna, the consciousness of Christ, is not so much so that this deity had to teach. And when we say "deity," you also are a deity. When one looks, and when we say the "consciousness of Krishna," the "consciousness of Christ," when one sees within himself and can reach full and total consciousness or awareness, he has awareness of the past and of the present and of the future. He has a total awareness — a oneness with the original vibratory force which has become all vibratory forces that are around him. This has been achieved by others throughout the ages also.

What has made this sect [Christianity] so powerful is the fact that it was persecuted so strongly. That which is persecuted always rises — for to be persecuted is to cause friction which must be counterbalanced.

And yet, much was lost. If you must look to the teachings, look to the teachings of the Gnostics.

Now in Christ Himself, was He alive? Has He walked this plane before He was born to the Essenes? Yes, but it is not important to you where he walked or who he was, for this will not alter one thing, one jot, nor one tittle, not one iota, nor one small speck.

A Jewish participant found the references to Jesus as the "Christ" (i.e., the Messiah) "hard to hear," and asked, "Is the whole Jewish race wrong?" After an answer stressing, again, the universality of the Christ, The Eternals said:

The Jewish heritage is correct, the Christian heritage is correct, the Moslem heritage is correct.

The Christian heritage has not left the Jewish, they have simply added to it that which is good. The Moslem heritage has not left the Jewish, they have simply led their ways down their own path and added that which is good.

Therefore, the Moslems say that their Savior shall return with a shout, and a mighty shout. The Christians say that Christ shall come even from the heavens with a loud shout and a blowing of trumpets by the archangels. And even Krishna shall return in the like manner. How be it that if all of these agree, and even the Jewish scriptures themselves say that the earth shall roll upon its axis, and prophesy a time of peace, that this cannot be accepted? We have not overcome confusion by far.

SCRIPTURAL EXCHANGES

The Eternals commented at some length on interpretations of various passages from Christian scriptures. Here are three typical exchanges.

Could you give us an interpretation of the Beatitudes [the remarks of Jesus in the Sermon on the Mount — Matthew 3:12 and other references]?

This was the sole purpose that we are gathered for, in essence — that we might bring about a knowledge of peace and love.

In Matthew 5, they talk about those that mourn being comforted. How shall those that mourn be comforted? How shall those who are hungry and thirsty for righteousness be filled? [Two questions; the answer has been combined into one.]

There is a balance and a counterbalance. All things are balanced. Therefore, if you are in a state of sorrow, you shall come to a state of happiness. If you are in a state of trouble, you shall come to a state of peace.

Second, there is altering of the consciousness; and if it be that the consciousness is altered and that all be set about as it said it would, then there will come a time — a glorious time — of peace, when all shall be in good and all shall be in righteousness. If this be so, then how will it be that they should be hungry?

How can we, as the salt of the earth, lose our savor; and where shall the salt be cast out? And how shall we be trodden under foot? [The reference is to Matthew 5:13.]

You look within and you see the kingdom. You believe it is within and then you turn, and do not believe. Again you have lost your savor. You have lost your divine heritage. You have lost that which you had found.

It is written that you can profane God, that you can profane the Father, and that you can profane the Son, but you cannot profane the Holy Ghost or the Holy Spirit and enter into the holy kingdom. For if you deny the power, the vibratory, the creative supreme power, the power, Holy Spirit power, Holy Ghost, or power — whatever you want to say — if you deny the power, then you cannot look within and you cannot attain that which is within yourself. If you do not attain that which is within the supreme light, then you are within the outer darkness.

SPIRITUAL EXPERIENCE

With the next two exchanges The Eternals invite participants to open a new door to the understanding of spiritual experience.

When and what is the kingdom of heaven?

The kingdom is now the kingdom within. In my father's house are many states of consciousness. And I go to prepare a state that you might have it for yourself. If it were not so, we would not have told you of the consciousness.

Who is your father?

Call no man "father" for there is none that is holy. We speak of the supreme vibratory force; that which was before that which is come into being.

Could you please tell us about the different heavens? You spoke of the Fifth Heaven, what are the other heavens?

The Fifth Heaven was an allusion to the Books of Enoch, wherein he spoke of traveling through the heavens. Don't think that your soul shall rest in Heaven. For ... if the kingdom of God — if the kingdom itself — dwells within your heart, within you, then you are there before all else is there.

Is heaven within us, is that what you are saying?

Did not Christ himself say the Kingdom of Heaven was within? [Questioner answers "yes."] If it is within, howbeit that it is up there in the clouds [that] your little gold harp and your set of wings await? Don't look for the "pie in the sky...." This is not where you belong, you are not "up there." And yet, when you claim your heritage — your divine heritage — and have full and total and complete freedom, and release — liberty of all liberties — you have total power and soar where you will.

As the tree falls, so it lies. And that is to say, in that state of consciousness [in] which you die, that state of consciousness [is that] ... which you are in.

FORGIVENESS

Please speak about forgiveness.

You must learn, in essence, to forgive yourself. To forgive yourself is to forgive all others.... Do not judge yourself from the beginning. Do not judge those around you and, in essence, you have forgiven them because you have never created that which would be forgiven. For all evil lies within yourself, as does all good. It is not what another does to you but what you have perceived and how you have reacted to it.

Religious teachings are full of the concept of forgiveness. Is that something man has put in?

No, but it is something that has to be spoken of in an abstract term. To truly forgive is to love and to not hold against. But once you have forgiven, you cannot say, "I have forgiven that person," for to truly forgive is to wipe the slate clean and it is no more.

I am still interested in the dynamics of forgiveness. Could you speak to us more about it?

To forgive is a very powerful thing. In order to forgive, you must totally — totally — remove all of the doubt, all of the grudges, that you hold against a person.

This has been said before: ... to say, "I forgive you," does not mean a person is forgiven. To forgive a person is to return them to the state that they were at before they did it. And in order to do this, you have to love them so completely that you can accept what they did without holding it against them. This has to be total and complete.

And with faith, where doubt — even the least shadow of doubt — constitutes not a slight lack of faith, but total, total dis-faith, total disbelief; so with forgiveness.

The least shadow of resentment, the least shadow in your mind, or even [to] remember the evil, is totally and completely bringing yourself to a point where you have no forgiveness for the person. For you can only do one or the other. You cannot forgive a person halfway. For to do that is not to forgive at all.

SOUL MATES

Could you please clarify the term ... "soul mate?" Is this a common experience?

When one speaks of "soul mate," one speaks of people who have what some would term "karmic tie," not of any type but of one that is favorable. Now, if you have a favorable tie with another individual, it can actually be not because you have done well in the past, but you have done evil, and then it must be counterbalanced. So therefore, when you say that you have a soul mate and you get along so fabulously, it might do you well to look into the recesses of your mind and to see what evil you have done in the past that makes you do such good now.

"Soul mate" is a misleading term in that it would lead one to believe that you have lived forever and ever happy with this person. That is not true. This does not necessarily mean that you are in a fairy tale with this individual, although it is also possible, if you are progressing and have another individual progressing with you, that you will choose the same planes together again and again. In this [case, the expression] "soul mate," in its essence and in its true sense, would be somewhat correct. However, you may be balancing a karmic trend, so to speak, of another individual, so the term itself is not always relevant in the way that it is used.

Do entities in these progressions tend to travel together or do they separate once they are out of progression and go their own way totally?

They travel together at times, if it is required by balance and counterbalance. If it is not required, then they will travel their own way if they choose to do so. But just as friends might choose even in this physical plane to walk together, so can these spiritual entities choose to walk together. This is of their own making and of free choice.

Can that companionship go through several progressions here on this earth?

It can go through as many as desired. It can go through one year, a thousand years, or ten thousand years, and it makes no difference.

PERSONALITY AND SPIRITUALITY

We all see ourselves as people with personalities. Do you

have a personality after you make the transition that's called "death"
in this world? Do you keep the personality that you have when
you are in the body?

You are asking about existence of personality as in continual,
onward and onward. That part of your personality which you now
reflect you shall maintain. It will not necessarily be the part that
will be lighting up the room, so to speak, the next time that you
are present in this plane.

Your personality is like a diamond and it has many facets cut
on it. And it shines and it sparkles according to the way the light
hits it. So now you may appear to have one personality, and yet
you speak of a different personality in death. You may have a
different personality in five minutes from now, or a minute past.

A person's personality is a reflection of his own truth, his own
knowledge and wisdom, reflecting that which is around him also.
So your self is part of your personality, and all that is around you
is part of your personality. It is not something that can be
separated nor divided. And yet only one small surface of it may
show at a time, or even in a hundred or a thousand years. And that
still leaves many sides to shine. But yes, even if that side is not
shining, still the rest of your personality is there. For if you're
looking at half a diamond, it does not mean that the other half of
the face or surface is not present.

LIFE RECORDS

*Do we, as humans, have a soul which is a ... form of life
energy?*

Your soul is your conscious energy, that record which is
recorded and not erased, that which is balanced and counterbalanced,
that which is remembered of beyond all time.... Your body has life-
force, but within this body itself you store information that will
move out of the body and continue onward.

*Is there a specific place in our body where this life information
is stored? Is that throughout our being or does it have a localized
center in the physical?*

It is not localized in the physical, itself, but it is localized in
the spiritual.

Where is it localized in the spiritual?

[The Vessel answers by drawing a circle with his hand around

201

the center of his chest.]

Is that what would be called "the heart chakra," that circle that you are drawing on your chest?

It is the door of the heart, the chakra so green.

And that's where our life records are stored, in the spiritual?

In the fire of the green. In the essence of the being. In the chakra of the heart. For from the heart comes love, and from the heart comes hate. And as you speak with your mouth, you reveal the very feelings that are in your heart.

And with your mouth, then, why do you curse man, who is made in the image of God? And yet, bless God, Himself? For is not to curse one made in the image of God as great a sin as to curse God, Himself?

Therefore, if you can bridle the tongue, you have mastered the heart. And to master the heart is to master all things.

PAST LIVES AND THE CONCEPT OF TIME

In ... Seth Speaks,[1] and the different Seth books by Jane Roberts, an idea has been presented that all our past lives are happening all at one time. That all our previous lives are, right now, happening all at one time but at different levels. Is this so, or is this just a confusion of concepts?

It's immaterial in the spiritual world. Time does not exist to start with. Time is simply a manmade device. Time is created that you might control your life a little better. First you see that the sun sets and rises, and you have night and day. And you say, "Time is a day and a night." Then you divide it, "Well, I'll do this when the sun is in the middle of the sky [pointing], and I'll go to bed when it sets here [pointing] in the evening." And you divide it yet again, "When the sun — that precious little light — has come up, just where I can see it over the trees, I'll eat something. Then I'll go out and do some work. And by the time it gets right there, straight up over my head, I'll be hungry so I'll eat more."

And it continues, until you no longer control time, but it controls you. "I must do this when the sun rises, and as soon as it gets to the point of noon, I *have* to have something to eat or my stomach will absolutely collapse." And time doesn't even exist. For what was, still is. And what is to be, has already passed.

202

You said earlier that a few people here present have had lives in the Middle Ages in a monastery....Is one part of them still there?

A diamond has many sides. You may only see one side at a time, but the other side is still there, and still where it was, when you walk around it to look at the other side. [Author's note: To put it another way, the past, present, and future form a single crystal. The past is just one facet.]

In other words, you are saying that that is a reality at some level?

As real as the flesh that you have on your bones. [Author's note: This was a difficult concept for us to comprehend, as our questions reflect. Even the reply, "As real as the flesh on your bones," was not a fully clear statement, as we were also told that all is an illusion, or "unreal."]

If time does not exist, and there are many facets to our being, as there are facets to a diamond, and you have spoken of the facet that is showing, is it possible to go back or to cross from facet to facet or is only one showing at one time?

It is not the normal reality to cross from facet to facet? Yet this is done quite frequently.

Is it a skill that should be developed, or an ability to try and develop?

Most would term it a "gift." And yet a gift must be worked at hard to develop it to its potential. Sometimes you can jump from facet to facet, or from time to time....

If it is true that all time is nonexistent, can a person be progressed so that he can experience his future life, as he can be regressed so that he can experience his past life?

Do you desire a cryptic answer? Then one you shall have. Yes. [Laughter. Earlier in the session, someone had commented that many answers were cryptic.]

Endnotes:

[1]Jane Roberts, *Seth Speaks: The Eternal Validity of the Soul* (Englewood Cliffs, NJ: Prentice-Hall, Inc., 1974).

Chapter Twelve

READINGS

Build the spirit and the soul to last through eternity.
The Eternals

When The Eternals spoke to a group, we called the session a "Teaching," and the information that came through was general, intended by The Eternals to benefit humanity at large.

As our work became known, people also requested personal readings. They wanted The Eternals' counsel on health, finances, relationships, and past-life ties with loved ones in the present. Some asked about their soul's purpose and their destiny in this lifetime. One or two even wanted to know, "What question should I be asking that I don't even know to ask?" Naturally, very few people came for readings who were happy and content — about the same, I imagine, as go to their doctors when they are in good health.

Daniel offers us a glimpse below of what it is like to be a channel and give psychic readings — the price one must pay in knowing others' pain, in offering wisdom that can be scoffed at or not perceived. He says:

"The responsibility that goes with doing personal readings is awesome. Most people don't turn to a psychic until they are on their last legs. The majority are depressed, ill or terminally ill, or suicidal. They have been failed by conventional help, and I'm a last resort. It makes me realize my good fortune, but I carry greater sorrow for my fellow man every time I do a reading.

"For every person that can accept the unknown there is a person who fears the unknown. It can be hard being rejected for your abilities. Working with my wife, I healed an aunt of a serious illness by balancing her energy flow. Jesus gives me the power, but I seldom get to see my cousin now, since I'm the oddball who sees lights about people.

"Everything has its price. Half the people I meet look at me as if I'm a hoax. The other half seem to think I'm prying in their minds, seeing deep dark secrets. Of course, I'm not a hoax. I believe in what I do. As to seeing deep dark secrets, I'm too busy tending my own life — thinking about what I'd like for supper.

"What has made me feel best about the readings is the lives we have helped. I guess being able to give urgent and lifesaving information in several important emergency cases has been our crowning achievement.

"And I must admit being in the Light and being able to see the Light with the eye is a joy beyond words."

I, myself, have been to some of the top psychics in the country for personal readings and professional discussions. This was always a rewarding experience, and the information was usually very helpful. Even information that did not seem accurate at the time later proved true.

But the reading may or may not satisfy the recipient. The questions are always answered, but not everyone can, or will, *hear* the answer. Some cannot use it. Receiving guidance and counsel and then doing something with the information are two different things; not even Cayce's readings were followed by all recipients.

For those who are able to hear, a reading is like going to a much wiser source of information than most of us have available to us (going straight to the top, as it were). Advice comes from a loving but detached source, more objective than a friend and more unbiased than a specialist.

WHAT HAPPENS AT THE READINGS

The personal readings were separate from the group work. A few people met with Daniel and me at my home. Most submitted written questions (we had discovered in our early experiments that Daniel and The Eternals could communicate with questioners telepathically). In this case, the questioner stayed at home, resting quietly at a prearranged time, and we did the reading "long distance."

The general format of a long distance reading was this. After Daniel reached the Hall of Records I would say:

You will have before you the soul, body, and enquiring mind of _____ (name), present at _____(address). He/she was born _____ (date and year). Please give a full mental, physical, spiritual, and emotional reading for this entity; giving that information that will be of most benefit to him/her in life. Afterwards answering questions he/she has submitted.

Generally, The Eternals began with a full physical, mental, and spiritual evaluation, with personal counsel and guidance. This part was a monologue and usually lasted about half an hour. In the next half hour, The Eternals answered questions. (I read them if the subject was not present.)

Attending the readings and Teachings was not new or startling for me, although each one was most impressive. For some people, attending the readings and teachings was a big step into trust and courage. One woman, a teacher, explains it this way. (She is speaking of the Teachings, but her feelings express common reactions to the personal readings too.)

"When my husband and I were invited to witness the readings by Daniel, we were not sure what we were getting into. Neither of us had been exposed to anyone under hypnosis, much less to someone who was speaking for other beings in such an intense and electrifying manner.

"We were both unsure of whether we wanted to become

206

involved in such a strange happening. After much thought, we decided that life was too short to miss an opportunity offered at our door step, so we went.

"We were hooked at the first meeting. Tuesday nights became the focus of our week for the length of the time that the readings lasted — two or three months. At times, we were merely interested in what he said, at other times amused, and other times intensely horrified and depressed at his visions of the future. Never had we experienced such a mind-opening and thought-provoking series of meetings as was offered when Daniel gave his teachings and answered questions by those present. We were glad to be a part of it."

The readings and Teachings were serious, but not somber. As I've said, there was much laughter, many funny episodes. The Eternals had great compassion for those who hurt, and, it seemed to me, hard words for others who needed shaking up. I wish I had space for all the readings; I have tapes of more than 100. I have chosen two.

The first was given for twins who live in Maine. Their parents owned a health food store there, and the twins proposed to build a healing center in conjunction with it. They asked many questions about bricks, mortar, and land; they wanted to build first and teach later. The Eternals weren't interested. "Start now," The Eternals said, in effect. "Give classes and workshops and healing programs with whatever facilities are there now."

I tried to do my job as a guide and stay out of the controversy. The interplay continued for several sessions. "The Wood Cutter," the story I have excerpted from the sessions, seems to me to be wonderful advice to the twins. It seems to hint that they must go deeper to find ways to build their building.

This lesson was helpful to me, as well. The story told me to have courage and faith, to go deeper into my search into the mind and soul, and it hinted strongly that I should not be concerned with my early successes, but rather continue to learn for greater gain.

THE WOOD CUTTER
February 21, 1984
Independence, Virginia

There is a man. There is a man. He goes forth. He goes forth. He goes forth to cut wood. There is a man, he goes forth to cut the wood. He is a poor man and he has only been making ends meet. This man has been making his living — but barely.

There is a man. There is a man who goes forth to cut the wood. He labors hard from sunrise to sunset, and he cuts his wood. And he cuts his wood at the edge of the forest. Every day he cuts his wood at the edge of the forest. He cuts his wood and he cuts his wood — day in and day out. Calluses and blisters. Rain and sun.

One day while he is cutting, this hungry wood cutter — one day while he is cutting, this hungry wood cutter who has naught, who has not been looked upon by fortune — one day, he is cutting, cutting at the edge of the woods, and by him passes a man of wisdom who says, "Wood cutter, wood cutter, if you would have wealth, why do you not cut deeper in the forest? Why do you not go deeper?"

Now the wood cutter — the "lumberjack," as he would be called — thinks of this as he is going the next day, and he does walk deeper. Yes, he walks deeper into the forest, and what does he find? There is a tall stand of trees — sandalwood trees — and he cuts them. He cuts all that he can cut. He cuts all that he can haul. And he moves them to town. He takes them to market and sells them.

Now fortune has looked on this man. He has got quite a gain for going deeper. And the next day, he goes out and he starts to go deeper. And coming again to the sandalwood trees, he says, "Did not the wise man say, `Go deeper'? He did not tell me to stop at the sandalwood trees. He told me to go deeper into the forest."

So the man who had cut wood walked deeper, and he walked deeper into the forest. And what did he find? He found an old, abandoned, deserted copper mine, and he filled his pockets. He stuffed his load. He loaded his wagon to the fullest — all that he

could carry, all that he could haul, all that he could move he took
to town. And he was rich, rich — yes, very rich — he had much
money now.

And the next morning he got up and he walked past the
sandalwood trees, and he walked past the copper mine, saying yet,
"Did not the wise man say there was more to be found? Is this not
what he meant when he said, `Go deeper'?"

And deeper yet he went — a day finding a silver mine, then a
gold mine, then mines of diamonds and gems, then ruby. And then
he was rich, wealthy indeed — beyond all means of richness.

And so it is with the quest, the quest for knowledge and truth
and light. And when you go forth — when you go forth, then you
shall find. And if you do not stop, becoming overwhelmed and
overjoyed, and full of pride at your first exploits, if you do not stop
when you attain a few trifling powers, if you do not stop at the
copper mines, then you will find the gold mines. And soon you
will find life, overflowing and abundant, through the truth of the
knowledge that shall be found. And so it is with the seeker of the
truth.

The second excerpt is a reading The Eternals gave me. I
wanted to gain insight into myself and my reasons for
choosing my life's work. I include it because the reading is
the first time The Eternals specifically discussed a past life.
Before this we had heard about balance and counterbalance
— reincarnation, in general — but not about a particular life.
The reading is especially good with the preamble warning
about taking past lives in their proper context.

READING FOR HENRY BOLDUC
September 20, 1983
Independence, Virginia

*In which endeavors or work would I be of most service to
mankind?*
Of where would I be of most service? First, when a person is
alive on this earth, if he lives a good life, he is of service. If you

do not do that which you can do, you are not of service. The answer, in effect, is that you must do all that is in your power to do good — do good to yourself and to your fellow man. When you are doing well to all those that are about you, you are of service. It is not a matter of occupation to be of service to your fellow man.

Though certainly you might say, "Oh, a doctor, when he heals the man who has been in an auto accident, is of more service than the man who sweeps the street." Yet if there is a man keeping the street clean, then one might not [have to] swerve to avoid a piece of litter and crash into the side of a building and have to be repaired by a doctor. Therefore, there is no great job nor little job. Therefore, there is no large event nor small event, but all are equal. And in all that you do, and in every endeavor that you take, if you do it to the best of your abilities and with the greatest love toward mankind that is possible, if you are consistently outreaching — then you have served your purpose and you have done well and moved forward, for this is the progress that one should make.

Could I please have some insight into my past progressions on this planet?

Have you a time period? Or a highlighted area, or specifics that you would rather explore?

[This question momentarily disoriented me, as I did not have a specific time in mind. So I stammered, and blurted out my question, as I knew for sure the Roman period was a troubled epoch of my soul's experience.]

I would be in questions as to the Roman times, as the Roman era.

For what value the past would be, or for what value the past *is*, first let us say this much: in progression, though you be progressing, you are not what you were, nor were you what you are. This is not said to be confusing, or to sound as if we cannot give you the answer you are seeking. This is said to make you aware of this much — you are under a state of constant change, and what I shall relate to you, or *we* shall relate to you, is of no effect in the present. What you have done in the past, even five minutes ago, is of no effect to your present situation inasmuch as two things. True, there is a balance and counterbalance effect, and you have set, by your past situations, your future situations and present situation. But the past *is* — therefore it cannot be corrected and it cannot be relived. And the past is a time that is not. You cannot go back to it and think for guidance, for you are not the same now as you were then. These are the two things that we must make clear.

Now we see you, and show you yourself, in a short tunic tied about the waist with a red strap. Yes, and the curly hair and the large, broken nose — half Jew and half Roman. You died there for your outlook — preacher of faith — not a kind death, either. And much of this has been [alleviated], and taken from you out of kindness, for it is not for you to remember how you were taken apart. But what is for you to remember is the goodness that you did. You counterbalanced, or you outweighed by your own upright piety.

Were you not the most righteous of the Pharisees? Were you not the most pious and bigoted? This was the reason that the effect was had. And when you became otherwise, were you not just as righteous? And were you not just as pious? And did you not propound yourself in just the same way? If it had not been for the Roman blood, you would have died much sooner. You had their rights. What would you like to know about this time?

Is there anything that was set in motion then that has an effect now? I understand that we are not now what we were. Are there any carryovers or any part of my inner psyche that is reliving this in any way?

Your trouble is this. Inasmuch as we have already said, piety and bigotry were so strong, the heart was cold and callous. Yes, there is an effect and there is a reason. But it is not what you would suspect. This is the reason for the gentleness. This is the reason for your love of humanity, and this is the reason for your kindness. See, this is the counterbalance, the soft, the easy. This is the reason for the liberal, the easiness. This is the reason, but it is also overplayed, for things have been let slide. Things have often gone too far, and you have let others go their way often too long. But yes, this was the balance and the counterbalance of which we spoke. And it is there, but at least the death shall be more pleasant. You don't need to worry about being scattered.

This is the balance that we speak of, and this is all that you need to know of that balance. We tell you not to worry about the trivial. For it matters not of the status of the past, but that which you do in the present. Look to do good and your balances shall be weighed and not found wanting.

[Life has its interesting moments! And this was one. I was preparing to end this session. In other parts of the session I had been given information about my health and guidance about my work. I was well-pleased, and the cassette was nearing its end. But the Vessel was making some unusual faces and was obviously still looking at or working with something. In the months to come I would become familiar with even the tiny signals a channeler sends out — but in this session I wondered what to do. Trusting my intuition, I turned the tape over and asked the following question. I am certainly glad I did; a whole series of powerful messages of ancient history came through and I was given great insight about the origins of my work and my reasons for doing it.]

What other information are you processing, or working on?
I'm working through the era and time of Egypt. I'm working through the most holy sanctuaries under the head of that which would look as a pharaoh, sitting upon the body of an animal, entering through the doors to the holiest of temples, into that known as the "shrine" — the most holy and the most sacred. I'm looking upon that which you were at that time. I am reliving that which you were at that time, feeling it, that I might tell you the balances of it. This is more of what you sought after, even though you could not tell me what you sought.

For in the time of the sun and the moon, and in the time when the stars ruled — when they sought the guidance and the truth of those stars and the planets—when that man was educated beyond that which we will ever have in our libraries, in the time when the mind was expanded greatly, you, Ram-shad-ic-mon-tale-hep-muth, were of the temple. And there you served, and you carried the lamps before all the altars. And you spoke and learned of the holy rites and of the words of the past, and the gates and doorways into the eternal present.

This is where you learned the secrets of the mind and that which opens the mind. If you knew now what you had [in] the past before you changed, you would not believe nor comprehend that which you knew. You would not be able to even understand what you had hidden in the recesses of your own mind. But you had power and it was of no use. And that is why, now — without power — you must be *of* use. This is what we make clear. For you have asked, "Why am I involved in this endeavor?" You had power and were of no use to men. Now you have not power, and shall be of use. Yes, that is how it shall be. For you wore the most holy robes and burnt the lamps before the altars. You stood at the feet of the most holy men in the land and you shared the bread and the table of the most powerful of the land — and yet did nothing. Now you have not power, nor the persuasion, and yet that work which you shall do shall be large.

Have we told you all that we should, or would you like to know more of this period?

I would like to know more, please.

Ask in specific, and we shall tell.

I don't know what to ask.

Well, let us start by telling you this much: there was the Pharaoh and he ruled the land, and he was considered the head deity. But he looked to his religious leaders of that time for guidance. That made you a very strong influence for him — third most powerful in the kingdom that was ruling the world. And you did nothing for anyone except yourself. You saw to it that the priests were well-fed. You saw to it that they had land and cattle. But you did not do anything for anyone who needed your help.

We speak to you of a time period when you were dressed in red and green stripes upon white, over the head. Being with a band around the forehead, you are dressed in the most holy and sacred robes of blue. And you were the most influential one who ever bore the lights before the altars of the — shall we say — holy shrines.

You lived in a time when man was advanced. There were

libraries. The language and communication was beyond what is even comprehensible now. The hieroglyphs that you have seen written were not the crude language that some assume, but conveyed many times more than you can ever think of conveying with abstract words. For they were even more abstract, and their formation was even more difficult.

You lived in a time when counting was far beyond what it is now, and the calculus and the mathematics of this present time do not even approach — for a man could work, mentally, what one could now do in the computer age upon the screens. They stored in their minds things that are now stored in storehouses — and because they looked deep into themselves, they had the power and the strength to do all that they desired to do.

There were people — those few chosen select who were initiated into the temple — who had the power over their bodies and minds and all that was around them. Even Moses himself was trained as you were, and look at the power that he had. See what we say? You were a great man and did nothing.

Shall we go further?

Please continue, yes.

Then we shall tell you also, you wore bands of gold about your arms and there was a wide band about your neck. And you wore a seal, so that when you spoke — then you sealed the document with that seal which was upon your ring and upon your cylinder — and no man could undo that which you did, save the Pharaoh ... and he would not have dared, for you were the holy oracle — the lamp bearer, the light bearer, the spokesman of those to whom they thought they had access.

You saw the armies destroy and oppress the foreign nations. You saw them take them apart and waste them totally, when you could have saved people. You saw them desecrate, when you could have had it kept and used.

You lived in a time when things were built in a way not now known. But also, much was done by forced labor and you did nothing to break this labor. You lived in a time when the great stones were moved on rollers by the backs of slaves. And men were pulled into service, willing or not willing.

You lived in a time when the females, the most glorious and wonderful, were considered to be almost of a god-gift. And the males, though they were the rulers and the kings and the powerful, looked to the fertile and knew that the females were the same holy stock.

You lived in a time when you were dressed, and dressed well. There was nothing to bind the movements; the belts tied about the waist were wide. The chest was bare when it was permitted. The formal dress draped loosely and comfortably, and your feet were well protected, though not inhibited for they were only covered from underneath.

We cannot even convey to you the knowledge that was kept. But you could look upon another man's mind, speech was not all that was known. We do not tell you that speech was any less, nor was there an extreme ability of telepathy — this is not what we're telling you — but people were highly observant. They could look upon each other and they knew the needs and desires. They knew the thoughts from that which had been thought — that which a small child knows, but is quickly unlearned, they had learned to keep.

This was the time. This was the time. We leave you now from this. We part, and put our blessings upon you. Rasha-he-rashn-ne har-han ish-ar-na ra.

[Years before, when Patricia and I were traveling around the country, we were sitting on the beach, watching the ocean. Suddenly I had a flash of a different time and place. Here, as nearly as I can recall the words, is what I told Patricia about this flash, which I hardly remembered until The Eternals related it to me in fuller context.

I was in Egypt on a hilltop or mountain top, but it was a hill that had a level enough spot on the top for a few chariots and an unpaved road going to the top. The land was virtually desert, with scrub and some mud walls, but basically flat. There were two opposing armies to the right and left and a major battle was about to begin. But even before the battle I knew for sure that "we" were to win it — and we did, by day's end. We had done something

215

previously to insure this success, as I had predicted we would.

I knew I was in the presence of the Pharaoh and a few other powerful rulers and advisors. We were safely away from any possible fighting and a special bodyguard was at the base of the mountain or a big hill. I deduced that I had a position of power or influence just to be there. There was a strong and cool wind. I did not feel like a warrior or military person in this scene. I was happy to be outdoors and to watch the action.

So let the last words be from The Eternals.]

You would not learn all that you need to know immediately. Some of this will come to you when the time is right. And when the time is right, all of it will come to you. Did Christ speak with stories to make things more clear? Did He tell stories because He wanted people to understand his every word? No. The stories were cryptic, and in them were hidden the messages that were of truth. He told the stories that everyone would be confounded and few find the truth.

Even so, this is given to you, and to those without, who would search and can find. Yet all is not given freely. Does this not imply work on your part? Work it implies. And work there must be. For nothing is given freely. For all must come with effort. And yet, everything is free if you will simply expend the effort to receive it. For it cannot be bought with money, only the effort of the spirit.

Chapter Thirteen

PRETTY FLOWER MAKES HER APPEARANCE

The secrets of the universe are not really secrets; they are simply unrecognized.
Pretty Flower

A new door was already opening in my life. I was still acting as guide for Daniel Clay as he gave the personal readings requested of us through Ageless Expressions. But Daniel was preparing to guide most of the sessions himself. He had long ago been told that the day would come when he would leave the "crutch" of hypnosis behind and move at will into the Hall of Records. Now, as this book is written, I no longer work regularly with Daniel, although we remain good friends; his wife reads him the questions people submit, and he continues to give personal readings through Ageless Expressions.

As Daniel made this transition, another friend was reentering my life. I had met Eileen Rota years before at The Adventure, my house in Massachusetts. In December of 1984 she was visiting us and asked for a reading from Daniel. She followed its suggestions, which had to do with certain health problems and received much benefit.

In January 1985, she visited us again. During this visit,

217

she asked me if I would be willing to repeat the Cayce and Daniel procedure with her. I was not looking for new projects; I was busy with two manuscripts and the antique business. But the question was in my mind: Could the experiment with Daniel be replicated or was it a rarity? I had no doubt that Daniel and I had duplicated the Cayce experiment. Now I wondered if it could be done regularly with others. Cayce often said that everyone can do this work, but saying and doing are very different. Here was an opportunity to test Cayce's statement.

Eileen and I had worked together off and on for 10 years. I had guided her through past-life regressions and had made self-hypnosis cassette tapes for her and her family. I felt comfortable with the groundwork we had done. Also, she had conducted many of her own soul development projects, such as automatic writing, and she occasionally offered psychic readings through palmistry. She was not a novice in soul exploration.

So I agreed to try the Cayce procedures with her and on January 20, 1985, we began. Eileen, Ann and I retired to my office and the comfort of dim lighting and a recliner chair. We surrounded Eileen, in this and every subsequent session, with protection — White Light and prayer — so we were confident that no unwanted energy would enter. After Eileen was in a trance and going to the Hall of Records, we all waited to hear what was going to be said. We waited. And we waited. Then, just as I was going to begin the return procedures, Eileen said a few words. Soon she started chanting; then more release through tears. I closed the session, guiding her back down through the levels and through the wake-up procedure. It was a beginning; not a session that offered any profound information, but neither did Daniel's early sessions. What was important was that Eileen felt an energy come through her and then leave again. *That* was important.

Several entities presented themselves at different times during the first two sessions. Finally, one, a male, described himself as the "bridge," and stated that he would not appear again. Then another entity, an old woman, came through. I asked, "Do you have a name that we could call you?" And we were told, "I would have to tell you the English, as I don't believe this vessel is prepared to make the throat sounds of my real name. My name is Pretty Flower."

Now that we were introduced to her, we wanted to know about her. We wanted to know exactly who or what we were communicating with. We asked her for information and what she told us is "The Story of the People." Before she tells it, however, I want to include an exchange that took place midway in a session. I mention it now because it forms one of the fundamental themes of Pretty Flower's message. I asked Pretty Flower,

Can you give us more insight about yourself and about The People?"

....Well, we would clarify one point and that would be that at these gatherings, the energies channeled have been called "Pretty Flower," and we have been most happy to be included in that vibration. And it would be a moot point that the energy of Pretty Flower is in existence only and solely at this gathering at this particular time. And of previous times, there have been a different vibration, and we could continue to call that vibration "Pretty Flower" if you wish, but it is simply a combination of vibrations which occur.

[In other words, Pretty Flower is saying that she is Pretty Flower, but she is also a *combination* of energies. She will return to expand our notion of her, which is often stated in terms of the universality of all energies, many times again. Then she delivers a gentle, conceptual prompting:]

And as the vibrations in our lifetimes, so to speak, as on this earthly plane, you could continue to view lives as different times. I will try to put the facts according to your beliefs ... [but] I think it would be a difficult situation, so we would have a little bit of changing of the beliefs, so to speak, merely as a way of accommodating the information which would proceed. Would that

219

be too complicated?

[I think the key words here are, "you could continue to view lives as different times." In other words, *we* may speak of individual times and energies, but, according to Pretty Flower, there are no different times; all times and all energies are one. She continues:]

....The conceptual misconception arises when we think of past lives and the present life as being distinct and separate spaces of time. Now as we continue, you will be most enlightened to learn that past lives are not past, they are happening as we are here. It is most easily described, I believe, by the terminology of "dimensions."

Now, in the dimensions that pulse, we have a way of relating to them, and it seems as though you have chosen to call them "past lives," which is perfectly all right, as long as the understanding is there that it is not something that is over with. It is almost like an overlay. It is almost like using tracing paper.

So, for the level of understanding in this early session, Pretty Flower was going to attempt to phrase her facts in our language although it might also require a change in our own belief system. So she asks, "Would that be too complicated?"

I answered: "So far it sounds okay. I hope I can accommodate my new beliefs to the relativity of lives and our understanding of the sequence of lives in the earth. But I am eager to change my beliefs as the awareness is made known. Is that clear?"

And she said, "I believe I am in understanding of what you are saying."

THE STORY OF THE PEOPLE

Can you tell us of the life that you lived? Can you give us some understanding of yourself, of the life of Pretty Flower? Is there anything you could speak to us about?

Oh, my, there certainly is much. As it is possibly quite

evident, that I had existed many years ... when the tribe of my father — I was born to a chief, he was young and fiery and my mother loved him very much, and we were holy people, as we all are. That is a lesson in itself. But we were holy people and we were living upon a hill ... very broad at the top and ... the grass was very green. And as I grow, I find that I have many questions; many, many questions. And I ask the medicine man of the questions and he says to me, "Because you are the chief's daughter, I will answer your questions." And I laugh at him. He thinks he is so big. And I see in his mind that he is a kind man and he is of great medicine and he is also fearful of his own death. So I visit him often and I see his mixtures and he begins to teach me. Now you must know that that is a taboo because I am the chief's daughter. However, I do continue, as it is my place to learn of potions, to learn the tying of the medicine bags, to learn the placements of bones, and to learn the magic of feathers. These all I do learn. Now, you must realize, that many are in awe of that — It takes some time and it is in secret.

Now, my mother, my dear mother, has a hint of what is transpiring and she asks me would I not learn to sew? And I say, "Mother, I do not care to learn to sew. I will spend my day with Nmlmchuque [phonetic], the medicine man." And she looks at me with fear in her eyes and knowing that it is as it is.

Now, our tribe is a healthy tribe. We have much to living; we are not warring people, we are peaceful. And we do much with the stars. And we do much in the cave of the crystal. The medicine man is not allowed in there, but I am because I am a woman. Only the women are allowed in the crystal cave. And we are there for ceremonies of replenishment.

And there is much happening in our tribe. We are communicating on many levels with many of the people who presented themselves in this very physical room in which we sit [referring to some of the people present during our session]. This is not the first time, certainly, that all of us here have experienced each other together — in one form or another. And that, in a sense, was the purpose of the room, the chamber from the crystal cave. There are many stories to be told, many.

Could you please tell us ... in what geographical location was

this place that you lived?
    In Arizona.
    What tribe were you?
    The tribe is the Zulie Tribe, and that's not the tribe that many are familiar with us. They have given us many names and some of the Indians themselves purport that we never existed. We were not among them in the forms that they were used to seeing.
    ....There are many ways, as you know, to travel, and so we traveled many times with the use of our spirits. And we took those opportunities to teach those of the tribes surrounding us. We communicated through their medicine men, when their medicine men were of the state that ... could receive our messages. Many times we spoke through the chiefs. There were many powwows and many magical moments, and it appeared that those tribes were able to hear our messages through magical moments, so we used those times to present guidance for their preservation.
    Yes, we were the people ... on our hill, and we were also not on our hill. We have been able to function in many dimensions. As you know, this is not the only dimension happening at this present time.
    And that was of teachings. Teaching ... you know, not by books. Teaching and allowing people to love and to be married to the earth and the mother pulse of the earth to exist in them too. There are many lessons to be had.
    And what year was this?
    As relating to your calendar, the moons are many — could I calculate that? — Seven hundred and two we have coming to me. I have no idea what that is, as I do not relate so to your years.
    You said some of us were together ... in the same tribe?
    Well, we have had many lives, all of us here. It comes down to concepts, you see. As we are here in this very space, we are also elsewhere — in many other spaces, and in some of those we are more together than in others. It is an example of drawing the mandala. As you have a central point and you draw the lines to form the circles upon circles, the lines cross, many times. And we are the very lines. Is that a story enough?
    I don't understand. Are we like the spokes of the wheel going out from a mandala?

Well, there are many "mandalas," you could call it. It happens once again from the center of you — your love center — and as there are waves coming from you, the waves happen to generate over to this wonderful young man, and his waves happen to generate over to yours, and again and again and again, and as those waves are touching each other, we are together. Now, that is admittedly a very simple answer, but, in a sense, that is how it works in the entire universe. It's something to meditate upon, if you desire. If you would meditate upon it and return again, I would be happy to talk with you about what has come to you in meditation....

Would you speak more of The People?

The story of The People has no beginning and has no end. We are simply The People. And as The People, we find that we are vibrating in a purpose. And the purpose requires that we assume a form, and we vibrate the messages of the Truths to those beings who are able to receive the messages of the Truths.... The Secrets of the Universe are not secret; they are simply unrecognized. That is why they are unknown. Nothing is keeping them secret from anyone else. When we open ourselves to the Secrets of the Universe and the Truths of the Universe, we simply open. The Truths are simple. They are not complicated at all.

We have spoken in the past, as we have existed [as] The People in many different forms ... in the form of a nation ... of a tribe, which would be the same. And in that tribe we have found that we are able to perceive the many vibrations of what is called "man" and the "earthly plane." We have ... worked through the many vibrational levels in learning the presentations of the Truths ... and found many manners of channeling these Truths.... We would find that this information has been presented to many medicine men. And we would be at this time telling that "medicine man" is a term that would be being used for all in that field.

There is never one purpose to one action. The dimensions of the vibrations are total and complete of the entire universe. And as we have spoken in the past, a tiny tear from the leaf of the tree, when it drops to the earth, there is a vibration and a marriage from that tiny drop. And the marriage is experienced throughout the entire universe.

We would find that the energies of Pretty Flower and the other energies of The People would have presented themselves at different times, so to speak ... and in different locations, so to speak, for different peoples, in order for the passing on of the stories of the Universe. We as The People presented ourself to those tribes entitled the "Mayans," ... to those people who are termed "Atlanteans," ... to those peoples who have been termed the "Mongols"; we have presented ourself [to all peoples, and we mention those names because they are most familiar with this gathering.

There are many purposes of the vibrations of The People. We would be standing with you if you would but ask. We are without number. We are unlimited. And we come bearing Light and Love. The People are present on the vibration of the earth in physical and in spirit form, that we may serve. And there would be a simple request from The People, and we would be present in assistance with anything! The purpose of The People is to uplift the vibration of the planet toward the Light of the Universe and to experience the One Vibration of the I AM.

DIFFERENCES IN THE CHANNELING

As each person is unique, so is each person's channeling. I had started Eileen's initial session by doing exactly what I had been doing with Daniel. But right from the beginning I realized that what was happening with Eileen and Pretty Flower was very different from what had occurred with Daniel and The Eternals.

Eileen worked at a very different pace from Daniel. I had to go much more slowly. She breathed very deeply and shook, but had little uncontrolled vibrating. There were tears, but tears of release and relief rather than of sadness. She recalls, "The first time Pretty Flower entered I experienced a shaking within my being. I sobbed aloud, and all the while inside I prayed that I would get out of the way and let the channeling happen."

The most obvious difference was between the entities coming through. The Eternals are forceful, energetic; even

224

macho. Pretty Flower is gentle, humorous, and nurturing. Her voice is always gentle and sweet and often the meter of her words is poetic. Participants in our groups tend to feel peaceful and at one with themselves in her presence, just as they are stimulated and challenged by The Eternals.

In subsequent sessions I learned or relearned the techniques and procedures that facilitated Eileen's channeling by listening to her expressions of voice, body, and vocabulary and by studying the tapes to become familiar with these expressions. I used her own words wherever possible to give suggestions. Some of the most helpful and necessary suggestions were about trust, healing energies, and gentle transference.

Pretty Flower, herself, had suggestions — often strong ones — about how I could modify my procedures. For instance, to enable The Eternals to enter through Daniel, I always took him through the Cayce levels (see Chapter 8). I continued doing so with Eileen until she suggested we leave the levels out and allow Pretty Flower to "simply enter." In other sessions she told me fine points of procedure and timing. For instance: "In the future we could spend a little more time with the opening, after the entry of the White Light." Another time she suggested changing a procedure "so that the waves of blue light may carry the vessel out in an easier manner."

She also wanted more time to meet the soul energy of Eileen during the process of entering and exiting. She said, "There is, upon entry and exiting, a spot or a vibration where we happen to meet. And it is most pleasurable. And we could, if we were not in a hurry, pause at that moment to embrace. And the trust is built even more, as the embrace increases the expansion of the chakras and allows a healing and alignment to take place." What was happening, Eileen told me, was that she and Pretty Flower met and danced together, faster and faster each time until it was as if they created a vortex. Then Pretty Flower came in as Eileen stepped aside. By following Pretty Flower's advice and giving more time during their meetings, I was able to help

225

Eileen let go more easily and allow the channeling to happen.

After about 12 sessions we had fine tuned our method for accessing Pretty Flower. These are the suggestions we used.

SUGGESTIONS FOR ACCESSING PRETTY FLOWER

... In due time, in your own time, a minute, an hour, a day, a week, a month, some time, your subconscious will reveal its gifts to you. In a dream or a daydream, when you are not especially thinking about it, new understanding, new levels of perception, new awareness of yourself and of others, new information will come that you may process and use to your highest potential — information to help you achieve the highest ideals you have set and you are actively working toward.

And you may, once again now, begin the process of opening yourself to the White Light. Surrounding yourself with healing love, surrounding yourself with trust, begin the process of opening the chakra centers. Begin first by opening the crown chakra and letting in the healing light. Fill the head chakra. Allow the light to move down the body, into the throat chakra, the heart center, the solar plexus area, the cells of Leydig, all the way to the reproductive system and continuing throughout the body internally.

Now surrounding the body externally with the White Light. The White Light fills all the empty places. With trust and belief in the power of love, you begin to feel the love energy flowing. Love fills your being as you begin to go to that inner spot of innocence and trust.

And soon the White Light becomes an intense blue-white light. And the waves of blue light carry you out in an easier manner and allow for the opening of the energy that comes through you.

You begin to see the old woman. You beckon to her; you welcome her. At first she is but a small speck and then she begins to grow larger and larger until the presence of the spirit of Pretty Flower is in front of you. You begin to step aside, motioning her to come ahead, giving full permission, with love and trust, to use the temple of your spirit. You are now totally immersed in the Light.

And now come the wonderful angels and spirit friends and you realize that you are not alone.

You continue to trust and allow the trust to build. And upon entering, there is a spot where the two of you meet and you pause at this moment to embrace. And the embrace increases the vibration of the trust and you hold hands and dance together joyfully, and this allows the proper alignment to take place. You have reached that spot of innocence, that holy place.

The transition is now completing. Love continues to pulsate and permeate in and around your being. You are in tune with the vibration of the universe. You are in tune with the healing process. Focus only on Pretty Flower at this time. And now the transition is complete.

You may use this time for chanting to totally align the energies. You are vibrating in truth. Or you may use this simply as a time of quiet, to align the soul energies.

And when you are ready, we may begin communicating. We welcome you to this gathering and this place.

Once Pretty Flower's presence came through, she moved the recliner into a more upright position. Usually she asked for permission to "make a sound," a chant. Her chants were remarkable. Each one was different. Some were soft and elongated, some high and piercing, some low and guttural. They were often accompanied by hand and body movements; Eileen says sometimes her whole body vibrated with the sound.

THE EXITING PROCESS

The exiting process is similar to the process of entering, but in reverse. Pretty Flower puts the reclining chair back into a more horizontal position and breathes a deep sigh. Through the many sessions she has explained that in exiting she goes to a different vibration — one other than Pretty

Flower; the exiting is easier in this manner.

At the end of many sessions there seemed not to be a full closing of the crown or topmost chakra. Eileen would be back, but not yet fully awakened. During one such session she gestured in a fretful way with her hand to her forehead. (This is another kind of situation in which my experience and attention to the vessel are important, for Eileen could not seem to speak to say if something was wrong.) Guessing the cause of the trouble, I went to her, placed my hands on her forehead and said the words, "Closing the crown chakra now — allowing the crown chakra to close...." This action seemed to be effective in the balancing of energy and in closing. (Later on, Pretty Flower, herself, directed that the crown chakra remain open, and today Eileen reports that it does, with a sensation she describes as a continuous, slight, mentholated tingling, a sensation that increases during meditation or during sessions, and decreases during other daily activities. She says, "The Blue Flame sits atop my head always.")

Other than that, there was almost never any physical contact with the vessel throughout the sessions. In fact, I am careful to monitor a group to see that no individual comes even in close proximity to the vessel to disrupt her energy or aura field.

Here is the exiting process that I used with Pretty Flower and Eileen.

Thank you for this sharing, communion, and marriage of the gathering.

Please begin the process for this gathering to be completed — preparing for the proper entity to return to her physical body in her temple. Surrounded with trust, with the remembrance of surrender, allow this celebration to be completed. We thank you for this time of sharing, this time of learning and growing and fun together. Allow the old woman to become smaller and smaller. Allow the souls on all levels to bid farewell. And as you part, there is a moment of embrace. With trust and with love, the transformation becomes complete.

Coming back — through the light, bidding farewell to the angels and spirit friends in the fullness of joy, with permission, with trust, and with full determination. Vibrating in strength and in harmony, slowly begin the process of closing the chakra centers. Beginning at the reproductive center, gently closing of this center and the cells of Leydig. Closing of the solar plexus; once again the closing of the heart chakra, the throat chakra, and leaving the head chakra, the crown chakra open. Returning to normalization, the chakra centers of the being.

A gentle closing, and allowing the soul entity of Eileen to return into her proper temple, her proper vessel. Realigning the soul body with the physical body, and the mental body. And each time we do this work, there is a healing. And each time, the going out and the coming back in, the opening and the closing, become easier and easier.

You are fully oriented into the present. Continue the alignment process. This is _____ [date], in _____ [city or town], _____ [state]. Are you ready now for the counting up exercise? [Vessel raises a finger to signify agreement.]

We will proceed very slowly and carefully. I will count from one to ten. At the count of ten, you can open your eyes, be wide awake, feeling fine. Feeling better than before. I will count now. One, coming back. Two, coming up very slowly. Three, coming out. Four, feel total normalization at every level of your being. Five, feel the life energies returning. Six, feel the circulation returning throughout the being. Seven, coming up to your full potential. Eight, with total equilibrium and lightness. Nine, revitalizing; and ten, energized and wide awake. Just rest for a few minutes.

Chapter Fourteen

A TYPICAL GATHERING

The love that passes between each other is the greatest
work on the vibration of the earth.
Pretty Flower

At the beginning of a few sessions Pretty Flower said that there were other beings or soul energies besides herself who wished to speak through the vessel. "We are crowded in here," she complained. I responded, "Although there are many energies and entities who have much valid information to be spoken and to be shared ... only one can speak at a time. Therefore it is our choice and our desire that only the spirit of Pretty Flower speak to us now." Eileen told me that at this suggestion a clearing took place. "I felt that I would explode," she said. "But when you said those words, the others left; the exiting was gentle, but swift and clean."

Working with Pretty Flower, as working with The Eternals, required a new vocabulary to understand the messages fully. Each session was referred to as a "gathering." A group meditation or guided meditation was a "communion" or a "marriage." Pretty Flower usually asked each person, "How are you vibrating?" A translation could be "How are you feeling?" or "How are you?" But a very different use of the word "vibration" usually referred to a specific lifetime — that is, "in this vibration" meant "in this lifetime." The process of going to or, more correctly, accessing Pretty Flower was called the "ceremony," although the word was used in other ways, too.

Although each was different, we soon came to recognize and look forward to typical parts of a Gathering. There were six: introductions, stories, "traditions and ceremonies," meditations, personal messages, and leavetakings. One flowed seamlessly into another. To give you the flavor of a Gathering, this chapter is, itself, a sampling.

INTRODUCTIONS

Gatherings with Pretty Flower started with introductions. People usually introduced themselves and said a greeting; Pretty Flower recognized newcomers and asked them about themselves.

These introductions usually initiated a period of naming. Pretty Flower often gave participants new names, asking for permission first. We came to realize that these new names were often names the person had had in a previous life or lives. She usually named the women, often giving them nature names, such as "Sister of the Howling Wolves," or names pertaining to a beautiful part of the universe, such as "Shining Star." Often she told a story or made a comment about the name.

If the participant was a man, Pretty Flower acknowledged the present name or gave a different name in English. In rare instances, she gave a man or a boy a nature name. In general, however, she did not consider it proper to name men, herself. With warriors — that is, men — naming was a private, almost secret matter. It seemed only a warrior could bestow the name of the warrior, and the giving of the name was a teaching of truths connected with that name. Nor could Pretty Flower teach what she had not experienced. So in our sessions, when she wished to give a man a name, she often made way for a warrior, who came through to bestow the name.

In the introductions, Pretty Flower had comments and

insights not only for individuals within the Gathering but had messages for the Gathering itself. Following these she would chant — and as I have said, these chants were wondrous in their variety and expressiveness.

THE LITTLE STORIES

After the introductions and chants, Pretty Flower usually told what she called a "little story." Some are short, some are quite detailed. I think storytelling is valuable, as each person perceives the nuggets of truth at his or her own level of comprehension.

Pretty Flower encouraged us to share her stories with everyone, young and old alike. Here she introduces the stories, telling us what we need to know about them and cautioning us not to compare one's level of understanding with another's.

There are many beings in many forms throughout the universe telling stories to the people. And there are many who hear, and many who seem as though they do not hear — and have heard. There would be no judgment in any dimension as to those hearing the stories and how they understood them. There would be no comparisons.

There would be simply the channeling of the stories to the people... telling the stories to the people, the children. We would be finding that innocence within self, and in finding the innocence within self, we would find the greatest strength. And from that innocence, we could read the stories for the people, and then we would be vibrating the story. Strength comes from the innocence within — not in the fists without. There is no need to fight for anything, as the universe is ours because we ARE the universe.

....There are many, many ways of sharing of the stories with the people. The most important factor is to know that we are all the same — those telling the words, and those hearing the words.... We are the story.... Those writing the music and those hearing the music. We are all the same. We ARE the music.... We are the sound of the Wind Spirit through the trees.... We are the sun.

And know that the manifestations and the character of those

beings around are the manifestations of ourselves. And as we look around lives, we find that we see a mirror in every face we look. And there would be total love, unconditional love in the innocence ... in trust.... Every possible thing that has ever been conceived, directed, talked about, thought about, not thought about — is within. Everything! Everything — is the universe. And I AM the universe!

Pretty Flower's little stories seem simple, but they pack a powerful wallop of truth. She once said, "Sometimes even the most simple statement must be surrounded by the flowers of gold so that the eye of man might be attracted to the simple statement."

THE STORY OF THE CAMPFIRE

Well, I believe we could begin. We might begin with a little story. A story that's concerning the campfire itself.

The campfire has a center of hot coals,
Hot coals there is in the center.
And around the hot coals
Are the kindle that is not quite burned.
And around the kindle that is not quite burning
Are the rocks, and they are hot.
And then around the rocks
Is the hearth, is the earth.
It is quite like our hearts, you see.
In the center is fire,
And then as we come outward
Things get a little cooler.
We have a choice, you see.
We can allow that heat to become greater
Without a fear
Of burning ourselves.
Without the fear
Our flames become greater,
As our love becomes greater,

And it expands and expands.
So that our entire beings
Are filled
With hot flames,
The power of love.

Now we have a conceptual misconception here. It seems that there is a belief that love is soft, and it is. However, the source of love is that fire within us — the great power of the White Light. And we can trust, and we can let that power grow and envelop us and all around us. Thus we create the world in which we live.

It all seems like a simple story and those who hear it might say, "That's a cute little story." However, what might also happen is, those hearing the story might decide to practice the principles of the story.

There is much to love in this room, and an expansive meditation would certainly benefit many, and the flowing would be even greater. It is a pleasure to be among you.

TRANSPLANTING THE TREE

Sometimes, when working with an individual in the gathering, Pretty Flower would weave a story about that person. The following story evolved in such a manner. A woman was struggling with the realization that she was going to have to leave a man. She asked what she should do.

It is a time of transition, is it not? It is very difficult. As we go through changes and transitions, it is like a tree being replanted. First there is the pushing away of the topsoil. And then there is the pushing away of the middle soil. And then we get to the root of the matter.

And sometimes the roots surprise us that they are running so deep and long, and we find that in some cases, we can dig away the roots and we can pull in those pieces to be with us. And there are other times we find that we may have to clip the root at the furthest point out, so that we may pull the tree.

And we can always gather part of the Mother Earth and surround those changes with the Mother Earth vibration. We ask for an envelopment around that part of the tree and around those roots, and we have an assistance... those beings lift us, as trees, out of that spot.

Have you ever seen a tree walk to a new spot? No. There is total trust. It is beyond us, my dear. We simply let go and allow the energies to pull us along, and lo and behold, here we are as another tree in another place, and what has happened? Loving hands have prepared a place for us. A special place, otherwise the special hands and the loving hands would not have removed us with such care.

And so the new place is prepared, and the earth has been pushed aside, on many levels. And there is space for the very long roots to find a home. We find that we, as the tree, are placed in the new space with part of our old space. Remember the Mother Earth has enveloped us. And so we are placed in a new spot with part of our old blessings comforting us so that we may have some associations with which to feel our vibration. We are beings which require a vibrational acceptance of the spot in which we are.

So, as we, as trees, feel the love and the contentment, and the joy with which the new place has been prepared, we slowly learn that we can trust and we can let go from holding our roots so tight to us, from fears. And we find that we could possibly release, and we could allow our roots to experience a little of the new soil, a little of the new vibration.

Remember, roots do not sprout in seconds; it takes a little time. And remember that those loving hands who prepared the space, those friends, also prepare those tools that help us to stand so that when the Wind Spirit comes along, sometimes without realizing his own strength, that we have helping hands to keep our position in the new space. We can rely on those tools; we can rely on those friends; we can rely on those beings so that our trust grows. It is not something that immediately happens, and that is probably very good for us.

In the new space, there is wonderful air. There is wonderful food for the pores of our bodies. There is wonderful sights to see. And the Wind Spirit blows through our hair, freeing us from bondage, and allowing our wings to unfold. And lo and behold, a new freedom and a new vibration, greater and more filled with joy and light than we have ever experienced and that we could ever conceive to experience, unfolds. And the tears and the mourning that you are feeling is wonderful. And I am most grateful that you are sharing yourself with us. You are very generous to be here. It is most wonderful that you are here. And I weep for joy that you are here, my dear.

[She chants.]

We will wash away our beings with our tears, my dear. [She weeps.] And we will share in our mourning, for the time of growing, and there could be a realization that in growing, we are not becoming stuffy adults, my dear. In growing we are allowing ourselves to be the children that we are. We are allowing ourselves to let go of the rules and regulations which tell us that we must be this way or we must be that way. We let go of those rules and regulations.

[She chants.]

CEREMONIES AND TRADITIONS

Sometimes, instead of or in addition to a story, Pretty Flower presented material we called "ceremonies" or "traditions." These involved a change, during the session, to a different entity, often a warrior. The warrior spoke of his own ceremony or tradition, which involved warriors. (Remember, Pretty Flower spoke only of ceremonies and traditions that were her experiences and truths.) The warrior's voice was deeper than Pretty Flower's. He sat erect on the chair (she had a tendency to curl into the chair), commanding great energy and force.

At one Gathering, a man asked for the teaching of a ceremony. A warrior "appeared" in full strength of his being and began this great teaching.

THE DANCE OF THE BEAR

One moment, there would be a change of energies. One moment. We would begin at the beginning, which would be the Dancing Bear.

There would be a purpose to the Dancing Bear, which would be at the discretion of that being who would be surrendering to the Dance of the Bear. The purposes are many. And at the base of all the purposes the Fathers of the People would have the recognition that there is deep within their breasts a desire to be one with the universe. And so, the Dance of the Bear — whether the purpose be to gain possessions, to gain love, to gain that being to be at your side forever, whether it be for riches — the Dance of the Bear teaches us to relinquish those desires and recognize that in our breasts we have the desire to be one in the universe. Those who are being taught the Dance of the Bear know these facts and they also know that whatever their wishes are, will be fulfilled in the dance.

And each comes with a tiny secret in his being as to what that great wish would be. And even though he knows that those wishes will be dispersed, and the one wish in the breast to be one with the universe will remain, he still carries the wish in the hopes that perhaps he might be able to carry that wish through the dance to the end — so that the wish might be granted.

And some of the wishes are not what we would call "poison wishes," some of the wishes are for the health of the grandmother. There are wishes that we would think of in that term so there would not be a judgment of any man or being upon any wish that he thinks that his neighbor might have or upon any wish that he might have, in the back of this being, where secrets are being kept.

And so we prepare for the Dance of the Bear.... And as those wishes come forward, we allow them to be in our presence. And we weed our gardens, and we come to those wishes which we will not allow ourselves to pull from the garden. They will not budge! Those wishes are the truth. Those wishes are the ones we cannot relinquish; try as we may, they remain with us. And we would be truthful beings, and we would know that there would be a wish for something that our being would judge as wrong and we still have that wish, even though we say, "I do not wish that." It is still there in the garden and will not be budged. And so, we come, after a period of being with ourselves, to a time when we recognize the truth about ourselves and we recognize most of the wishes that we cannot simply abandon.... And those Great Fathers and those

Teachers ... would advise those who are preparing their first time for the Dance of the Bear, that if there are many wishes, there are many purifications through the Dance of the Bear.... The young warriors ... know the intensity of their Dance of the Bear.

And, when the time and the courage seem to come together, there would be a cleansing of the being within and without.

[The warrior then goes on to describe the purification mixtures from the earth which were to be rubbed onto the skin of the young warrior, and the choosing and consuming of the root which would "pull the poisons" from his body and inflict great pain. After this internal cleansing would come the external cleansing of the body with water and sand.]

And then the Fathers of the tribe would be standing in a circle near that spot and they would open their circle for the warrior. And he would come forward. And there would be on his body placed a skin of the Bear. And the Fathers of the Tribe would be in Holy Ground, and the warrior would be in the skin of the Bear, and the Dance of the Bear would begin the moment the skin of the Bear touched the skin of the warrior. And the energies of the skin of the Bear would be in the skin of the warrior. And the warrior, being the first time, would feel the electricity of the movement. And he would be aware that he is in the energy of the Great Bear.

And his dance would begin.... As the paws and great claws of the Bear touch the ground — and the arm of the warrior is the arm of the Bear — the warrior [begins] to dance around around around.... And in the movement of the Bear, the wishes of the warrior come forward to his being. And shake his head though he may, those wishes will not go away. He feels those wishes pounding in his very being.... And he knows that his body is being pulled this way and that way and there are movements he knows not. There are sounds that come from his being he knows not.... And the Bear dances and dances and dances.

And the Bear takes the claws of his being and he pulls at the flesh that he might remove those wishes. The warrior knows in his being that the Bear, the Holy Bear, is purging his being of those wishes so that something else might be there.... And that process continues for as long as it may take, for the wishes of the man are great.

And there is a moment when the being of the warrior knows that he cannot hold on to those wishes one moment longer. And he throws them away. They are not there! And his being is purged of the wishes of man. And in his breast, a great fire builds and builds and builds. And he feels that the energies of his being, of the warrior, are building and he knows that his spirit is one with the universe. And in that taste of that vibration he knows that nothing will replace that vibration. To be in the presence of the Universal Energies of the Fathers — nothing will take that place.

And when that realization is here [marking the drawing of the circle, star, and pyramid on the forehead], the energies of the Bear have completed their work and the skin of the Bear simply falls to the earth, and the young warrior is carried by the Fathers to the Holy Grounds. (We would not speak of the Holy Grounds at this time. There is much healing to be done in the body of the warrior as there are many spaces on his body where the gouges of the claws have removed his flesh and his wishes.) And in the Holy Grounds, there is a revitalization of the body of the warrior.

[She chants.]

THE QUESTIONS

The remainder of most sessions was filled with the many and varied questions the participants had about life. Participants asked for guidance on physical, emotional or spiritual matters; queried her about herself; raised questions about a past life or lives; and asked for comment or guidance on questions of public interest. Sometimes she answered matter of factly; many times she answered in parable or story form; but she always had a message or reading for each questioner. Throughout, she frequently repeated the idea that past, present, and future are meaningless terms: all lives are one. She also reflected (here and in other readings) The Eternal's view that lives balance one another.

At times she spoke of the "Great Cristos," but she usually kept her teachings open to encompass all faiths and denominations. To me, this has been wonderful, because there are people who are not open to the "religious trappings" of other channelers. Her source surely is of the same light and wisdom, but she presents it more universally. People of other religions have expressed appreciation of this fact. Many recognize Jesus and His message, but they may have been born to another faith and wish to continue the religion of their parents and ancestors. Surely one should not have to change religions in order to accept ancient truths. By not limiting her teaching, Pretty Flower in fact opens the doors of spirit to many more seeking persons.

It seems that Pretty Flower's work during the Gatherings was to free people from the burdens they had chosen to carry upon their backs. Sometimes during the questions and answers she would help someone to see what their *real* question was so that she could work with belief patterns. She would get to the basic question and then, when the truth had been exposed, would call it all "fantasy." Then she would talk about reality and about us as creators of our own realities.

At other times she would lean forward in the recliner and look directly (even though the vessel's eyes were closed) at someone and smile her smile of love. Then she would say, "I could answer the questions you have asked, but what is that worry that you are carrying deep within your gut? Let's talk about that."

The following exchange summarizes much of Pretty Flower's philosophy.

A 15-year-old boy says,
I am asking for guidance. I want to know if I should ... try to figure out things or just to let things go.

When you conceive, a seed is planted in your being. And the seed grows, and grows, and opens. And the thoughts come forward as a great tree. And you can be in the center of the tree or you can pluck a fruit, eat it, and try to figure out what the center of the tree is by the fruit. Or you can *be* the tree.

In the next reading, Pretty Flower talks to the parents of a boy who, when he was about two, was almost electrocuted in an accident involving Christmas tree lights. Though paralyzed, he had regained limited movement and speech through intensive physical therapy. When Pretty Flower gave this reading for his parents, he was about five.

READING FOR DANNY'S PARENTS

....We would find that the wonderful vibration of the boy, Danny, would be trying to make a decision whether to remain on the vibration of the planet Earth or not. And we find that the challenges that he has set upon his soul for the vibration of this time have been many.... And we would find that there would be much love surrounding that being. And that he would be working within his being at the lessons of expressing love. And he would but respond to the sounds of love.... He would but respond to the elimination of the rules and regulations for a short period only to be able to be — just to be. And he could but be in the outdoors — just to be.

And there would not be a concern for what he can do or what he cannot do — how he could perform in one instant what would be almost expected of his brother; in another form, what might be expected of himself. For he is but vacillating between beliefs that are present around him.

And if he could be allowed to vibrate as himself. And would be that the mother would be with him and that they could be atop the mountain —and that they could make sounds together with the freedom within. And that the sounds would be whatever would be coming forward. And that the man, the man of sound within his life, the man who loves him with tenderness, the man who caresses his being, would be the greatest channel of love for the child.

And there would be, if possible, the environment of the country. Of the mountains, of the waterfalls, of the furry animals — so that the spirit friends, and the angels, and all those beings could vibrate with him.

We would find that in previous times, the boy existed as man in the civilization of Rome and that there was much time on the chariots. And we would find that in another time, in the time of

Atlantis, there would be a type of transportation also that he would be involved with. There would be many other times when there would be a type of transportation. Gliding above the earth and rolling upon the earth, with which he would be involved.

And we would find that there would be many lives and many times where there would be great companions, and they would be amongst the greatest leaders of the earth. And that, in one form or another, that he would be a companion and trusted friend of many. That he would be at times, the secret companion of many. That there have been in many times and in many parts of the earth, many secrets that he has held within his being. That he has functioned in the vibration of truth, that he has functioned in the vibration of honor. That he has functioned in the vibration of light.

Know that the choices are made before we even enter the vibration. And then there is an awareness and an acceptance of those choices. And we could be speaking to that wonderful vibration of the young boy, and we could be saying, "This is what you have chosen, my dear. And you are doing great work. And the vibration of the universe is within you. And all those who come in contact with you are blessed for simply being in your presence. And that we love you even beyond ourselves. And that we receive the love, ... the truths, ... the honor, ... and ... the light that you are radiating to us. For you are as you are, a light upon the earthly vibration. And many purposes are being fulfilled, even as we speak."

There could be a time when there would be a traveling to the Western states and there the young boy would experience a vibration of memory from a previous time. And there could be a vibration together as family. And awarenesses would be opened....

And to those people living in the vibration to know that they have the blessings of the universe. And that they are fulfilling many balances in caring for the young boy.

I would be making a sound for the wonderful young boy. [Chants.]

I would say again and again of the wonderful boy, Do not communicate with him as if he does not understand you. He understands more than you know. His understandings are greater than your knowledge. He is a gift and we are aware that you are in that belief yourselves, but that you would be hearing it from the vibrations of those beings who would be surrounding the blessings of the home for the care and protection. Know that the burdens of life are lifted from the very beings. And that you may, if you choose, walk in the light of the universe and vibrate as one.

One moment, please. [She chants.]

The boy is the bird, and the mother would know the meaning.

GODS PURPOSE FOR US

What is my purpose and how can I assist in it?

Well, everything usually proceeds as it should. However, sometimes we choose to sit down and sometimes we choose to walk along, and sometimes we choose to get in our canoes and let the river carry us along.

Now, there is much happening in your life and it seems to me that you have collected (not to take this in a negative sense but simply as a statement) — you have collected some baggage. Now, if you would choose to travel down the river with this baggage, know that it is quite a job to fit it into the canoe. So it may require a slow trudging along the river bank. It is simply a choice, you see, as you well know, that one could allow the baggage to travel along in its own canoe.

Does this baggage have a name?

It is called "man." It is called "any being or any creature or anything about you that is more important to you than spirit and your uniting with spirit."

Then there is a choice that that remain the supreme priority and everything else then proceeds as it should. When we sit down to figure out how we can fit all the baggage in one canoe, we forget to leave room for ourselves and we end up trudging along the riverbank while the baggage floats on the river.

What does God want me to do? What do I need to know about this present lifetime?

My dear! Know that we all, every being on the vibration of the planet Earth, in spirit form and in physical form, know everything there is to know, have the complete knowledge of the entire vibration of the universe because we are the I AM. The only difference would be, my dear, that some are a little more awake than the others to the fact that we are the I AM. And when you ask, my dear, what God would want for you, you are asking yourself what you would want for yourself. As we are the I Am.

Let go of the piddly stuff that you surround yourself with.... You believe that there are a certain few who are so enlightened that they may leave while the others burn to a crisp! It is time to abandon those chains. There is no need to be bound into the position you place yourself of a lesser being even though your star is shining bright.... Within every being is the Light of the Universe. And we all are the same. There is none better and none lower or higher or any of that stuff that we seem to be reading about in the pages of some of the propaganda.... We are human beings on the vibration of the Earth and our purpose is to vibrate. And our purpose ... would be that the food for the being comes in spirit form, and that we are the spirit form.

....All those beliefs ... and fears are not even large enough to cause your notice if they were under the tiny fingernail of your baby finger. They are nothing! And you are everything!

CHANNELING

I would like to try channeling to reach teachers and guides who could be of help in my life. Is this a path I should try?

You could use this as a tool. You need to realize that you *are* a channel, as you speak. As you speak with all those you come in contact [with], all those people in this community — you *are* a channel. As your very presence is there, blessings are bestowed upon them.

If you desire to take a more active part, and be as you suggested, then I suggest the following:

One, daily meditation. Two, a realization that whether one channels or not, one is a holy woman. That is a big step, my dear. Channeling will not make you a holy woman. You *are* one. If you choose to offer yourself in service for channeling, try and see if it fits. It's like that pair of pants. See if it fits. Try it on for size knowing that it will not make you anything you are not already.

DAILY LIFE

As the participant, a college student, asked the following question, I answered to myself, "Well, just do less." But Pretty Flower had a different, more holistic view.

I'm trying to balance full-time work with full-time school, and it's putting a tremendous strain on me, and I must reconcile it. And I don't know how to balance it and not run myself into the ground, and I'm looking for an answer.

We would be finding that in the dimension of the daily living, that there would be the consideration for the mental, so to speak, and there would be the consideration that would be the studies, and there would be the consideration for the physical. There would be a slight emptiness for the consideration of the spirit.

And when you speak of balance, you have absolutely said the correct word. For balance is what is being sought. And that we could be functioning within the mental dimension, and we could be functioning within the physical dimension, but we do not function in any without spirit.

For that is the essence of our being, the food and the strength, the nourishment that comes from spirit. For as we are vibrating within the day, we find that on personal strength that we become weary. That we become as you have stated: "How can I be studying when I'm so tired? How can I be working when I should be studying?" Back and forth, back and forth — when there could be a recognition of the center. Even in the busy schedule ... there could be a moment where we could reconnect ourselves, so to speak. Do you hear the words? — Reconnect ourselves, as we have separated ourselves to the mental and the physical and we are actually one — with spirit. So that we would find that in the day ... there would be a connection with spirit. And that there would be a connection with the I AM. And that could happen in one moment. That could happen in what you would term "five minutes," one long meditation, or just as we are walking up the steps, we could be saying, "I open myself to the awareness I AM." And the strength pours forward, for from the center comes everything.

We would be in awareness that we create our own reality. So

that if we would have the belief upon rising from a rest that we have received the proper amount of rest and nourishment in physical, mental, and spirit form, [then] we could have that belief carry us through the day. However, if we awaken and we wonder if we have enough rest, and we look at the clock and say, "Oh, no. That was only four hours," ... [then] there is a tiredness, and there is a worry.

And we would in the remembrance [know] that the strength comes from within. We are the strength. We don't go searching somewhere for it.... And the simple connection with that realization will allow the flowing to happen and that you would be filling your being — filled to the brim — and overflowing with the excess that would be pouring about you in the blessings. For not only is it untrue that we do not have enough, the truth is that there is great bounty and abundance — so much so that it overflows our very being and spills out as blessings upon the planet. And we but simply open ourselves to the awareness that that is the balance we are seeking. And that at any time, if you would be opening yourself, that we would be beside you. And would be knowing within your very being that we do not exist alone. For we are everything. We are everything. We *cannot* be alone.

VIOLENCE IN THE WORLD

I am asking about the way the world is going and about the violence. I wonder how that is going to be in the future. Is it going to resolve? Will we blow ourselves up? Are we going to see the other side of it without mangling ourselves?

....Would you be remembering (as we have spoken together in the past), that the future is the present, and that we would be creating from within what we would term "reality," when it, in fact, is fantasy. And that we would be in the cycles ... and circles together, (balance and counterbalance) and ... when we realize that we are in the circle, that we have the opportunity to be stepping out of the circle ... and to be coming awake, and to be aware that we are creating. And those that travel in the circles and the cycles are completing the cycles over and over and over again and again. And the balance and counterbalance continues and continues.

And the violence balances the peace, balances the violence, balances the peace. And that we have the awareness that that is what is occurring in the fantasy called "reality" on the planet called "Earth." And that when we are concerned of the violence, that is a genuine concern, for there is a remembrance of being in the cycles. And the remembrance is part of the concern.

There could be statements of who would win what battle. There could be statements of government as have been made by many other peoples. There could be statements of the economy, so to speak. We are feeling that that information brings us to the very edge of continuing in the circles and the cycles. And that when we are angry because someone else is fighting, guess what we are doing? We are dipping our finger back in the cycle. And we are forgetting who we are and what we are.

....We do not even need to be in the cycle of concernment about the balance upon the planet Earth, for we have been fed this information by the people who have been involved with the violence and the balance and counterbalance of the violence. And they report to us about the violence! And we have been trained to pay attention to it. ....[But] it would not be our purpose at this particular time, to be placing ourselves within violence.

....For when we read the newspapers and when we read the reports of the violence happening in the fantasies of the warmongers, when we read those reports, we follow like mice, we follow like robots, for the words entice us. They are masters of control! They are masters of control! And we would but remember that we have a choice — the blessing of the great universe in the human being — that when we are awake, we recognize that we have a choice. And that we can, once again, drop it like a hot potato. And we can enter our beings, once again, and settle in, so to speak. And vibrate within the one.... for becoming one and being one, and coming to full center and vibrating so that we are the vibration is fulfilling the purpose.... And then we are as we are to be.

When we become aware of the vibrations within our being, and we are getting to know self, so to speak, we could be connecting with other parts of our being — not only the violence. For when we activate the magnets of our being, we attract. We

247

simply open to that information. We would know that everything about us would be but fantasy. We live within the dimensions of the planet Earth and we are multiple beings. And that we are spirit! That which we pay the most attention to would be the smallest part of our being. That which we care the most for, sometimes, would be but the vessel. And that the vibration within and the spirit within is that which we are. The body, as we are well aware, is but passing. For the spirit is and was, and always will be.

If violence is one edge of the pendulum, and peace is the other, is the middle neither?

The middle is everything. In the middle is everything. In the middle is the I AM. Everything.

So we should seek neither the violence nor the peace?

We do not need to seek. We simply open. Everything is within. Everything. We have a great struggle to break from the belief pattern that we are seeking. For in that belief there is a type of action that happens away from self.

We would but recognize that we *are* the journey within. We are the very journey. And that we are the creators. And that is, what is about us is our creation. And that we could begin by taking full responsibility for self. That no one "makes me mad." No one "makes me sad." "He gets me angry." We all know those feelings and those statements. "You make me cry." "I weep for you." We would find that we could accept the responsibility, each and every one of us, for self. And we could accept the responsibility for being within the spirit. And we could let go of the attachments to the tiny cycles and circles, and bigger cycles and circles — that we could vibrate as one. For it is the purpose that we vibrate as one.

When we are in the purpose of uplifting the consciousness of the planet Earth, would one be thinking that we would carry it upon our being as Atlas? No. We would but vibrate within and we would recognize that we are the I AM.... It is not a struggle to learn about it. It is not a matter of will. It is not a matter of study. It is simply asking, simply making the statement, "I open myself that I might recognize deep within my very being that I AM." When we practice that, then there are many, many awarenesses coming forward, for the belief patterns flood in. And we could but watch them flood in and not attach to them, but recognize that they are but belief patterns. And know that, even as we *are* this very second, that we are perfect, that we are exactly as we would be at this very vibration. There is [now] full acceptance of self, an opening that "I'm okay." "I am as I am right at this moment. This is me. And deep within my very being I have opened to the recognition that I AM."

I am fearful for the violence in the world. And for the violence in myself.

This is a great realization. Great progress has been made. It is a great realization when we see and recognize the responsbility for creating our own realities ... that we all are creating our realities. And that, in the reality as we experience it, there happens to be news coming of the violence that is happening elsewhere.

It is to recognize that there is a balance. And sometimes the purpose of the news of the violence happening elsewhere is to allow us to purge ourselves of the violence that is happening within so that we might learn forgiveness of our very selves, so that we might learn understanding of our very selves; and in understanding, then we do not require that we be understood. We simply understand.

And in the world of violence and in the world of peace is the central point. And we can choose to experience either or we can recognize that in the center we are married and we are in the pulsebeat of the universe.... We are simply responsible for opening ourselves to be channels of love.

....And when I say "we" I say that there is not one person in this room who this does not apply to. We can use the news of the world to stop the flow of love from being channeled. We can use any reason because we are human beings, and we are learning how to open and channel love. So, when we are walking down the street, if we hear people arguing on the same sidewalk, it is quite a challenge to continue to channel love. And that is the challenge that we have all accepted in one form or another, as we are on this path and we are the path.

It is not an easy task to let go of the concerns for the violence that is happening in the world. The easier way to let go is to recognize that when we are concerned and overwhelmed with the violence of the earth, we are, in fact, in it. And it is us. And we are it. And we learn to be in touch with the violence within ourselves. So we can choose which vibration we wish to exist in, as we are not responsible for the balance and counterbalance that happens in each and every being's life. We are simply responsible for opening ourselves so that love can flow, and all the anger and stomping of feet, of the awareness of what is happening on the sidewalk or in the other part of the worldly vibration is our humanness — that [is what] stops us from being channels of love.

We can be here and be channels for the love of the universe or we can be on the other side of the earth, having our face blown from our heads, or we could be exploding something within the body of another person.... I do believe that you deserve to be here. And that you can forgive yourself for being here and not there.

LOVE AND RELATIONSHIPS

You said earlier to open oneself to love. And I find if one does that, that one can become vulnerable and be hurt. It is something that concerns me.

Well, what you have described is certainly what happens when love is flowing.

Now the reason that the hurt happens is because of some human traits that we are learning to change. One is that when we love we love with expectations.... And when we care, we want the best. And when we want the best — you see how it goes? On and on it goes. Now, as we love, we love as channels. We are the vehicle for love, and as we raise our energies from the love center, and we include the eye, then we see love as it is. And as we are bound in this earthly plane, to some extent, we tend to surround our love with our emotions, and we ask as a test of the love, we ask that a little hurt be bestowed so that we can see how great the love is. It is an interesting cycle.

And, my dear one, I do suggest you ditch it. You need not test. You are very sensitive, you are loving, you are kind, you would not hurt a flea. Recognize that the source of love is not you. The source lies in the universe — the great love, the great protectorates, the great hearts and eyes, those who see all and know all, and love all — even the maggots, love even the killers, love even those who hate us, and love even those little children. That's what love is.

And do not feel that you are ... lesser for my saying this to you. I say the truth to you because you are about to whirl and change. It is a great love that will be flowing through you.

Would you guide me to understand about my soul mate? How will I meet her, etc.? [The questioner is male.]

It seems that there could be, within the being, a little bit of expansion of beliefs. There would be a term "relationship" and there would be the term "soul mate." Now, how would you feel if you were to learn that your soul mate, the soul mate of this particular lifetime, would be a man? Now, that changes the idea of the relationship a little.

....Now, it seems as though there is a desire to have a relationship that would be very deep with one particular being. And we have on this planet the time of expansion. (Now, that certainly would not mean that you would gather yourself a harem!) However, there seems to be in each relationship, so to speak, a wondering in the back of your mind, "Would this be the one? Or would this be the one?" Or, "Maybe tomorrow I will meet my soul mate." And that we are simply stating that, truthfully, in this lifetime, we would find... that your... soul mate is in masculine form.

We are all soul mates, so to speak. There could be a woman who would be standing at your side, and as an equal, would be partners in life. There are some relationships where one being would be more taking care of the other being, and know that that would be in process a type of balance and counterbalance of what you term "other times." And also know that it is time in this particular vibration for you to be standing in partnership which would be affording you the greatest freedom from self, as the beliefs that you have set within your being as to what role you would play with a woman would be needing to be changed before that relationship would evolve. It is a ... process of looking within and recognizing that the fulfillment of needs within lies in the relationship with whatever you might term "your God." And then, the fruits of the earth are yours.

251

GUIDED MEDITATIONS

Next in the Gatherings came a guided group meditation, an experiential treat for all present. Almost every Gathering included one; each was different. Sometimes we sat in a circle holding hands. Sometimes we stood. Sometimes she asked us to look into each other's eyes. Sometimes she said each person's name aloud. Each communion was guided by her slow, gentle, loving voice encouraging us to allow the process to unfold.

The meditation which follows would be far more interesting to experience than to merely read. So, if you would like, you may read the Meditation *slowly* into a cassette tape for you and your friends to enjoy together. If so, you may wish to decide beforehand on a group chant to do in place of Pretty Flower's at the end of the session.

MARRIAGE OF BREATH
A Standing Meditation

I would ask if you would wish to partake of a union on different levels, of the beings present in the circle.

What we would suggest would be that instead of holding hands, that we could place our arms about each other. Would that be possible?

And in that space, there should be comfort, as this would take a few moments. If you would adjust your feet so that you would stand firmly ...

And I would simply suggest that there is a joy in the center of every being, every being. And, because there is a joy in the center of every being, there is a joy in the center of those beings present here.

And as we recognize that joy, we can, without wills, determine that there is an opening, and we can say to ourselves, "I open myself," and if you so choose, one might say, "I open myself to the White Light of the Universe." And if we were to decide to say, "I open myself to the White Light of the Universe," then we could let go of trying to open, as the process simply happens. We could

252

even say, "I surrender to the White Light of the Universe in full trust and love."

And know that, surrounding your beings on the outside of the circle of your beings, stands another circle. And in that circle are the angels with their magnificent wings and with their wonderful blessings. And as they are present around you, they embrace you ever so gently.

And as they embrace you ever so gently, you can know in the very depths of your being that you need never be alone. In fact, you can know that you are never alone. The guides around you are here for you. And they have come to present their vibrations for your feelings that their vibrations and your vibrations would encompass a marriage.

And as this marriage is taking place, with our wills and without our wills, it is simply a union. It is the type of union that happens as simply as when we open our eyes in the morning, and we know that it's morning..... It is as simple as that.

And as the union confirms the vibrations within and without, we are most filled with joy that you are trusting of the White Light of the Universe, and the Blessings of the Highest on High have showered and are showering themselves upon you, even as we vibrate together in this room.

And the blessings of the Highest on High can fill your beings to the brim so that when there is breathing, there is breathing in of the blessings that have flowed from one of the others. And the breathing out is breathing out of your blessings married to those blessings. And as we breathe in, we breathe in the blessings of the Highest on High. And when we breathe out, we breathe out the blessings of the Highest on High married to our own vibration. And we are the Highest on High. And we are the I AM.

And if you would remain as you are for one moment, I would make a sound for you that would be the sound of the marriages that are taking place on many levels, and the blessings that are so bountiful, vibrate and make a sound of their own. One moment please. [She chants.]

THE PARTINGS
Finally, she would take her leave with a blessing and a chant.

We have done much work here this evening. Our concept of work may change ... as we learn that work itself is a letting go of the conception of work. It is not a nose-to-the-grindstone, it is a letting go, and experiencing the wonders and the vibrations in the simplicity of joy and choosing to focus ourselves on the joy.

Often there were individual blessings and parting messages. Here is one for a man.

When you put your head down to sleep this evening ... there would be a blessing for you, as you are in the vibration of the spirits of the universe. Sometimes, the vibration is so subtle that we don't recognize it. But it is there. And you would know, even as you are drifting off to sleep, that many hold you in their arms and that there is much love pouring forth to you.

Chapter Fifteen

THE DOOR OF TRUST

*The longing to be in the great, wonderful universe
would be the longing to journey deep within our beings.*
Pretty Flower

After Eileen and I worked together in January of 1985, I rested, studying and assimilating the information that had come forward in the Gatherings and savoring the experience itself.

Eileen, back in her New Hampshire home, was not just resting. During the six months before I saw her again, two significant things happened: Pretty Flower came through without a guide, and Eileen began to work with a new guide.

Pretty Flower's appearance solo, so to speak (to use her characteristic phrase), occurred in a most prosaic way. Eileen was to be one of the subjects of an article about childhood psychic abilities and she had asked a friend to take pictures of her to go with the article. The friend later told me this story.

When they finished taking the pictures, Eileen spoke casually about her feeling that Pretty Flower was almost ready to come through unassisted. "I wonder if she would do it now," she said to the friend. "I'd love to have you take pictures of her."

"Try," said the friend, poising the camera and fiddling

255

with the exposure settings. Eileen closed her eyes and let it happen. In only a few minutes — two, perhaps — her eyes closed. Her face, hands, and body assumed Pretty Flower's characteristic posture. Pretty Flower spoke, introducing herself and telling a charming 20-minute story for the friend before leaving again of her own volition.

The friend was flabbergasted (she had had no experience with channeling) and had just enough wit to continue to take pictures.

And Eileen was elated. Pretty Flower had come through on her own —without any formal, guided procedure. This meant Eileen could continue to work in New Hampshire without my presence as a guide. This she did, holding one or two sessions a week for groups near her home, working to become an ever clearer, more open channel for Pretty Flower.

EILEEN'S NEW GUIDE

Meanwhile, another person was beginning to take a role in her development. Brock Hood had known Eileen for some time in other circumstances. Their communication began with hypnosis and continued with past-life exploration. When he heard of her work as a channel he was eager to learn more. He attended a few group sessions, but he wanted something more than the group could offer. He began coming to Eileen's house once a week, every week, asking if she would channel. Brock wanted to work with Pretty Flower directly; later, of course, they realized that he was asking to do the work of a guide. He studied hypnosis techniques and learned to communicate with Pretty Flower, learning her language and way of answering his questions. A strong foundation was built, and they learned much together. Eileen trusted and respected him.

WAITING FOR PRETTY FLOWER

In June, Eileen and Brock visited us in Virginia for a week. His purpose was to begin work on opening himself in order to channel; her purpose was clear, too, as you will see

256

in a minute.

What a week it was! Brock and Eileen told some of their friends about the visit. We told some of our friends. Suddenly, spontaneously, more than a dozen people came.

We worked and we played. European friends, an Austrian and an Italian who were traveling cross country, extended their stay at our house. Helmut led a group that worked on opening to the energies of the universe by assuming positions he taught while making the sound of runes. To demonstrate the power of the runes, four people picked up our friend, Dan, with two fingers each! They tried it three times and actually carried him around the deck with their fingers. Robert, our Italian friend, who speaks almost no English, wanted me to hypnotize him, and though I normally don't do such stage-type work, I did so, and succeeded in spite of the language barrier.

Daniel Clay came by one day and I guided him in a group reading on our deck, the first either of us had done outdoors. We had a brainstorming session to percolate ideas for a school for prophets and guides; you will read some of the fruits of that session in the next chapter.

I guided Brock through an amazing past-life regression and through his first time channeling. The reading was clear and we were all excited for him. He was as ready to channel as to guide.

I guided seven or eight major sessions that week; other people guided sessions among themselves. For me, the most incredible sessions were the ones with Eileen. As I said, her purpose in coming to Virgina was clear. Pretty Flower had told her what it was. She — Pretty Flower — was ready for a full entry into Eileen's embodiment. Pretty Flower had asked Eileen to come to Virginia and work with me on this new and intensive procedure.

What it meant was this.

Until now, when Pretty Flower came forward, Eileen stayed in the background as much as possible. She was aware of Pretty Flower's entrance; they met, embraced, and danced together. Then Eileen made room for Pretty Flower, becoming part, as she says, of "a Blue Mist at the top of my head." Pretty Flower then made her appearance to the rest of us, the two of them coinhabiting Eileen's body.

When Eileen returned fully from her trance, she remembered some, but by no means all, of what Pretty Flower had communicated to us. In other words, until now a part of Eileen's consciousness had monitored the sessions, although there were gaps in which she had no awareness. Now this would change. Pretty Flower had requested Eileen's full body during the sessions. It was time to allow a full entering of Pretty Flower and exiting of the consciousness of Eileen. Eileen was prepared for and accepting of the necessity for a full exiting; indeed, she was eager for it to happen.

THE FIRST FULL ENTRY AND EXIT

On the afternoon of June 12, Eileen, Brock and my wife and I went alone to a quiet room; we did not ask the others to be present, as we were attempting a major change and wanted as little distraction as possible. Also, we were not sure what form the transition would take.

Pretty Flower had long ago requested us not to use the Cayce levels when guiding her entry. For this session, however, she had asked us to use them, so I guided Eileen in opening the chakra system and on through the levels as Cayce had described them. Next I guided the entry to Pretty Flower and requested a full entry.

EILEEN
June 12, 1986
Independence, Virginia

THE ENTRY

[After hypnosis.] Please begin with the opening, the gentle opening of the crown chakra. Opening the crown chakra to the White Light of the universe and begin allowing the light to come through strong, brilliant, radiant, filling the crown chakra, in

258

perfect harmony, radiating fully. [I continued in this manner to guide her through the opening of the remaining chakras. See chakra illustrations.]

And slowly the White Light becomes a blue-white light; wholly, with trust you surrender to this spot of innocence, deep, deep in the glow of the blue-white light. The entire being is filled with the blue-white light, strong, safe. The being is filled with light. And if this is a good time, nod your head that we will continue. [She nods.] Thank you.

[I then guided her, as Edgar Cayce had traveled while in trance, through the various levels of seeking the Light. See "The Cayce Levels," Chapter 8.]

There is a full and complete entry of Pretty Flower in her highest essence in the fullness of her being.

[So far everything had been familiar, even normal. Beyond this, however, I had no idea what to expect or do. It took time and it was like groping in the dark, literally and figuratively. But clearly, my first job was to be sure the complete transfer of energies between Eileen and Pretty Flower was taking place. I then continued.]

There is a complete exiting of the body vessel — Eileen — as she makes room and parts temporarily for the full entry of Pretty Flower. The vessel spirit, the vessel being, the energy of Pretty Flower makes a complete and full entry. And in the fullness of life, a total and complete entering with no diversions, but always coming straight into the light. There is warrior strength on each side, in front, and in back to protect you, in many dimensions. There is the full protection, the full trust. And when you are ready, please tell me how you are doing and how we may assist this process.

[There was no signal, so I repeated myself. Eileen's body vibrated, but Pretty Flower still did not make a sound. So I said...]

If this is a good time, use the attunement of sound to fully balance the energies.... As the alignment becomes complete, continue to use the sound to fully balance the energy. We welcome you. We are pleased that you are here.

[Now Pretty Flower did speak, but in a constrained and difficult way. I continued.]

Spirit has fully entered flesh. You are very welcome. The soul body is full. The vessel body is full. The mind body is full.

Is this a time that you can speak? Hello, Pretty Flower.

[She can scarcely speak.] I have been making this transfer many more times before and would be complete. For the vessel is still in what — [she struggles to speak] — transformation which — a binding effect, so to speak.

All the energy about to enter.

[Now Pretty Flower actually screeches. Eileen's body shakes and contorts. She speaks about Pretty Flower in the third person.] She wants out, so to speak, and finds the door closed! And is knocking, knocking on the door to be out! And it would be closed, so to speak! So we find a great deal of tension occurring!

I understand. We will work with this. We will make the opening of the door easier, with trust, with proper technique and suggestion, with our fuller understanding we will make the door open easy and allow her to depart happily, safely.

She would be happy to be leaving at the moment. However, the door is not to be found, sadly to say.

[Obviously there was trouble. Somehow, Eileen was not able to leave her body totally. Later, she told me, "I was in the Blue Mist at the top of my head, and I was frantic! I couldn't find the door to leave, and I was pounding on the top of my head, screaming, 'Let me out! Let me out!'"

At the time I couldn't hear her screams, of course, but Pretty Flower's choking and screeching and the vessel's agitation gave me the clues I needed to know what was amiss. This is where years of experience pay off. Giving the suggestion for Eileen to "leave" her body was not working. I had to approach this in a different way. Inspiration came — I told Eileen to go deeply within herself. In the next few sessions I perfected the wording, but the concept remained: to go deeper within, to a safe and comfortable place, rather than go away from herself. (My suggestions are meant for Eileen; I am talking here to Pretty Flower, naturally. In the next few exchanges, the two of us are working to help Eileen.) I continued.]

The door, if I understand correctly, is to be found inside. The door is deep within, and the door is at that place of trust. The door is called "trust." And as she finds that place of trust, she sees the door.

Would you say that again, please?

[I repeated the suggestion and did so again after she asked me to proceed a little slower.] Tell me when she finds the door that is marked "trust." [Pretty Flower signals by raising her finger.] Okay. Now she places her hand....

[Pretty Flower interrupted me.] Now that would be, so to speak, backwards.

[I puzzled for a moment over this; somehow, then, I knew what she meant: The letters on the door were reversed.] We'll find the door where it's spelled correctly. Find the proper door. Bypass the diversions and find the real door where trust is spelled correctly: T - R - U - S - T. Find the real door, and tell me when you have accomplished this. Tell me when she has accomplished this. [She raises her finger.] Thank you. Now she places her hand upon the door, upon the latch. Then she slowly....

It's a very big door. [Huge, Eileen told me later.]

She slowly, with full strength and courage and determination, opens this door and realizes that the vessel body is full, that she is not leaving the vessel empty. She realizes that two are occupying the space for one. So she opens the door, carefully, safely, slowly, using her full strength, which is considerable. Now tell me when she has opened the door. [Raises finger.] Okay, thank you.

Now with full understanding and awareness, she slowly steps through the door. She allows herself, her will, her strength, her essence, to step through the door, through the threshold, into the place of trust. And tell me when she has accomplished this. [Pretty Flower signals again.] Thank you.

Now in the place of trust, there is full safety. The place of trust is simply a place to wait while the vessel is filled with her friend. She has made room for her friend, Pretty Flower, and she allows the door to close temporarily so that Pretty Flower may use the vessel. And tell me when this is accomplished. [She signals.] Okay.

Now in the fullness of light, Pretty Flower uses the vessel body. Her spirit body is attuned to the physical body. You may speak if you would like. There is a fullness of entering, a balance of energy. Welcome. Greetings. Allow the vision to become fully clear. [Pretty Flower was now clearly present. I then greeted her.] It's nice to see you.

Thank you.

You're very welcome.

Now I'm fine.

Pretty Flower made a sound. And then, to our astonishment, she opened her eyes and stood. She looked all around and looked deeply into my eyes. Then she returned to her chair, breathing a deep sigh.

Let me explain why this was such a change. I recognized when Pretty Flower was present because she laced her fingers together and placed her hands in a certain clenched position. In our earliest sessions, she clenched her hands so tightly that they turned blue, and she hunched over in such a tight and rigid position that Eileen's neck and shoulders needed massage after the session. Once, early on, I noted the blueness of the hands and asked Pretty Flower if she wished to change her posture. "Why?" she asked, and I explained. She assented to the change and I gave the appropriate suggestions.

Gradually, in subsequent sessions, the tightness passed. (Once she said sassily to me, commenting on the relaxed position, "We're getting good at this, are we not?") But her hands and feet were almost always kept in a special way, and her eyes were always closed.

Now major changes had occurred. While Pretty Flower could barely speak at this intensive level, she could, and did, open her eyes. She studied the room and the people. When she looked at me I felt very uncomfortable, for I was looking at the eyes and body of Eileen, but it was definitely not Eileen walking around, and it was not Eileen inside her eyes — it was a different soul.

The process of change was profound. The closest I can come to describing it is when I remember the birth of my son. In 1969, my wife, Linda, and I were alone and we delivered our son. She had had two previous children from an earlier marriage, and this was an easy birth. Eileen's sounds and the sounds of new life coming forth were similar. And as I think of it, a new life and opening to a new level of life are similar transformational experiences: birth and channeling. This was like the rebirthing of a soul.

Perhaps the form we used previously was partly responsible for not having a full entry, because the answer was not to go "out" or "aside," but rather to go safely and securely deep within. Or perhaps both Eileen and Pretty Flower needed more than a year to become accustomed to the preliminary steps of the channeling adventure. Whatever the reason, we were now embarking on a new dimension in Eileen's channeling.

THE EXIT PROCEDURE

Presently, after about 20 minutes, Pretty Flower said, "I want to go." I responded:

Okay, I thought so. Please become comfortable. Allow the vessel to become fully comfortable. Go in peace and joy. Thank you. Bless you, dear sweet soul. Thank you for coming and visiting, gentle soul. We will look forward to seeing you many times, and sharing, and communicating, and laughing.

Allow the body to become fully comfortable. Allow the body to rest. And slowly, very slowly, allow the Door of Trust to reopen and allow her to enter through the door of trust, where you are both together. Where you come together, maybe dance together. She enters through the Door of Trust, and you embrace. And the vessel remains full with the energies of both of you.

But soon it is time for Pretty Flower to depart, that she may return as is desired in the fullness of time and place and circumstance, when she is invited to return through this vessel. And the vessel Eileen returns with fullness of strength into her temple. And there is a return going through the levels.

....And as the tiny dot of light, moving to the level of intense darkness and loneliness, as if it were a universe of darkness. But on the beam of light you safely enter your physical body. And the

263

dot of light grows and fills your being with the life force.

The chakra center is ablaze with White Light. The entity of the proper vessel, Eileen, enters with fullness of energy, in balance and harmony, in healing. And Eileen seats herself carefully within her vessel of being, within her body vessel.

You are very welcome back. And you begin the slow process of gently, gently returning to normalization. Your chakra system, leaving enough open that the physical body may work with the energy and grow through this experience. Leaving enough of the energy open to maintain health, healing balance. Allowing the light to become dimmer so that it is not too bright. Finding the full and total level of balance, that level of normalization, and allowing the centers, the reproductive center, the cells of Leydig, the solar plexus, the heart chakra, the thyroid and parathyroids of the throat, the pineal, the third eye chakra, and the crown chakra, to full normalization.

There is the full and complete reentering of Eileen. The full and complete departing and saying thank you to Pretty Flower. Rest for a few moments. Allow the balance of energy. And as you are ready, signal with your hand and we will begin the count-up exercise. [After some time, she signals.]

....It is June 12, 1986, in Independence, Virginia, and she is fully orienting into the present — aware of the circumstances and the time. It is approximately 4:10 p.m. in the afternoon. You have done very well today. Take your time, take your time. And as you would like, signal me with a finger, that we may proceed. [She signals.] Thank you.

....In a little while, when you awaken, you will feel better than before, energized, revitalized, recharged. The energy field in and around your body will return to full normalization. Allow the closing of the brilliant light so it may be to a point that it is healthy and beneficial....

I will count now... [and I counted her back into consciousness].

WHAT HAPPENED NEXT

This session and the subsequent full-entry sessions that followed prepared Eileen and Pretty Flower for the next phase of their work.

Brock had observed and learned more about guiding. The procedure I initiated in this intensive transitional session and refined in several subsequent ones in Virginia is used by Brock and Eileen today as they work together. They have refined the process still further, but its basic form is the same: Brock guides her to the Door of Trust, and through it, that Eileen may exit and Pretty Flower may enter with full-body synchronization.

Eileen describes her consciousness as "walking down a path" once she enters the door marked "Trust." She enjoys her journey, while Pretty Flower does *her* work. At the end of each session Eileen hears herself being called and returns through the door and into her own awareness.

Pretty Flower, too, is learning the uses of Eileen's vessel. Together, Brock and Pretty Flower enjoy walks into a forest where she works with him in a natural setting, expounding on her concepts of beliefs, creation, and unconditional love.

During the sessions, Pretty Flower also enjoys full body movement, telling her stories with much animation. Frequently, she asks participants to move around, too. In a recent session, for instance, she asked people to change seats about half an hour into the session. Several people had questions about their health. She asked each one, in turn, to come to the center of the circle, where she walked all around them, placed her hands on their bodies, made motions over them and chanted, giving tone alignments. At the end, she asked them to stand and gather together in a circle around her. After giving a blessing to each one, she taught them to bestow the Blessings of the Universe on each other by kissing palms, foreheads, etc.

I had the opportunity to hold a seminar with Eileen and Brock later that summer. I spoke on hypnosis and channeling, after which Eileen channeled Pretty Flower. It had been just a few months since I last worked with Eileen so I was amazed at the remarkable ease with which she now channeled.

265

Illustration #10
The chakras or spiritual centers.

As guide, Brock opened the session by reading a very short procedure to Eileen. Where we had once used a 20-minute procedure, now it was barely three to four minutes before Pretty Flower said the words so familiar to my ears, "One moment. We would be arriving, so to speak." Then she sat forward on her chair and looked around at us all with her wide-eyed gaze.

I could feel a breath of fresh, vitalized energy enter the room with her presence. "Hello my friends," she said. Then, with quite animated body movements, she told a delightful story, after which she spoke with each person individually. When she stood and walked to one woman, she walked with grace and sure steps, quite unlike the first few we had shared together. Where once I carefully prevented people from coming too close to her body (to protect the energy flow of the chakra system), now she embraced them and often placed her fingers on the third-eye area. She called different people forward and then made those deep, resonant tones, still as beautiful as when I first heard them. Quite a few times she leaned her head back and filled the room with a loud, boistrous laugh. I had to laugh just at the experience.

She turned to one woman who came to the session wearing a neck brace and asked if she was ready to release her pain. When the woman said, "Yes," Pretty Flower moved her hands around the woman, sometimes close to her body and sometimes further away. Then she said three times that the woman was healed and touched the edge of the woman's blouse. The woman removed her neck brace and rolled her head around. "It does feel better," she said. Pretty Flower perkily replied, "Of course, you are healed!" The woman smiled and Pretty Flower added, "It's this little healing spot you have on your shirt!" We all laughed together. (When the session was over, the woman left her neck brace behind, no longer having any use for it.)

The session lasted two hours. Then Pretty Flower sat down, closed her eyes, and breathed a deep sigh. The facial structure so common to her slowly left and Eileen's face reappeared. Brock simply counted up from one to ten and

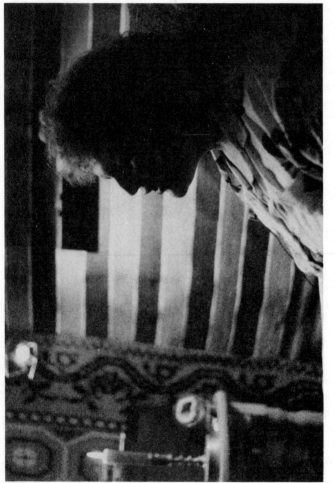

Illustration #11
Eileen Rota channeling Pretty Flower.

Eileen returned to full consciousness. The whole session and procedure was smooth and untroubled. It was a joy to see how our work had progressed.

Pretty Flower can guide her own entering and exiting process now, but Brock still guides Eileen through the Door of Trust. The vital need for a guide is always present and Brock continues this important work. Eileen has told me that the process is easier now that she has no recollection of the sessions. She has no emotional involvement and her critical conscious mind is not in the way; by totally detaching, she channels more purely and elegantly.

Eileen and Brock journey around the country, offering Gatherings for all who wish to share in the blessings and teachings of Pretty Flower.

Chapter Sixteen

VISIONS FOR THE FUTURE

I cannot think of permanent enmity between man and man, and believing as I do in the theory of rebirth, I live in the hope that if not in this birth, in some other birth, I shall be able to hug all humanity in friendly embrace.
Mahatma Gandhi

There are valid concerns about conducting age regression and channeling experiments, or doing any other kind of soul exploration, in safety. Evil exists. I have not found it; I have not looked for it. As you continue the work, as you look deep within yourself and reach out to light you will learn and grow in safety.

A few people fear the idea of exploring their inner minds. This is a well-founded fear for them; we all have certain fears of the unknown. But let me illustrate my response to this with a recollection from my youth. The Red Cross offered free swimming lessons near our home. My mother had a great fear of drowning, so she said on numerous occasions, "Don't go swimming until you know how to swim." The only problem with her admonition was that later in life both my brother and I almost drowned because we had never learned to swim. She wouldn't let us go until we knew how, and we never learned how because we never went. Learning is a better solution to ignorance. Just because we don't fully understand something doesn't mean we should reject it. Rather we can learn and grow to understand.

Yes, there are cautions and obstacles to soul exploration. The biggest problem, as I see it, is the ego. In regression, a person with a powerful past, for instance, may wish to recapture that time again. But people cannot ride on yesterday's glory, nor are they locked into yesterday's tragedies. The person who boasts, "I am the greatest," is as out of balance as the person who whimpers, "I am less than nothing."

And then there's the temptation to think we are somehow more spiritually advanced than others if we can recall past lives at will. For all of these reasons and more, the Cayce readings advise not to dwell only on the past.

In hypno-regression, the potential exists to merge one's past and present into a whole person greater than his or her various parts (lives). It has been a transformative spiritual discipline for me, a tremendously valuable tool in helping me to bring the pieces of my own puzzle together. For example, in so many past lives war tantalized me — foolish as a moth attracted to the flickering flame of a candle — with its promise of excitement, glory and importance. But the consequence was self-destruction.

After death, I chose to cleanse my soul's scars by reincarnating into a life at the other extreme — that of the monk. Naturally, after the far too quiet life as a monk I longed for *action*. I seemed to bounce back and forth, in seesaw fashion, from monastery to warrior. But this was my way of finding balance through experience.

Recollection of my past through regression has given me a glimpse of wisdom. Now it is up to me to put that wisdom into action by choosing neither extreme — but a path of peaceful adventure. Surely the goal of regression is to *balance* the extremes and build our humanity.

I trust I am gaining respect for those who plan and work ceaselessly for peace. They inspire me to make peace in my everyday world without thinking I have to hide away for a lifetime in some dark, cold abbey. An adventurous soul needs light and fresh air!

GO WITH CARE

One definite problem I have observed over the years in a relatively few number of people is what I call "addiction to readings." "Readings addicts" develop an insatiable appetite for readings. One or two readings isn't enough for them, they want more ... and more ... and more. When more is given, they ask still more questions. Unfortunately, they request another reading before fully acting upon the information they already have. They are never satisfied.

In a recent extreme case, a man I met would rarely make any decision without first checking with "the Source." Perhaps he was afraid of making a mistake — a noble concern but unrealistic. Trying to avoid all mistakes is like trying to avoid rainy days. Rainy days are inevitable just about everywhere except in the most barren desert. Deserts become wastelands for *want* of rain. We can gain valuable experience by learning from our mistakes. Success and failure are but experiences — it is experience that builds wisdom.

Readings are helpful — guidance is good, but *all* things should be in moderation. A few readings may be inspiring, but a dozen may be overwhelming. Readings are holy experiences, magical moments where the veil of eternity is momentarily lifted. A reading is a soul study that needs time to be assimilated just as a meal needs time to be digested to nourish the body.

Another problem to watch for is what is called "self-fulfilling prophecy." This is where you may have been told something is going to happen, and although you do not necessarily believe it will really happen, you take the steps, consciously or unconsciously, to *make* it happen. A positive example of this would be if you were told you would be starting an exercise program soon, noticed an ad in the paper, and joined up.

When suggestions (whether given in a negative sense

or not) are used to create negative actions or conditions which would not have evolved on their own, we have examples of negative self-fulfilling prophecy. An optimistic person might be able to turn a negative suggestion into a positive one, but another (through fear or lack of trust in self) could fall victim to the suggestion and create problems that were not intended to be part of the original game plan.

There is bound to be criticism of an idea when it threatens a basic belief pattern. This is certainly the case with reincarnation, though the situation is compounded when others assume one can return as a butterfly, or mule, depending upon one's "just reward." Imagine the threat to traditional Christianity if speaking in tongues were found to be ancient languages spoken by these people in past lifetimes!

I think much of the criticism projected towards the belief in reincarnation and the seeking of knowledge through past-life regression and channeled material is a result of:

(1) misuse of information given in a reading

(2) over-use (addiction) of information given in a reading and/or

(3) the substitution of another's will for one's own. If someone else is determining what you do and how and when you do it (whether it is your mate or your guru, whether it is a leader of a cult or a person from whom you seek readings), you can bet you are not in control of your own life and not being guided by a Higher Source.

Getting "sidetracked" *is* a real fear for some people. Personally, I believe that people can get sidetracked with an imbalance on any spiritual path.

Then, how *do* we find our spiritual balance?

First, we develop the desire to listen to and open to the Divine within. Second, we learn to trust ourselves. As in any personal growth venture (emotional, social, spiritual or whatever) this is a trial and error procedure. We begin on a practical level by mentally evaluating the information available to us. Then we seek guidance from the Higher Self, through prayer and meditation. This requires a true listening to that inner-self guidance. Then, using our best mental and intuitive faculties, we make our own choices.

This is healthy, this is balance, physically mentally and spiritually.

And, I think the issue of trusting ourselves is the very reason behind the stress in the Edgar Cayce readings on self-guidance. For when we open ourselves to the Divine within and act on the promptings received, we further develop that ability to trust ourselves and our own judgment. We then have the wisdom to discern what is Divine and what isn't. When we side-step this process by substituting another's judgment for our own, we delay the development of self-trust and lose faith in our own ability to make decisions. *That's* when we are vulnerable to imbalance — vulnerable to others' opinions, directives and judgments; vulnerable to self-doubt and any other potential sidetracking on the spiritual path.

Realizing that we have the ability to tap into the highest guidance available, through the Divine within, is surely a reassuring thought — truly a gift, from what The Eternals and Pretty Flower tell us.

Now, the way we reach the Divine is a personal choice. There are many paths to God and each is a valid path. Each person finds his or her own path and stays on that path for as long as he or she needs to. Kahlil Gibran said, "We have eternity." For some, the path may lead to development of intuition; for others it may bestow the ability to accept the wisdom from a channeled reading and put aside the rest; for others it may be the development of channeling. This is certainly the way Daniel and Eileen began their journeys.

Inevitably all paths lead to the God within. As we evolve as souls, we come to forks and crossroads and take new paths. Again, the best path is the road of Balance — encompassing many of the spiritual understandings. Prayer, meditation, self-hypnosis, play, song, dance, work, etc., are all paths to God — the more variety a person's life has the better. But the soul whose focus is *just* prayer, for example, is as unbalanced as the one whose focus is *just* hard work. Balance and moderation are the keys.

WHAT ABOUT CHANNELED MATERIAL?
Certainly, not all channeled material is accurate, any more than all news on television or in newspapers and magazines is accurate. Channeling can be as clouded as a news story because the same words, images, and events can be interpreted differently by different people.

In a recent channeling session Daniel addressed this very issue:

One must not look far to find why there are contradictions within channeling. All channels will taint the materials that come through. If you listen to the channeling of a Zen Buddhist, it will sound much different from the channeling of one who has spent his lifetime building clocks in the clock factory and knows nothing but the language of the tick-tock. So it is [that] there are contradictions through the impurities of the vessels through which each channeling must come. And if one desires to believe strong enough, that also shall taint. There are many who are learning to channel, and as they learn, they must learn to sort out impurities. But these come through even the most well-experienced, even as the most éxperienced baseball player still misses grounders and pop-flies upon occasion.

There are still personal prejudices and personal biases which will sift through the individuals through these channelings. That is why each and every individual should channel within themselves and receive of spirit of self. Only by self-revelation can one know of spirit and truth.

It has been said in the Bible that "By their fruits you shall know them." But again, this requires personal discernment. If we are not balanced ourselves, we may not be aware of imbalance in a channeler's works or actions. There are as many grades of channelers as there are grades of people's actions.

The fruits — the work and teachings — of Daniel and Eileen were positive and beneficial influences on us. Often spontaneous healings, on many levels, occurred. And we

275

knew these channels as *people*. We were aware of their purpose to help others in their search for spiritual understanding — this, in addition to sensing the Light about them.

A very important consideration to keep in mind when studying or evaluating channeled material is that the information was originally given for a specific individual. The caution here is that the channeled material may not be valid for anyone but the one who received the reading.

Of course, other material can be relevant to many. And where personal information or guidance is similar in a number of readings, a certain "statistical relevance" is indicated although there is no absolute rule here.

OPENING TO CHANNEL

When I work with people to develop their ability to channel I look first to see how strong is their desire to be of service to others; then I gauge their desire to seek and to be open. What I'm looking for is, *Why* do you want to channel? Do you want to channel to help mankind, to learn and grow, to become a more whole person, or is it just to impress people with your new hobby? Because in channeling the ego can be a tremendous stumbling block. The goal here is to detach *who* you are from *what* you are doing.

Edgar Cayce's readings lend some fascinating clues as to why the purpose in channeling plays a vital part in one's ability to access Higher Sources. Apparently, *with an unselfish desire* on the part of the channeler *to help others* and *with the desire to be a channel through which the highest spiritual forces can manifest*, the probability of channeling quality material is greatly increased.

Also, when the seeker (the person requesting the reading) is open and receptive to the information being channeled there is a far greater potential for a good reading. Interestingly, the readings indicate that the right purpose on the part of each allows the seeker and channeler to actually commune on a soul level during the exchange. No wonder a reading can be so on target!

Proper preparation is vital in channeling, just as it is in regression. (You may wish to review this section in Chapter 7.) My "training program" requires inner exploration and spiritual disciplines (e.g., exercises in hypnosis, age regression and chakra attunement) developed through working alone with hypnosis tapes and with me. Over time this allows a mutual relationship of trust and compatibility to develop between the channeler and myself. Through practice we learn and grow together refining our techniques and procedures. (I have included CHANNELING GUIDELINES in the Appendix for those of you who are interested in the specifics of proper foundation work and the potential hazards to avoid in opening to channeling.)

Actually, my job is to be, for the vessel, the link with earth reality. My attitude is one of respect for the source and the information. The vessel and I take neither credit nor blame for information that comes through. This keeps our egos out of the way. The information can be evaluated and weighed by intelligent and neutral people to determine its value. Prophecy of future events can be filed to see if later it proves correct. I simply support the natural process of what is happening without judgment.

I believe it is mandatory for vessel and guide to work together many times before channeling experiments are conducted. This lesson was brought home to me as recently as July, 1986, when I worked much too soon with a new student, Roger Hunt. We had worked together only twice before. In our first session we went through the chakra opening process. In the second we went through the Cayce levels but without attempting a reading. In our mutual eagerness we went too fast. Roger was very willing, but still had doubts as to whether he was ready and able to channel.

If we had had a stronger foundation, we could have avoided an experience that frightened him. As it was, while he was in a trance I could see he was processing a lot of feeling and emotion. But he did not speak. Then, after a few minutes, he asked for help to come back to familiar reality. I gave appropriate suggestions; he followed them and returned without panicking.

Roger started the session by seeing what looked like a normal house cat, but the cat grew to be larger than a tiger. Roger fled and became lost in a wooded valley. His subconscious mind protected him from becoming permanently lost in the woods. He prayed aloud for help, "Father, take me home." And I guided him back slowly and safely.

Roger's self-doubts projected themselves as frightening visual images. He did not describe them as he was viewing them; if he had, I would have given appropriate suggestions.

As a result of this experience, we decided to build a much stronger foundation by working together on easier projects first. Two weeks later we did, in fact, do a regression session. It proved to be one of the most interesting, fact-filled sessions I ever conducted. (About a year after the regression Roger wanted to proceed with the channeling work. It was a wonderful success and once again taught me the need for patience in spiritual work.)

Roger's case is unusual. Neither Daniel nor Eileen experienced anything like it in the beginning sessions. Nevertheless, I could observe strong effects during their first sessions and both of them described intense experiences. But they persisted in the work and the difficulties lessened.

Some people experience unusual reactions as the chakra centers open. For instance, as you may recall in Eileen's early sessions, the crown chakra remained open, and she found the sensation very uncomfortable. Though not quite "returned" from her hypnotic state, she was able to motion to me that the center was open, and I could relieve her discomfort by putting my hands on her head and giving her suggestions to close the chakra.

Other people have strong reactions to the experience of traveling through the levels and layers of the mind. Still others are concerned about the validity of the information they channel, wondering if it is contaminated by their conscious minds. To me, these obstacles are like tests to see if the person really wants to continue with the work.

In December, 1987, Daniel Clay channeled for a large group of people in our home. The session was so interesting, I would like to share some of it with you. It also nicely reflects on the information just presented on channeling. I asked The Eternal, "What recommendations do you have for individuals who channel, and how should they go about it?"

There are very few recommendations that would be of great importance. There is one recommendation that is of the utmost importance. That is: you should do so with love. Anything that you seek with love and you do with love then returns with love. Anything you do for glorification of self or for the gain of self within the physical would also be bound to become a balance against your own being, and would be a greater burden than it would be a gift. All that is done with love and with light ... is surely ... within love and light. If you have love, then surely you would live a life of love and prayer and meditation. Meditations and prayer are surely that which would lead you to that which you would seek.

That which many would call "prayers" and "meditations" are a very limited scope of what meditations and prayers are. For your meditations may be your writings. Your meditations may be your readings. Your meditations may be your studies. Your meditations might be your favorite relaxing moment, with your favorite relaxing beer. Meditations are those times when you are able to align yourself at one and become in harmony with truth.

So it would be that prayers are not just those times when you are thrown upon the ground in great distress. Prayers are also those times of joy when you smile and you shout. Prayer is also those times of wonder. Prayer is those times when those glorious thoughts thread through your mind. You must realize that your spirit round about does commune continually. The electro-plasmic field of your own personage is in continual prayer and in continual communion with those round about.

Our free will gives us a big responsibility on the Earth

plane. It implies that we have choice, ever, and thus our thoughts and actions become our own responsibility, as The Eternals and Pretty Flower so often remarked.

When we use our mental faculties to evaluate, while listening to our intuition, I think we're really on to something. And when we receive guidance for our greater good, we use our free will to choose to follow it or ignore it. You have the choice to put your life on hold, or you can live each moment to its fullest. When all is said and done, the wisest person is the one who listens to his or her own inner counsel. The person who lives life fully and accomplishes much is the one who learns to access his or her own quiet, still voice from deep within.

UPDATES ON EILEEN AND DANIEL

Traveling all along the East Coast giving readings and group sessions, Eileen and Pretty Flower have made lots of friends. People have opened their homes to Eileen and their hearts to Pretty Flower. Eileen has told me many times how amazingly generous people have been.

Daniel Clay is also busy traveling and presenting workshops and channeling sessions around the country. He's reaching out and helping many people.

I have always thought that one of the great lessons in the School of Life is to learn generosity. In observing the work of Eileen and Daniel Clay I am constantly amazed as to how giving people are to a worthy goal or ideal. I've observed many forms of generosity that are far more important than just the financial. There are emotional, physical and spiritual aspects of generosity.

Often generosity is in the accepting — not just giving. A group of people have even volunteered to work and compile a book of Pretty Flower's teachings. It is a precious and wonderful book called *Welcome Home: A Time For Uniting* (Sand Castle Publishing, P.O. Box 629, Virginia Beach, Virginia 23451). People *asked* to be of help with transcribing, typing and the many aspects of birthing a book.

Although volunteers and helpers are much appreciated,

both Eileen and Daniel Clay have been careful to avoid overzealous "groupies" on one extreme, and crotchety "debunkers" on the other extreme. For Daniel and Eileen both, I have carefully noted that their channeling has been a spiritual *process* not a single event.

Recently Eileen told me that she is now taking a six-month break. These are her words.

Now I'm taking the time to integrate my own experiences which occurred during sessions. My views on what it is that we actually do during channeling have changed and broadened. Instead of viewing Pretty Flower as a personality of spirit which enters my being from without, I realize that I am opening to a Universal Truth and Source from within. As we have always said, "the journey is within," and with that in mind, I'm more able to live the teachings which I have channeled. I realize that Pretty Flower and I are One in the same.

Eighty-five percent of my regular day is spent in the state of alpha and I really enjoy it. I have a more universal way of viewing the people and occurrences in my life. I'm just taking a little break so that I can stop and "smell the flowers," and do what the teachings have suggested to many: I've let my little child-self out. We're skipping down the path together and I'm having fun!

UPDATING MY WORK

Much of what I do daily revolves around regression research projects. This work changes and evolves as new discoveries are made.

Though I was reluctant in the past to guide personal regressions in a group setting, I now guide one personal session as part of my full-day workshops. Participants learn more from observing than from discussion alone. Participants also experience a group past-life session similar to the format in "Accessing Your Souls Memory." (See the Appendix.)

In regression sessions people are able to fit together the jigsaw pieces of their puzzled past. But more importantly they discover the positive patterns of their past, the gifts of

281

their soul and the wonderful talents deep within that they may not have known about.

A person's first regression session may be like looking through a glass, darkly — later he or she may come to see themselves, fully, face to face. Regressions can also help unravel the mysteries of history. We have all heard of Mozart, who had a prodigious gift for music before he could talk or of the brilliant children who enter college at 11 or 12 years of age. Where do these things come from? Look at my friend who in his subconscious explorations discovered an unsuspected talent for mechanical things; he is now happy in a job he once scorned in his father's garage. How do we explain these things?

There is far more depth to the human mind than we can possibly imagine. The best way to learn more is to search, experiment, and explore for yourself.

There are benefits from understanding. This is a holistic, long-range study we are doing. It can bring benefit to our lives as we fine tune the gifts we have and use those gifts to help others. It is a work of great responsibility and integrity.

This work requires vision and foresight. The future is being built by our thoughts and actions today.

THE DREAM OF A SCHOOL

My vision is to see study groups and schools formed specifically to teach people to channel and to be guides. Perhaps the textbook could be called *A Guide for Guides*.

Though we do not yet have an official school, you can begin now on your own. The time is ripe. Find other searching souls and questioning minds to work with you. This is easier than you think. Go to classes in related topics in your area and start talking to the people there. You will discover that there are many, many other people searching for answers.

You are not alone. If there are no yoga, meditation or psychic development classes in your area write to the Edgar Cayce Foundation, the Association for Past Life Research and Therapy,[1] or a similar national organization.

Most of all, you need to begin — right where you are at. This work is a creative journey into your inner mind. It is an adventure into self-discovery, and no one else can do it for you. Does exploring new dimensions seem like a risk? Then consider taking a risk. Risk like this evokes courage and maturity and can bring healthier self-esteem. However, if your inner guidance says no, then don't try to push the river of your soul; there are no shortcuts to maturity.

I was barely 15 years old when I started my spiritual adventure — not yet victim to "set-in-concrete" thinking. Thus, not realizing I would fail, I went ahead and succeeded. Youths have the natural courage and adventurous spirit that sometimes become hardened and cynical as people age.

Mind belongs to the people who improve it, study it and most of all explore it. Hypnosis is one of the best tools to explore and understand the mind. Hypnosis, used spiritually, is one of the best approaches to soul exploration. And the young people — or at least the young in heart and mind — will become the leaders and vanguards of the new age. Pretty Flower put it this way: "In the innocence of the child is the foundation of the wisdom of the universe."

I hope I have inspired you to begin looking deeper into your inner mind. I hope you may even wish to journey within and explore your soul memories, to gain access to your higher mind, and to discover your soul's destiny. But before you do, there are some specific recommendations I wish to make.

Psychic development is not an end in itself — it is just one step toward spiritual growth. There are many other steps and many other paths to self-betterment. The goal is to become a whole person, mentally, physically, and spiritually. When you set your goals and ideals in life, please include steps to help all aspects of your growth. Continue your education. Strengthen your character. Integrate your personality. Volunteer for community work, join a health club or fitness center. Build a healthy mind and a healthy spirit.

Age regression and channeling are doors to the New Age just as the ships of the fifteenth and sixteenth centuries opened the way to the New World. Then, as now, some people have fears and doubts of the unknown and the unexplored. Today we smile to think of the absurdity of the belief that ships would fall off the edge of the world; we grin at the legends on the old maps that say of the uncharted, unknown seas, "Out here be monsters." But there was a time when both were common fears.

My quest has been, and still is, unveiling the mysteries of the mind, unlocking the secrets of the ancients. In my search I have gained knowledge and experience. Through persistence and perseverance I have received spiritual guidance. My goal is now to inspire you and encourage you to explore the richness and magnitude of your own mind and soul. Reading about new things gives you knowledge. Working with and applying your knowledge builds wisdom.

The ancients hid the secrets of the universe in men's minds. Now is the time to bring them out of hiding. And please — write and share some of your discoveries with me.

Henry Leo Bolduc
Adventures Into Time
P.O. Box 88
Independence, VA 24348

Endnotes:

[1]Association for Past Life Research and Therapy, P.O. Box 2015, Riverside, CA 92516.

APPENDIX

285

ACCESSING YOUR SOUL'S MEMORY

The following transcript is an entire present and past-life regression session for your personal use. You may simply read the material out loud, or you may tape it for yourself, a friend, or for a group. If you want to record it, use a 90-minute tape so you will not have to stop in mid-session to turn the cassette (the material takes about 45 minutes).

Read slowly and clearly. You may wish to practice first, perfecting your timing and the modulation and pitch of your voice.

(Full procedures for making your own self-help, self-hypnosis tapes are included in my book *Self-Hypnosis: Creating Your Own Destiny.*)

ACCESSING YOUR SOUL'S MEMORY
Start reading or recording here.
I'm going to count downward from ten to one, and with every descending number, slowly blink your eyes. Just look forward or upward. Slowly blink your eyes, in slow motion, with every number.

[Slowly.] Ten — nine — eight — seven — six — five — four — three — two — and one. And now you can just close your eyes, and you can just keep them closed. And I will explain what that was for — that was just to relax your eyelids. And right now, in your eyelids, there is probably a feeling of relaxation, perhaps a comfortable tired feeling, or a pleasant heavy sensation. Whatever the feeling is right now in your eyelids, just allow that feeling to multiply, to magnify, and to become greater. Allow your eyelids now to become totally and pleasantly relaxed. Now, this is something that you do. Nobody else can do this for you. You're the one who does it. So just take your time and completely, and pleasantly, relax your eyelids now. And as you relax your eyelids, you can allow that feeling of relaxation, that is now in your eyelids, to flow outward, in all directions, as in imaginary waves, or ripples.

Allow a feeling of relaxation to go outward to the entire face area. Just think about relaxing the face. Enjoy the relaxation going outward to the entire head area, relaxing the head. Feel the relaxation going to the neck and to the shoulders, down the arms and into the hands. Welcome a wonderful feeling of relaxation going down the entire body, to the legs, the feet, all the way out to the toes. Your body may feel heavy, or it may feel light. It may be perfectly still, or you may notice subtle movement.

As you completely and pleasantly relax your entire body, you can just slow down a little bit. Just allow yourself to slow down a little bit. And later, as we go along, you can slow down a little bit more and a little bit more. And, in a moment, I am going to count downward once again from ten to one. And this time, with every descending number, just allow yourself to slow down a little bit more with every number. And at the number, one, you can enter your own natural level of relaxation.

I will count very rapidly now: Ten, nine, eight, seven, six, five, four, three, two, one. You are now at your own natural level of relaxation. And from this level, you may move to any other level, with complete awareness, and function at will. You are completely aware at every level of your mind. You are in complete control at every level of your mind. You can accept, or reject, anything which is given here today.

You are in complete control. This is something that you want. It is here, and it is now. Eager to learn. Eager to explore. And let us begin now by comparing your mind to the surface of a quiet pond. On the surface, everything looks peaceful and still. But below the surface, there is great depth and much happening. My voice can be as a breeze, whispering in the trees along the shore.

Everyone does not realize his or her full capacities, and you have to discover these capacities in whatever way you wish. And, one of the things I would like you to discover is that your own subconsicous mind can listen to me and also deal with something else at the same time. Perhaps you remember doing this as a child, gazing out the window while the teacher was talking. Or walking with a friend, and talking with that friend at the same time. Two separate things, yet happening at the same time. You don't have to think or move about, or make any sort of effort. You don`t even have to bother trying to listen to me, because your subconscious is here and can hear every word. It's okay to let go. You are in a place where you can safely let go and just relax now.

You can take a deep breath, and you will note that a drifting can occur — that there is less and less importance to be attached to my voice. In due time, your own time, a minute, an hour, a week, a month, some time, your subconscious will reveal its gifts to you in a dream or in a daydream when you're not especially thinking about it — memories of other times and other places, memories you only thought you had misplaced, experiences you only thought you had mislaid. And with this new insight, comes new growth and new understanding. And stored deep in your subconscious are wonderful memories. Your subconscious can call upon and access these memories and bring them back with you later.

So, by looking deeper into the recesses of your own mind you can see your soul's vision and hear the voice of your heart. Later you can apply this knowledge to better understand yourself and your world. And, in a moment, we can begin a series of exercises into memory, perception and recall.

Can you remember a time in your life when you really felt safe and comfortable?

[Pause]

288

And you may begin now going back to about the time you were 18 years old — choosing a pleasant, happy memory of about the time that you were 18 years old. You will find that it is very easy for you to do this — choosing one specific memory or one specific event — and just simply focusing on it, looking at the people around you, then looking at yourself.

I will be quiet and give you ample time to simply enjoy this event. You may hear voices, you may see or feel the people. It may be in vivid color, as in a cinema movie. The images may be black and white, or just vague outlines. You may hear memories whispered in your inner ear. You may only sense the memory. Sometimes a certain smell will trigger the memory. It really doesn't matter how you perceive your memory. You're about 18 years old now. What is happening?

[Long pause]

Now you may continue back, going back now to about the time that you were 5 or 6 years old. Again, choosing a pleasant, happy memory, an impression, an episode, an experience, of about the time you were 5 or 6. Focus on this memory, look at it clearly. See what you were wearing, sense or feel the people around you. Look and listen to the information. Reach down deep and feel it, and I will be quiet.

[Long pause]

Now continue back, going back now to about the time when you were 4, then 3, then 2, and now 1. And going now to the time of your birth. And going beyond this even. Going to that very warm, very safe, and very secure place, where nothing can harm you, where you feel loved and surrounded by warmth. This is a time of forming, a time of growing, a time of movement, and really a time of preparation. This is a good time, and you can go beyond this even.

Going now into the Blue Mist. And the Blue Mist surrounds you and protects you. You are very safe and comfortable here. The Blue Mist is a time of inner peace, of quiet movement, of gentle sounds, and easy rhythm. The Blue Mist is really the avenue of the heart to the infinite. And you like it very much here. You can experience real peace, total peace, and quiet. And you are very comfortable here, and yet a part of you longs for something more. At first, only a small part of you longs for life and longs for movement. And this longing grows within you, and it becomes a strong desire. And this desire allows you to look outward, and you look out toward the horizon, and you see a light as if you were looking through a long tunnel. And you realize that the light is good. So you begin moving toward the light. You are traveling on the pathway of the heart — the avenue of the emotions — flowing, growing, going toward the light. And the light comes in through the top of your head and fills your entire being with light. The light heals you. The light protects you. The light surrounds you, as you feel the life energies flowing throughout your being. And as you mentally look down at your feet, notice what you are wearing on your feet. Plant your feet firmly upon the earth. Without analyzing, just look at your feet and mentally record what you sense or feel. You might wish to say this to yourself internally, quietly to yourself, or simply make a visual recording of it.

[Pause]

And now continue looking slowly up the body, at what you have on the bottom half of your body. Feel the texture, if there is fabric or material; see the colors. Continue looking up the body now, and look at what you have on the top half. And now look at the entire body and I will be quiet for a moment.

[Pause]

Notice any jewelry, anything on the head or anything you may be holding in your hands. Focus on a good, sharp, clear image. Process this material and make a record of it. Look at the entire body, and I will be quiet for a moment to give you a chance to do this.

[Pause]

Now, in your mind's eye, slowly look around to see where you are physically and make a mental note of what you see. Are there trees or sand, buildings, lakes or streams, the ocean? Look around and record what you perceive. And again, I will be quiet, that you may make a full turn, looking in all directions, making note of important things that you see. Encode the message and put it in a language your conscious mind will later understand. Record it to bring back later.

[Pause]

And now, you may look for other people. You may look to a time when you may see yourself near or with other people. And make a note of these people, encode these impressions and feelings. Perhaps there is someone special — someone with whom you have a close bond, an affinity, or a strong vibration. Look around. Perhaps there is a child, an adult, someone special, someone who has great meaning to you. Record this feeling and impression. If you listen quietly, you may even hear their name[s] being spoken.

[Pause]

And now you may look at a vehicle of transportation, something that you might have ridden on or in, something that feels comfortable when you sit on it, or in it. Or something that someone else is using for transportation. Make a note of the methods of transportation.

[Pause]

And at this time, you may also wish to taste something. What is it that you eat? Can you smell the food cooking? Are you able to taste it? Make a note and record this information.

[Pause]

And now, if you listen quietly, you may hear your own name being spoken by a friend or someone calling out to you. What do they call you? What are you doing? What is your work or profession? What are you learning?

[Pause]

And as you look for clues, can you tell where this land is? What would you use as a name, what is the land called? What is the name of this place? Perhaps you can perceive what century or what year this is. Record this information.

And now you may move to a major event in your life, a time that has important meaning to you, and focus on what is happening.

[Pause]

What happens next?

[Pause]

And what is happening now? What are you doing?

[Pause]

And now, in a detached way, as a bystander, look at the time of your death. Death is simply the next stage of life. What events led to your death? How did you die? What do you do after you die? Look at the death experience and assimilate its lessons and its message.

[Pause]

What is the reason or purpose for this life? What are the soul lessons? How did you grow in this time and place? Was anything left uncompleted? What made you the happiest in this life?

[Pause]

And now that you have this information, bring it together into a vivid symbol or word picture, or an image, and wrap it in something that you are familiar with that you may bring it back with you in a little while. Bring it into a symbol, into a word, into a clear vision, and encode it in your mind.

Most important of all, now, is to mentally look into your own eyes, and the eyes of the people that you have seen, those that you have loved, that person who was special to you. Look into the eyes of everyone you saw and send love from your eyes into their eyes. And as you do this important step, as you bless them and send them your love, they begin to fade. And as they begin to fade, let them go. Release them, bless them, and let them go as they bless and forgive you. Let the veil slowly drop. Allow the curtain to slowly close. Allow a full healing of this life and this time.

[Pause. In a group session, leave ample time to accomplish this important healing procedure. In individual sessions, the guide can now say, "And nod your head to signal me when you have accomplished this." Then *wait* for the signal-nod; some people take a few minutes for this step.]

And as you slowly begin coming back, traveling back through time, you can bring back with you all that was positive, and bright, and interesting, and important. Simply release and close the door on information that is not necessary for your soul growth at this time. Bring back something holy or special — something precious — a gem of wisdom, but only what you want. You will retain in your conscious mind only that which is important, helpful, and beneficial for you to retain at this time.

Now coming back through the light, through the Blue Mist, once again, traveling on the avenue of the heart, where all things are revealed unto you. Through that warm and safe place where nothing can harm you. Returning through the levels of the mind, to the clear recall of your own mind, and bringing back the information that you have recorded. Bringing that back with you that it may help you to grow and understand yourself even better. Slowly now, slowly coming back through the years of this present life to _____ (date), in _____ (state, city, or town). Plant your feet firmly into the present. Step into the present with fullness of strength.

And in a little while, when you awaken, you will feel just wonderful. You will feel better than before. You will be wide awake, clear headed, refreshed, and happy. Have you brought back something that is important, something helpful, something vital? Or have you allowed the door to close and the curtain to fall. It really doesn't matter. Your subconscious mind always protects you and knows what is best for you.

I will count from one to 10. At the count of 10, you can open your eyes, be wide awake, clear headed, feeling fine. I will count now. One — coming back very slowly. Two — coming out very slowly now. Three — coming up. Four — feel the life energies returning throughout your being. Five — feel total normalization and perfect equalibrium. Six — reenergized. Seven — coming up to your full potential. Eight — fully reoriented into the present. Nine — revitalized. And ten. Open your eyes, wide awake.

Your personal tape is now ready to use and enjoy. Remember, it may be a valuable experience to also keep a journal of each session.

CHANNELING GUIDELINES

1. For proper foundation work in channeling it is necessary to:

    a. Work with a guide during all sessions.

    b. Have worked regularly with cassette tapes, (either self-made or commercial).

    c. Examine the ideals and reasons for wanting to do this work.

    d. Prepare to make a long-term commitment.

    e. Get the physical body in shape in order to handle the higher vibrations. Take responsibility for physical fitness.

2. Without the proper foundation work, the following hazzards may result:

    a. Could stumble into lower astral levels, unknown and frightening levels, perhaps of gross matter. Some people who have rushed and tried to hurry the process have experienced this problem.

    b. Sometimes a channeler can become too sensitive. Some people have experienced other people's pain as well as their joy. In other cases, the channeler may take on the physical ailments and/or symptoms of the person for whom they are reading.

    c. It may magnify any health problems, mental, physical, or emotional, which may already exist.

    d. The channeler's ego and pride can be his downfall so that he or she could be led off the track instead of onto the right track.

e. Even the best of channelers have inner struggles and self-doubts in their work. This work is difficult even when the channeler is prepared. Without preparation and proper guidance — forget it!

f. Channeling is not an end in itself, it is another step in spiritual evolution. If we enter without preparation, we can hinder ourselves from experiencing our own openings and growth.

3. With proper preparation and a good guide, channeling can be an exciting adventure and a helpful and healing service to humanity.

PERIODICALS AND BOOKS ON HYPNOTIC REGRESSION

Past-life therapy is being used more every day and has become an innovative and important tool in the field of mind sciences. Professional past-life therapists honor confidentiality and are considerate and protective of the client's soul history. Past-life therapy is a valuable tool in the workshop of the mind, but it is not the only tool. The solution to every problem is always an individual one. Every subject has a "secret memory," as Carl Jung said, and in unlocking this memory is the key, the clue, to the therapist's success, no matter what method he or she uses.

Many excellent books and articles by nationally known psychologists, counselors, therapists, and doctors who use past-life research to discover the origins of patients' fears, anxieties, and habit patterns are now available. Here are some I consider excellent.

Periodicals:

Regression Therapy, the Journal of the Association for Past-Life Research and Therapy, P.O. Box 20151, Riverside, CA, 92516. Published quarterly.

The journal describes itself as "a professional journal with articles prepared by skilled professional people. The information in the journal is designed to aid the less skilled hypnotist to manage situations that may be encountered spontaneously at any time during the hypnosis of a client. Ongoing articles will keep the hypnotherapist informed on techniques to improve their service to humanity."

Books:
Note: These titles are from such Cayce Library categories as "Regression, Hypnotic," and "Past Lives Therapy," but there are hundreds of titles on past-life work under the general topics "Hypnosis," "Hypnotism," and "Reincarnation."

Thorwald Dethlefsen, *Voices from Other Lives* [translation by Gerhard Hundt] (New York: M. Evans and Co., Inc., 1977).

Bruce Goldberg, *Past Lives, Future Lives: Accounts of Regression and Progression Through Hypnosis* (North Hollywood, CA: Newcastle Publishing Co., 1982).

Peter Moss with Joe Keeton, *Encounters with the Past: How Man Can Experience and Relive History* (Garden City, NY: Doubleday & Co., 1980).

Morris Netherton and Nancy Shiffrin, *Past Lives Therapy* (New York: Morrow, 1978).

Betty Riley, *A Veil Too Thin: Reincarnation Out of Control* (Scottsdale, AZ: Valley of the Sun Publishing Co., 1984).

Brad Steiger, *You Will Live Again* (New York: Dell Publishing, 1978).

Dick Sutphen, *Past Lives, Future Loves* (New York: Pocket Books, 1978).

Dick Sutphen and Lauren Leigh Taylor, *Past-Life Therapy in Action* (Malibu, CA: Valley of the Sun Publishing Co.1983).

Helen Wambach, *Life Before Life* (New York: Bantam Books, 1979).

Alan Weisman, *We, Immortals: The Dick Sutphen Past Life Hypnotic Regression Seminars* (New York: Pocket Books, 1977).

Edith Fiore, *You Have Been Here Before* (New York: Ballantine Books, 1978).

WHAT IS THE REGRESSION PROCESS?

There are 14 basic steps to each regression session that I guide. The depth level of hypnosis varies with each individual as does the pace and timing. Each person responds with his or her own temperament, style and experience.

Here are the steps in their natural order. Each step flows into the next.

1. Hypnosis or Self-Hypnosis — entering your own relaxed, receptive, 100% natural level of mind.

2. Present-Life Regression — being guided back to recall and discuss pleasant memories from this life.

3. Prenatal Regression — passing through your formative months.

4. Blue Mist Experience — the time in between lives.

5. Past-Life Regression — utilizing your senses in the re-experiencing of stored memory.

6. Discussion — open-ended questions are asked by the guide during the regression. For example, "What happens next?" or "What's happening now?" and you answer them. Sometimes you may give a

wealth of information in monologue, with little prompting required.

7. Death Experience — a safe and positive way to complete the life's memory. As an overview, you can detach   and rise above the lifetime.

8. Soul Lessons — you are asked what you gained from the life, its lessons, the reasons, talents, etc.

9. Forgiveness — also called "Healing the Past." You mentally look into the eyes of everyone from that life and send love and forgiveness to them. You bless them, release them and let them fade.

10. Return through the Blue Mist — bringing back with you something special, a lesson learned perhaps.

11. Protective Suggestions — that you will retain in your conscious mind only that which is important, helpful and beneficial.

12. Return to Present — stepping firmly into the present in fullness of strength.

13. Wake-up Procedure — a process for total normal-ization and well-being.

14. Discussion and Evaluation of Session — the time to evaluate and discuss what has transpired.

The journey within is a sacred experience — a vision quest — to the center of your being. The journey is personal and different for everyone. You do not have to answer or explain yourself to anyone — you can evaluate your results for yourself, then accept the validity of your own experience.

Books & Tapes from INNER VISION

BOOKS -- *Check the ones you want*

☐ BORN AGAIN & AGAIN: How Reincarnation Occurs, $9.95
    by John Van Auken

☐ EDGAR CAYCE'S MASSAGE, HYDROTHERAPY
    & HEALING OILS, Joseph Duggan, MsT., $12.95

☐ PAST LIVES & PRESENT RELATIONSHIPS, $8.95
    by John Van Auken

☐ GETTING HELP FROM YOUR DREAMS, $9.95
    by Henry Reed

☐ JOURNEY WITHIN: Past-life Regression & Channeling
    Henry Leo Bolduc, $10.95

☐ THE INNER POWER OF SILENCE: A Universal Way
    of Meditation, Mark Thurston, $8.95

☐ FATIMA PROPHECY, $9.95
    Channeled by Ray Stanford

☐ MIRACLE OF SUGGESTION, $8.95
    Cynthia Pike Ouellette

CASSETTE TAPES -- *Check the ones you want*

☐ TIPS ON MEDITATION (2 Sides)
    by John Van Auken, $6.95

☐ EDGAR CAYCE'S REINCARNATION CONCEPTS (2 Sides)
    by John Van Auken, $6.95

☐ ADDICTIONS: New Ideas for Understanding and
    Overcoming Them, (2 Sides) by Henry Reed, $7.95

☐ AWAKENING TO YOUR SOUL'S MISSION (2 Sides)
    by Mark Thurston, $6.95

☐ HEALING THE WHOLE PERSON (2 Sides)
    by Harmon Bro, $7.95

☐ HOW TO DEVELOP TELEPATHY (2 Sides)
    by Henry Reed, $7.95

☐ EDGAR CAYCE PRINCIPLES FOR SELF HEALING (2 Sides)
    by John Van Auken, $7.95

*VISA/MasterCard orders Call Toll-Free 1-800-227-0172
or send check or money order to:*

INNER VISION PUBLISHING CO.
620 Sirine Avenue
Virginia Beach, VA 23462

Please send me the books and tapes I checked. I enclosed a check or money order for the full amount. I understand that INNER VISION pays all postage and handling costs. (Allow 4 weeks for delivery.)

☐ **Please Send Me Your Free Catalog.**

Name _____

Address _____

City _____

State _____ Zip _____